Hemingway's Cuba

Hemingway's Cuba

*Finding the Places
and People That Influenced
the Writer*

DENNIS L. NOBLE

McFarland & Company, Inc., Publishers
Jefferson, North Carolina

LIBRARY OF CONGRESS CATALOGUING-IN-PUBLICATION DATA

Names: Noble, Dennis L., author.
Title: Hemingway's Cuba : finding the places and people that influenced the writer / Dennis L. Noble.
Description: Jefferson, N.C. : McFarland & Company, Inc., Publishers, 2016. | Includes bibliographical references and index.
Identifiers: LCCN 2016047078 | ISBN 9781476666433 (softcover : acid free paper) ∞
Subjects: LCSH: Hemingway, Ernest, 1899–1961—Homes and haunts—Cuba. | Hemingway, Ernest, 1899–1961—Friends and associates. | Authors, American—20th century—Biography. | Journalists—United States—Biography.
Classification: LCC PS3515.E37 Z7469 2016 | DDC 813/.52—dc23
LC record available at https://lccn.loc.gov/2016047078

BRITISH LIBRARY CATALOGUING DATA ARE AVAILABLE

ISBN (print) 978-1-4766-6643-3
ISBN (ebook) 978-1-4766-2638-3

© 2016 Dennis L. Noble. All rights reserved

No part of this book may be reproduced or transmitted in any form or by any means, electronic or mechanical, including photocopying or recording, or by any information storage and retrieval system, without permission in writing from the publisher.

On the cover: Ernest Hemingway with books and his dog, Negrita, outside his home in Cuba (Ernest Hemingway Collection, John F. Kennedy Presidential Library and Museum, Boston); *background* map of Cuba © 2016 iStock

Printed in the United States of America

McFarland & Company, Inc., Publishers
 Box 611, Jefferson, North Carolina 28640
  www.mcfarlandpub.com

For Víctor Pina Tabío
and Kayleigh C. Ritten

Table of Contents

Acknowledgments viii
Preface 1

1. Cuba and the Ambos Mundos 5
2. Walking in Hemingway's Old Havana 18
3. Finca Vigía 46
4. Las Estrellas de Gigi 79
5. Tracking Hemingway Eastward to Santiago de Cuba 91
6. Tracking Hemingway Westward from Santiago de Cuba to Bahía Honda 127
7. Cojímar 144

Appendix A: A Short History of Ernest Hemingway 159
Appendix B: The Hemingway Women 172
Chapter Notes 186
Bibliography 194
Index 201

Acknowledgments

Many people have helped me in my journey to track Ernest Hemingway in Cuba; I could not have completed my voyage without their help.

In Cuba: I owe a great deal to my guide, interpreter, photographer and friend Víctor Pina Tabío. His knowledge of Cuba, his many contacts and his good humor during days when I surely taxed him with my constant changing of places to visit all proved invaluable. I could never have made any progress in Cuba without Víctor.

Other people in Cuba contributed to this work and are listed alphabetically and some also appear in the bibliography: Pedro Abascal, Habana; Ada Rosa Alfonso, Director of the Museo de Ernesto Hemingway; Prof. José Altshuler, Dr.Sc., Director of the Sociedad Cubana de Historia de la Ciencia y la Tecnología, Habana; José Armando, Dr.Sc., of the Biblioteca Pública, in Caibarién; Oscar Blas, San Francisco de Paula; Pablo Armando Fernández, Habana; Isbel I. Ferreiro, Deputy Director, Museo de Ernesto Hemingway; Esperanza García, curator of the Hemingway Museum in the Hotel Ambos Mundos, Habana; Gladys Gonzáles, former Director, Museo Ernesto Hemingway; Rosa María González, Directora, Alejandro de Humboldt, Habana; Dr. Roberto Díaz Marín, Secretario General, Sociedad Cubana de Historia de la Ciencia y la Tecnología, Habana; Prof. Elisa Serrano and her husband, Pablo Jane, of Habana, for all their good information and conversation; and Enrique de La Uz, Habana.

In the United States: Merri Ansara, Director, Common Ground Education & Travel Services, always made the arrangements for my smooth entry and exit of Cuba. At the John F. Kennedy Library, Hemingway Collection and archives, Boston, Massachusetts: Susan Wrynn,

Acknowledgments

Hemingway Curator, helped me greatly, as did Stephen Plotkin, Reference Archivist, and Laurie Austin of the Audiovisual Archives. Sara Kemp, Archives Assistant at the Philadelphia Academy of Natural Sciences, quickly provided me with material for my work.

Loren A. Noble not only put up with my journeys away from home while tracking Ernest Hemingway, she also read drafts of the manuscript and helped in the research. As I am color blind, Loren helped with pointing out the colors in my photographs of Cuba. Dr. Vincent W. Patton, III, Ed.D., MCPOCG (Ret.) has supported my work throughout the years. Saying thanks seems like a small gesture considering the magnitude of your help, Vince.

Monica (Moller) Ostrom gracefully consented to relate her interesting first assignment as a nurse in the Ketchum, Idaho, hospital with Ernest Hemingway as a patient.

The following people, listed alphabetically, read and commented on the manuscript: Bergen Spring; Dr. Thomas McCurdy; and Gregg Shield; Truman R. Strobridge listened and offered great advice. Their work greatly improved the manuscript.

Bergen Spring not only read the manuscript, but her outstanding art contributed to the illustration of this book. Tracy Smith, again, produced some excellent maps for the work.

Others in the United States, arranged alphabetically: Dr. Peter J. Capelotti, helped me in numerous ways, plus proving to be a good listener; the comments of the various members of the Hemingway Society's list have proved useful; the staffs of the North Olympic Library System, Port Angeles, Washington, and the Sequim Branch Library provided me with needed books and articles; the Port Angeles, Washington, McCulloch Tuesday lunch members: Carl Gay, Ray Gruber, John McCulloch, Dr. Thomas McCurdy, and Jim McEntire all listened to the constant stream of chatter about Hemingway without complaining; Taylor Paslay, Hemingway Preserve Manager, Hailey, Idaho, took time out from his busy schedule to show me through Hemingway's last home in Ketchum, Idaho; Robin Smith, of Robin Smith, Ink, helped immeasurably; Dr. William H. Thiesen for finding material on *Pilar* in The Mariner's Museum, Newport News, Virginia.

The writing of this book was akin to both the pleasure and work of landing a record-breaking marlin off the northern Cuban coast. Where it has merit it is because of the people listed above. Where it falters it is because I did not listen to their advice.

Preface

I can trace my interest in Ernest Hemingway to 1971 while still a career enlisted man in the U.S. Coast Guard. The icebreaker I served in had just come out of the Antarctic and arrived at Buenos Aires, Argentina, for one week in a standby status in the event of there being any vessel in distress within the southern icepack. With no library on the cutter, I had depleted all the books I had brought, reading many of them more than once. Upon asking a Buenos Aires guide about locating a bookstore with English language volumes, she directed me to a store on Calle Floridia, at the time one of the more fashionable shopping streets in the city. Among the books purchased was Ernest Hemingway's *Death in the Afternoon*. The purchase in this bookstore, the name of which I have long-forgotten, led to my first close reading of Hemingway and put me onto the path of his other works followed by biographies and some critical studies of the man. Along the way was the "discovery" that the writer had spent at least one-third of his life in Cuba. After the passage of over three decades of discovering Hemingway, retiring from the U.S. Coast Guard, obtaining a Ph.D. from Purdue University in U.S. history, I continued reading on Hemingway and consider myself a novice *aficionado* of the author.

In 2007, while undertaking a book on the U.S. Coast Guard's difficult mission of intercepting human smuggling into the United States, I was researching in Key West and, of course, took the time to visit Hemingway's home on Whitebread Street. By the time of this visit to his home in the Keys, I knew Cuba would take up a number of chapters of any book on human smuggling I intended to author. To discuss human smuggling out of the island country I needed research in the country and this required obtaining permission from the United States government to legally enter the embargoed country. The permission granted, in February 2008, I arrived in Havana and met with Víctor Pina Tabío, my interpreter, guide, driver, and the person who introduced me to Cubans and discussed general Cuban history and culture. In our daily meetings, we hammered out what I wanted to accomplish that day and the locations and people to contact to ascertain the needed information. In addition to my own walking tours of La Habana Vieja (Old Havana), we traveled to locations in other sections of the city, plus some of the locations along Cuba's north coast where smugglers picked up their human cargo, or launched their craft. As an aficionado I quite naturally tried to make time for at least a visit to Ernest Hemingway's home Finca Vigía (the Lookout or Watchtower Farm) at San Francisco de Paula, located in the outskirts of Havana. Víctor's suggestions led to an itinerary that not only fit in the visit to the Finca, but also allowed a rare chance to have a personal tour inside the house with the assistant director of the Museo de Ernesto Hemingway, plus enough time for a quick visit to the village of Cojímar, one of the locations where Hemingway moored his fishing craft, *Pilar*.

Throughout my research into Cuba in 2008 I could not help noticing two icons throughout Havana: Ernesto "Che" Guevara and Ernesto Hemingway. There were virtually no posters of Fidel Castro at any place where tourists might conceivably gather, but one could find either of the Ernestos on postcards, posters, and in books. By the end of the research period, it seemed to me that very little material existed concerning the locations frequented by Hemingway throughout Cuba, with the exception of his home and Cojímar. My time in the country definitely affected me, and I wondered how it had affected Hemingway's work and how had the various locations influenced the Nobel Prize–winning writer. After finishing the treatise on human smuggling, I began thinking more and more about Hemingway in Cuba. The historian Robert Caro, in a lecture on his magnificent biographical work of President Lyndon Baines Johnson, correctly mentioned the influences a specific place has on a subject. Recalling the lack of material on the various locations in Cuba that had anything to do with Hemingway, I decided to research biographies, plus his novels, and other works on Hemingway that mentioned, even if briefly, any location he may have visited. I then returned twice to Cuba to visit the sites. In general, the areas I searched stretched along the north coast of Cuba from Bahía Honda to the west of Havana and east to Nuevitas. The goals set for this undertaking were, first, to understand the particular areas and to see, as mentioned by Caro, if the places had any effect on Hemingway. The reader will immediately see that Hemingway, no matter where in Cuba, from the bustle of the streets of Havana, to his finca and to among the isolated *cayos* (islands), tried to learn from the people of Cuba and from the working class in general.

James L. Haley, in his biography of Jack London, *Wolf: The Lives of Jack London*, writes that an author, when writing a biography, should also "research *around* [Haley's emphasis] the subject." While this present work is not a biography, I feel that those individuals who had contact with Hemingway during his years in Cuba should be discussed in some detail. There is, for example, the story of U.S. Marine Corps officer John W. Thomason, Jr., who was the military attaché in the U.S. Embassy in Havana when Hemingway was planning his efforts in hunting German submarines in his fishing craft *Pilar* from the cayos of Cuba during the early years of World War II.

Another of my goals was to see if I could glimpse Cuba's history and people by traveling to the Hemingway locations. Along this line, did Hemingway apply what he observed from the country and the people to his writing? The short answer is to be found in reading *The Old Man and the Sea*.

The narrative of the present text will take an interested traveler to Cuba who wishes to cover Hemingway sites, both within Havana and far outside of the capital city, about two weeks to cover. However, for those whose itinerary is less than two weeks, there are three major sites within or very close to Havana that will take about a week and these are covered as well. I did not actually visit two locations. Chapter 5 explains the lack of a visit to one of the cayos along Cuba's north coast that had something to do with Hemingway. The book also does not describe this writer's efforts at fishing for marlin while in Cuba. The press of time and a small research budget prevented this, but those who have read at least *The Old Man and the Sea* and Hemingway's pieces written in the 1930s in *Esquire* on fishing for marlin can readily grasp Ernest Hemingway's love of the sea. Having read these writings, I did have experience at sea that helped me with understanding Hemingway's love of the sea.

It must be stressed that this book is not about the literary works of Ernest Hemingway, nor is it a biography of Hemingway; I leave both of these to scholars who have spent their lives studying the writer. The book is meant for the Hemingway aficionado; readers who are interested in learning more about Hemingway, and perhaps the scholar who may find something new in some of the locations along the north coast of Cuba. I have, for those readers possessing scant knowledge of Hemingway, a short overview of the man in Appendix A, and, in Appendix B, a short overview of the women in his life. In addition, those readers planning to travel to Cuba may find the descriptions of that country and its citizens to be of interest.

Since 2011 there have been some very interesting changes in the official relationship between the United States and Cuba. This may mean more travelers from the United States visiting Cuba and, perhaps, causing larger amounts of people at some of the sites. I have described the sites as I saw them at the time.

Four decades ago, when this writer's interest in Hemingway was first piqued, I was struck by the poor public image assigned to the man. He was, according to legend, little more than a hard drinker, a womanizer, and a braggart who routinely stretched the truth about his exploits outside of his writing. While there are, admittedly, elements of truth to all of these perceptions, a deeper level of research shows evidence of a more humane man. (For readers who wish more detailed information on Hemingway, his writings and some of his time in Cuba I have included a selected bibliography of the sources to which I referred.)

Hemingway's Cuba is, in essence, a voyage by a retired sailor with a love of Hemingway, the sea, Cuba and, most importantly, the Cuban people, who wishes to show Ernest Hemingway's haunts and how they perhaps affected his writing, while along the way gaining a glimpse of modern Cuba and Cubans.

◈ 1 ◈

Cuba and the Ambos Mundos

"Why do you want to go to that Communist country?"
"You mean you're going *alone*?"
"I would be afraid to go there by myself."
These were only a few of the many comments I received in 2008 upon announcing my success in obtaining a general license from the United States Treasury Department's Office of Foreign Assets Control to do research work in Cuba. My goal was to find some of the locations in Cuba used by human traffickers to smuggle people out of the country for a book on the subject. Because of my longtime interest in Ernest Hemingway, I also wanted to visit the two main locations of the writer's time in Cuba: his home outside of Havana and one of the locations where he kept his boat *Pilar*, Cojímar. Once my initial goal of completing my book was met, I then decided to do a second book, this one on the locations within Cuba that had influenced Hemingway. I also hoped to show a little of Cuba, its people, and its history. On each of my departures for this country, my acquaintances in the United States could only shake their heads at my impending danger.

After receiving a general license, the next step was to officially enter Cuba as a solo traveler. It was vital that I found a United States government-approved travel agent who specialized in travel to Cuba. I had the good fortune to find Maria Ansaria, of Common Ground Travel. She arranged the needed paperwork for the submission for a visa, a flight from Miami to Havana and lodging at the Hotel Ambos Mundos in Habana Vieja (Old Havana).

In 2008, the United States embargo allowed Cubans living in the

United States to return every so often; this created a number of regular charter flights for the short passage from Miami to Havana. At the time, the charter airline provided a small, twin-engine propeller craft, with, perhaps, no more than twenty people on board. With only a basic grasp of the Spanish language, the approach to José Martí International Airport brought to my mind all the worries and anxious comments made by my colleagues and friends. Some of the apprehension melted away when I noticed an older Afro-Cuban man sitting in the row across the narrow passage between sets of seats; his deeply creased countenance shone with a huge smile as the wheels of the aircraft touched the runway of the airport.

The arrival procedures in 2008 might seem unusual for most travelers in the United States. First, passengers disembarked the piston-driven aircraft directly onto the tarmac, no walking down a long jet way into the terminal. Once upon the tarmac, there were two large buildings. No signs either in Spanish or English, or painted arrows could be seen directing new arrivals as to where they should report next. My fellow passengers and I began a slow walk headed generally in the direction between the two buildings. After a hesitant few feet of walking, a door opened on the building to the left. A man appeared there briefly, and immediately all passengers began walking toward that entrance. Once inside the building, again without the benefit of signs, there appeared a long barrier, with small toll-like booths placed at intervals that turned out to be passport control. The official asked me if I spoke Spanish and with the reply of *muy poco* (very little) all the procedures were conducted in English. The number of travelers from the flight being relatively small, much of the normal paperwork and procedures after clearing the passport area was relaxed and went smoothly.

Flash-forward to the time for departing Cuba: I entered the small terminal, again with few signs of where to check in with the charter airline, or, for that matter, any airline. Looking around at a line of travelers waiting for something, I walked up to them and asked if anyone spoke English. Upon receiving "yes" from several people, it turned out many of those in line were Canadians; a few were missionaries from the United States returning home to Fida. The missionaries, in particular, proved especially helpful in explaining the procedures. I reported to the sole staff member and received a boarding pass. Following the instructions from one of the missionaries, I walked across the small terminal and paid a tax of $25 Cuban Convertible Pesos (CUC) and the official stamped it. I then went through passport control and eventually boarded the aircraft for Miami.

Two years later, José Martí International Airport had undergone many renovations that were designed to assist incoming travelers from Miami. This was, in large part, due to the new policy of allowing Cuban Americans to enter their native country as often as they liked. The numbers swelled so much that at least one air charter service rented a larger medium-range jet to fly the Miami-to-Havana route. Not only did this allow for more passengers, but also for more cargo being brought into the country by returning Cubans. By 2011, rumors were being circulated at the Miami International Airport that there were two aircraft for one flight into Havana: one for passengers, and the other for bringing in items for their families in Cuba—it was not unusual to observe a forty-inch television set being removed from the cargo hold of an aircraft. The amount of cargo being unloaded sometimes slowed the turn-around process for the flight back to the United States. With the remodeling of the airport, the checks through passport control and customs went more smoothly, with most officials speaking English. The exception to the rule involved Alan Gross, who was accused of illegally distributing prohibited satellite communications to Cuban dissidents. At that time—2011—baggage belonging to single passengers with United States passports was subject to close scrutiny.

Perhaps one aspect of entering and leaving Cuba with a license might seem unusual to Americans who have traveled outside their own country. Normally, a passport has a visa stamped in it, but because such a stamp would make officials at arrivals and departures from the United States heavily scrutinize the traveler, the Cuban government issues to those Americans with a license a small document in lieu of a visa. The passport-control official places the entry and exit stamps on the document, which is kept loosely within the passport.

After clearing all the officials and exiting the arrivals hall, the traveler who has flown in from Miami faces a loud, densely packed but cheerful crowd. The visitor moves along a narrow passageway in the group, as Cubans eagerly scan the faces of the arrivals. Having weathered the crowd, a cab is easily obtained. After a taxi takes to the main roadway outside of the airport the first sight for the traveler are the anti–United States billboards along the road. Once past these, the visitor in search of Ernest Hemingway's haunts now begins in the bustling capital of Cuba, *Habana* (Havana).

Ernest Miller Hemingway was born on July 21, 1899, into comfortable surroundings in Oak Park, Illinois. From the time he was a toddler until he left home at eighteen he spent summers at the family's cottage at Walloon Lake, near Petoskey, Michigan. There, among the woods, streams, and lakes, he developed the love of the natural world he would retain for the rest of his life. A very young Hemingway recorded in a small notebook that he wanted to write and travel and his early life seemed to be preparing him to undertake this boyhood dream. He volunteered as an ambulance driver in World War I and was wounded on the Italian Front while rescuing a soldier. Hemingway married Elizabeth Hadley Richardson on September 3, 1921, moved to Paris and soon became a part of the British and American writers in the Paris of the 1920s. The couple had one child, John, known as "Jack" or "Bumby." Hemingway's 1926 novel, *The Sun Also Rises*, announced a new voice on the literary scene. The author divorced Hadley and married Pauline Pfeiffer on May 27, 1927. Pauline's was a family of means. Whether this played a part in Hemingway's motive for marrying Pauline is not known, although it did free him from monetary worries. Pauline's uncle, Gustavus—"Uncle Gus"—made sure that his niece did not want for money. Shortly after their marriage, Hemingway decided to return to the United States. In March 1928, the couple sailed from Rochelle, France, on the Royal Mail ship *Orita* en route to Key West, via Havana. The writer John Dos Passos, a friend of Hemingway's, had visited the Keys on one of his trips around the United States and described the region, and especially Key West, as "something seen in a dream," which remains true in the 21st century. Dos Passos felt the sun would be good for Hemingway. The voyage provided the twenty-nine-year-old novelist's first introduction to Cuba.[1]

The passage to Key West, however, proved less than enjoyable. Hemingway, in a satirical note to Pauline, likened his room to a monk's cell where he felt he might spend the rest of his life attempting to reach Cuba. With Pauline six months pregnant with Patrick, she needed a rest in Havana. The couple stayed at the hotel Ambos Mundos, close to the waterfront. The hotel would see much of Hemingway over the coming years. After their short stay, the Hemingways continued their voyage to Key West on one of the four Peninsular and

1. Cuba and the Ambos Mundos

Occidental (P&O) Line ships that plied the waters between Havana and Key West.[2]

When Hemingway arrived in Key West in 1928, he had not gained great fame. True, he had a well-received novel, *The Sun Also Rises*, to his credit and a book of short stories, *Men Without Women*, but he had not gained the immense recognition he would in later years. On April 21, he wrote to Maxwell Perkins, his editor at Scribner's in New York City, to send him copies of his last two books as no one believed him when he told them he was writer. "They think I represent Big Northern Bootleggers or Dope Peddlers—especially with this scar."[3]

Hemingway began dressing informally, to say the least. One description has him with a knotted hemp rope used to hold up his trousers, or shorts. Instead of shoes, he wore moccasins sent to him from an old friend in Horton Bay, Michigan. Quickly becoming known as a character, Hemingway then turned his attention to gathering around him a close group of men, dubbing them his "mob." Members of the mob would eventually lead him to his passion for big-game fishing.

The first member of Hemingway's mob, Charles Thompson, came from one of the richest families in Key West. The Thompsons owned a ship's chandlery, an icehouse, a cigar box factory, and a hardware and tackle shop. They also controlled the Green Turtle industry in the Keys and Central America, processing their catch at their own cannery. A year older than Ernest, Charles stood almost as tall as Hemingway. Broad-shouldered with unruly thick brown hair, his wide friendly smile put people immediately at ease. A product of the New York City school system and the Mt. Pleasant Military Academy at Ossining-on-the-Hudson, he had served in the Army of Occupation in 1919. Ernest always gave everyone close to him a nickname, and Thompson became "Old Karl."

Hemingway drew upon everyone he knew for "bits and pieces" needed for his characters in his writing or to help him understand and master whatever subject then interested him. One of his great abilities was a quick mastering of virtually any subject. He seemed able to go from rank novice to an expert in a very short period of time. After their first meeting, Thompson invited Ernest and Pauline to his house for dinner, where the couple met Thompson's wife, Lorin.[4]

From Thompson, Hemingway learned tarpon fishing. A thirty-pound "tail-dancing tarpon coming out of the water like some silver dream, gill plates rattling and jaws shaking the hook" proved a far cry from trout fishing. The experience began his lifelong zeal for salt water fishing and the sea in general. Thompson also provided a needed link to the Conchs (the old line Key Westers). Michael Reynolds, Hemingway's prolific biographer, notes that if Ernest had not met Thompson he might not have returned to Key West to fish after visiting with Pauline's family in Arkansas. Similarly, if Pauline had not met Lorin, who was well-read and taught at the local high school, she might not have returned to Key West.[5]

One day, Hemingway convinced Thompson to leave his hardware business and go for a weekend fishing trip. They hired charter boat skipper Captain Eddie "Bra" Saunders to take them to some islands thirty miles west of Key West. The forty-two-year-old leathery-faced "white Bahamian" had migrated to Key West from Green Turtle Key, Bahamas. He felt at home in the waters stretching from Cay Sal Banks near the north coast of Cuba to the Tortugas. In a letter to his friend, poet and writer Archibald MacLeish, Hemingway wrote, "Bra is a bloody pirate but do you think he doesn't see nor feel." Leathery and gnarled from a life of working at sea in a semi-tropical environment and hands showing the beginnings of rheumatism, Captain Bra became the perfect study for Hemingway. Years later, in *The Old Man and the Sea*, he supposedly transferred the hands of Saunders to his character of the Cuban fisherman, Santiago, who fished from a small skiff in the Gulf Stream.[6]

The trip kept the party fishing mainly in the Gulf Stream, where Ernest took his first large sailfish. He constantly asked Saunders not only about fishing, but also the preparation. As the fishing party returned, Pauline and Lorin stood on the dock awaiting the fishermen. Pauline told Lorin that "she had never before seen Ernest so content."[7]

One of the more important members of the mob to play a part in Hemingway's Cuban years was Joe "Josie" Russell, born in Key West in 1890. He had worked for a time as a cigar maker until the industry moved to Tampa. The "red faced Conch ... owned two basic generators of income, a [charter boat] and a speakeasy." During the Prohibition years, Russell decided to cut out the middleman in supplying illegal liquor and became a rumrunner between Cuba and Key West. Hemingway later claimed Russell "was the first Key Wester to make the run to Cuba to bring back 'Hoover Gold,' as Josie called illegal booze." After the repeal of Prohibition, Russell owned a now legal bar that bore the name Sloppy Joe's. Hemingway, as was his wont, nicknamed Russell "Josie Gunts," while calling himself "Mahatma," "Ernie," or "The Old Master."[8]

Pauline insisted on visiting her family in Piggott, Arkansas. Ernest did not want to leave. Four weeks after their arrival he agreed that Pauline could travel to Arkansas, and he would join her later. Pauline's departure proved "one of the most significant occurrences in rooting Ernest to Key West."

During their time together, Hemingway had entertained Thompson with all the interesting people he knew from Paris and Horton Bay, Michigan. With Pauline gone, this proved the perfect time to invite his cronies to Key West. Ernest sent out letters to the painters Henry Strater ("Mike") and Waldo Pierce ("Don Pico"); Bill Smith ("Old Bill"), a boyhood friend from Horton Bay; and Dos Passos ("Dos"). By this time, Hemingway had his local mob in place: Old Kraut Thompson, Captain Bra Saunders, J. B. Sullivan ("Sully"), a transplanted Irishman who owned a machine shop; Burge Saunders, Bra Saunders's brother, also a charter boat fisherman; Jakie Key and Hamilton Adams ("Sack of Ham," or "Sacker"), both charter boat fishermen; and Earl "Jewfish" Adams, a newspaperman.[9]

These two groups, those from outside and the Conchs, made up "as grand a group of men as ever came together." The mob dined at restaurants, drank at bars, and fished. Between ramblings with the mob around Key West, Hemingway continued his practice of working early in the mornings on the manuscript that would become *A Farewell to Arms*. He wrote about winter in Italy with "the snow falling in his fiction and the sweat running from his brow" in Key West.[10]

Ernest and Pauline had lived in a number of rented houses until 1931, when Uncle Gus bought an 1851-era house in Key West for Pauline for $8,000 (almost $125,000 in 2016 dollars). The beautiful two-story Spanish Colonial home, at 907 Whitehead Street, was built by Asa Tift, a ship architect and captain, from Groton, Connecticut. Tift moved to Key West in 1851 with his wife, Anna, and daughter, Annie. Two sons were born after the family's move to Key West. Eventually, Tift lost his wife and sons to yellow fever. He remained in the house, never remarrying; he died in 1889.

Tift had the house constructed of white pine from Georgia, and limestone quarried on the property. It sits on almost an acre of land and stands away from the street. Tift sited the house on an elevation of sixteen feet above sea level, making it the second-highest elevation in Key West. Until water was piped into the island in 1944, fresh water was collected in two cisterns, one between the main home and carriage house and one on the roof of the main home.

When the Hemingways selected the house, it was in bad repair, but both Ernest and Pauline could see its potential and undertook a large restoration. Due to their efforts, visitors today can walk through the lush gardens and trees surrounding the house and see the home Hemingway lived in from 1931 to 1939. Pauline continued to live in the house until her death in 1981.

The house has wraparound verandas. The iron railings on the second story are redolent of those in New Orleans. Each side of the house has four large symmetrical windows with hurricane shutters that can almost be called doors.

Hemingway wrote in a studio on the second story of the building just behind the house. He gained access to it via an iron curved stairway until a catwalk from the master bedroom connected the studio with the main house. Visitors can see the room where Hemingway worked, with its crammed bookcases and hunting trophies hanging on the walls.

One of the stops for today's visitors to the house is the pool. Built in 1937–38 at the huge price of $20,000 (almost $350,000 in 2016 dollars), it "was the first in-ground pool in Key West, and the only pool within 100 miles." According to tradition, Ernest, protesting the huge expense, took a penny out of his pocket and slapped it down in the wet cement of the pool and said, "Here, take the last penny I've got!" Tour guides tell this story and point to the penny.[11]

For most of the Key West years Hemingway depended on Pauline's money. It was not until the publication of *For Whom the Bell Tolls* in 1940 that he could finally state he had now become a recognized figure in American literature and made enough money so that he did not have to depend on his wives—he had needed the small trust fund of Hadley, his first wife, and Pauline's money—to subsist while writing.

While calling Key West home, Hemingway began his legend. During this period, he produced six books, five collections of short stories, and a number of articles. In the story of Ernest Hemingway's life, his more than two decades in Key West is important.

In April 1929, Hemingway chartered Joe Russell's boat, the fast thirty-two-foot *Anita*—fast because it was also used for rum running—

1. Cuba and the Ambos Mundos

for a two-week trip to Cuba. Much earlier, Josie had told Hemingway about the large marlin off Cuba's north coast. On this trip he charged Hemingway $10 a day, with another $2 for a room at the Havana hotel Ambos Mundos and another fifty cents when Pauline came over, with the two weeks stretching into two months, the trip marking Hemingway's focus on big-game fishing off Cuba. The Ambos Mundos proved a good place to write, and he worked on the galleys for his work on bull fighting, *Death in the Afternoon,* and finished the short story, "A Way You'll Never Be."[12]

One of the first stops on the itinerary of anyone interested in Hemingway's time in Cuba should be the Ambos Mundos hotel. The dusty-rose-colored building, on the corner of busy *Obispo* (Bishop) and *Mercaderes* (Merchants) streets in Old Havana, was built in 1924. After the 1959 revolution, the hotel became a place for teachers and officials of the Ministry of Education. Now, with the interior completely remodeled, it still has much of the ambience of the Hemingway period. Today, a visitor can enter from Obispo Street or at the corner of Obispo and Mercaderes streets. If visitors enter directly from Obispo, they will see a bar to the left, with a piano facing the bar and a small café between the bar and Mercaderes Street. The reception desk is just to the right of the bar, and, in the modern era, there is a small pool containing some of the rare turtles of Cuba. Hung on the walls are large poster-sized photographs of the hotel's famous writer, and large, comfortable sofas and chairs scattered throughout the ground floor. The sight that some tourists immediately seem to gravitate to is the large caged elevator of the 1920s or '30s. It is always best to arrive early for a ride in the elevator before the crowds increase sometime around noon and continue until late in the afternoon. For those who do not care to wait for the elevator, there is a stairway with stone steps showing the wear of many feet that have made their way up to their assigned rooms. The second floor is taken up with a space for special functions or exhibitions, and above this, floors three, four, and five are for guest rooms.[13]

Room 511 is the special chamber of the hotel. Hemingway, as mentioned, came to this room when he lived in Key West and wrote between his hours at sea off Cuba's north coast. Before his divorce from Pauline on November 4, 1940, room 511 had become his residence and is now a small museum, looked over by Esperanza M. García. Today, the chamber seems rather small and Spartan, but this is as it would have been before Hemingway occupied it; however, once he settled in to live in the room, his future wife (his third), Martha Gellhorn, complained he was the most "unfastidious" man she ever knew, with fishing gear scattered about the small space. Hemingway said of the room that the bed facing the window was such that when "you sleep with your feet toward the east" the rising sun shining through the window will always awaken you. The room now contains a typewriter in a clear case facing a window that still provides the view described by Hemingway: "To the north, and to the east over the old cathedral, the entrance to the harbor, and the sea, to the east to Casablanca peninsula, the roofs of all the houses in between and the width of the harbor." To feel the impact of the room, a visitor in search of Hemingway sites should try to arrive early when Ms. García has more time to explain the room and the visitor can absorb it all without many people milling about in the limited space.[14]

One of the interesting aspects of Hemingway's stay in the Ambos Mundos concerns a story about the woman he began a relationship with while still married to Pauline. In 1931, Hemingway and Pauline embarked on the ship *Île de France* from Europe to New York. Pauline, seven months pregnant with their youngest son, Gregory, did not feel up to the normal shipboard merry-making. Donald Ogden Stewart, a longtime friend of Hemingway, and his wife also made the trip across the Atlantic on the same ship. Stewart's pregnant wife also did not feel much in the mood for celebrating. Left basically to themselves, Hemingway and Stewart "cavorted" with Jane Mason, the "beautiful and lively" wife of George Grant Mason, head of Pan American Airways in Havana. This marks the beginning of the Jane Mason affair.[15]

Born Jane Welsh in Tuxedo Park, New Jersey, on June 24, 1909, her mother, Betty Lee, was a singer from Syracuse, New York. Jane took the name Kendall when her mother remarried. She attended Briarcliff School and schools in Europe. Early on, she showed artistic talent but cared more for the social life. Jane was twice presented to Washington, D.C., society in 1926. At the end of the social season and at the age of eighteen, Jane married George Grant Mason, Jr. Mason was a graduate of St. Paul's and Yale and manager of the Pan American Airlines Caribbean area in Havana; he also owned half-interest in Cubana Airlines.

Jane was tall, with her strawberry blonde hair pulled back and knotted at the back of her neck. Her blue eyes set off a beautiful oval face with a "fresh complexion" and, at one time, she modeled for Pond's cold cream. President Coolidge's wife reportedly claimed her "the most beautiful woman to visit the White House." A friend of Jane once said of her, "Jane Mason not only drank a bit, but was one of wildest, hairiest, most drinking, wenching, sexy superwomen in the world." She was athletic, an excellent driver, loved to fish for marlin off Cuba, hunted big game in Africa and was an excellent wing shooter. She was "perfectly at home in the almost exclusive company of men and insisted on being treated by them as 'one of the boys.'"

According to Jeffrey Meyers, one of Hemingway's biographers, Jane could be high-strung and temperamental, as well as "moody and emotionally unstable." Prone to accidents, she reportedly "broke every bone in her body and had every conceivable illness." Jane wanted inscribed on her tombstone: "Talents too many, not enough of any." Interestingly, this complex woman became friends not only to Hemingway, but also with Pauline.[16]

Jane, Grant, and their two adopted English boys lived in Jaimanitas, the Western area of Havana near the present-day Hemingway Marina. Their two-story house stood on a large tract of land and numbering among their many possessions was a yacht. Occupied with his business, Grant left Jane to do as she wished. Grant and Jane, among others, fished with Hemingway on board Joe Russell's boat *Anita* during the last two weeks of April 1932. Pauline, who joined the group on the boat at times and then returned to Key West, did not seem to mind Hemingway's flirting with such an attractive woman, although in a letter to her husband she wrote, "Am having large nose, imperfect lips, protruding ears and warts all taken off before coming to Cuba. Thought I had better, Mrs. Mason and those Cuban women are so lovely."[17]

At this time Hemingway started making plans for his first African safari. As he worked in room 511, he heard a light constant tapping on his window. Throwing open the wooden shutters, he saw Jane standing there, having walked a two-and-a-half-foot-wide brick ledge five stories above Obispo Street to reach his room.

"Jane, my beauty! What are you up to?" Ernest asked.

"Oh, I was just in the neighborhood and thought I'd surprise you."

After climbing down into the room, Jane said, "I thought you might like to hear some of my ideas about your upcoming safari." In 2005, Hilary Hemingway, the writer's granddaughter, and photojournalist

Carlene Brennen collaborated on *Hemingway in Cuba*, with Brennen taking a photograph showing the ledge Mason allegedly traversed, illustrating that such a feat could be accomplished as long as the person was not cursed with acrophobia.[18]

When the Ambos Mundos was remodeled, the roof was made into two restaurants, one inside in case of rain, with the largest outside. When the caged elevator stops at six, visitors enter a covered vestibule where they can enter the indoor establishment or continue on and come upon an area that has a large panoramic view of Habana Vieja, far better than from room 511; this is now a regular stop for many of the guided tours of Havana. The vista takes in the cathedral, Moro Castle, located across the entrance to Havana's harbor, a large portion of Old Havana, the harbor, but also scattered in the landscape are glimpses of laundry hanging from some of the buildings, giving evidence that Habaneros do live in Old Havana, an area that the United Nations Educational, Scientific and Cultural Organization (UNESCO) has rightfully designated as a World Heritage Site. It is difficult to state whether it is best to take in this view during the brightness of a Caribbean day or in the tropical evening, but evening does seem a magical time as the sun begins to set and the vista spread out before you, resulting in an enchanting transition. The lights shining upon many of the buildings causes the structures to take on a golden hue. The observer can look out across the harbor and see Morro Castle, the fortification that has guarded Havana's harbor entrance since 1589, lit up and with a spotlight on a huge Cuban flag flying over it. Turning slightly to the right, the scene changes to the top of the golden glow of the Lonja del Comercio (former stock exchange) building, making its presence recognizable by showing off the statue of Mercury atop it. Finished with this scene, turn to the left and the twin towers of the old Cathedral will reveal the same golden aura. The newly arrived visitor cannot go wrong on the first evening in Cuba by dining in the rooftop restaurant of the Ambos Mundos. There, while gazing out over Habana Vieja with some seven-year-old Havana Club rum before and after dinner, the guest will hear the inevitable small Cuban ensemble playing the loud music they expect to hear and the musicians at their breaks attempting to tout their CDs.[19]

The person staying in the Ambos Mundos who is interested in seeing Havana without the crowds should struggle out of bed at 6:00 a.m.

and make the walk downstairs to the bar on the ground floor of the hotel and have a Café Cubano, basically a strong espresso. Cubans love to load the drink with sugar and rapidly gulp it down. If one does not care for sugar, then it is *"Café Cubano, sin azucar, por favor"* (without sugar, please). One cup will wake you up; two will clear out any remaining cobwebs. Once energized, start out the door into the nearest street, going in a different direction each day. The absence of crowds allows one to stop at various locations, especially those that have something to do with Ernest Hemingway, and spend time contemplating the location without the crush of the crowds that throng the major streets later in the day. (More on walks that feature Hemingway locations in Chapter 2.) Another interesting feature of early-morning strolling is to see modern Habaneros starting their day. For example, watch for children being escorted to school by their parents, or, if you are lucky, watch a class whose teacher has brought them outside and starting their day by saluting the flag and making recitations, while their smiling parents stand close by. One must look carefully to find the elementary and secondary schools in the Old Havana section of the city, as they seem to be located on at least the second floor of buildings and it is easy to miss the entrances. The early-hour ambles can make for a long day, but it does allow a visitor to slowly savor the city without the distraction of large crowds. Of course, these morning wanderings may be taken from almost any place one stays in Havana.

Hemingway aficionados can be excused for wanting to stay in the Ambos Mundos for the entire period in Havana, as it is an ideal location for visiting Hemingway sites or simply strolling in the old city. For variety, however, the visitor should seek out a *casa particular*, not only for variety and lower cost, but, most importantly, for a chance to get to know Cuba and its citizens better. (These establishments are also discussed in Chapter 2.) Whatever the decision, it is now time for the traveler to truly understand Earnest Hemingway in Cuba.

♦ 2 ♦

Walking in Hemingway's Old Havana

Each person who wishes to journey to Cuba to learn more about Ernest Hemingway will probably have many questions, but some will at least include the following four items. First, did the locations lead Hemingway to learn to love the country and its people? Secondly, and very important, did the locales affect his writing? Thirdly, do the locations help the visitor to understand something of Cuban history and the country's people as it did for Hemingway? Lastly, Hemingway's public persona has been that of a writer who drank too much and a womanizer prone to braggadocio. By examining the various locations in Cuba do they reinforce this stereotype?

I made a total of three visits of a little over two weeks on each trip to Cuba to attempt to answer these four questions. However, for those who have only one week in Cuba, there are three suggested must-see locations: Habana Vieja, the Museo de Ernesto Hemingway at San Francisco de Paula (Hemingway's home), on the outskirts of Havana and, finally, the village of Cojímar, approximately sixteen miles from Old Havana. Both the one-week itinerary and a longer trek are detailed. It is strongly suggested that any tracker, even one with an excellent knowledge of Spanish, obtain a combination driver/guide/interpreter and a rental car. I was fortunate to have Víctor Pina Tabío.

Once settled comfortably in Havana, the visitor may feel daunted by the population of the city of over 2.1 million people. The capital is divided into neighborhoods, such as La Habana Vieja, Centro Habana (Central Havana) and Vedado, to name but three, with Hemingway at

2. Walking in Hemingway's Old Havana 19

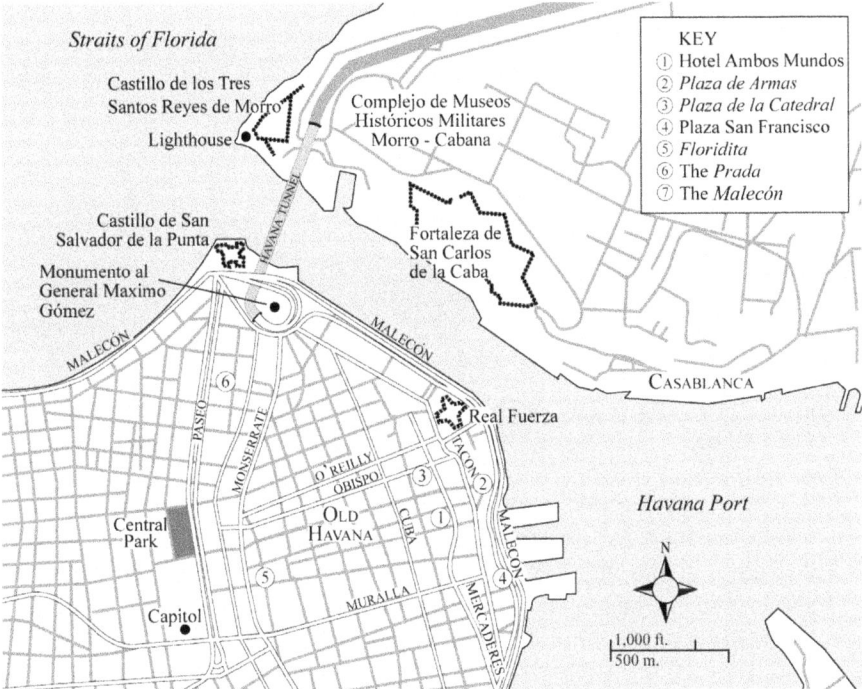

Walking tour of Ernest Hemingway in Old Havana. (Map by Tracy Ellen Smith.)

some time passing through most, if not all, of the many locations. However, within the entire metropolitan area of the city the neighborhood of Old Havana offers in one confined walking area the largest number of sites important to the writer; the Ambos Mundos is a logical starting and reference point. The entire area of La Habana Vieja can be covered easily within a day, even in the heat. If possible, the individual walks should be undertaken during the brightness of the day and repeated at night, as the different shades of light will reveal new views of the surroundings. For example, lights are trained upon the Lonja del Comercico in the Plaza de San Francisco as evening approaches and the building seems to take on a golden hue that is much different when viewed in the glare of the Caribbean sun.

The walker should begin by starting at the Obispo Street side of the Ambos Mundos (**1**) and walk eastward toward the harbor, crossing Mercaderes Street and continuing toward the general direction of the harbor. (**Bold** numbers relate to locations on the walking tour map.)

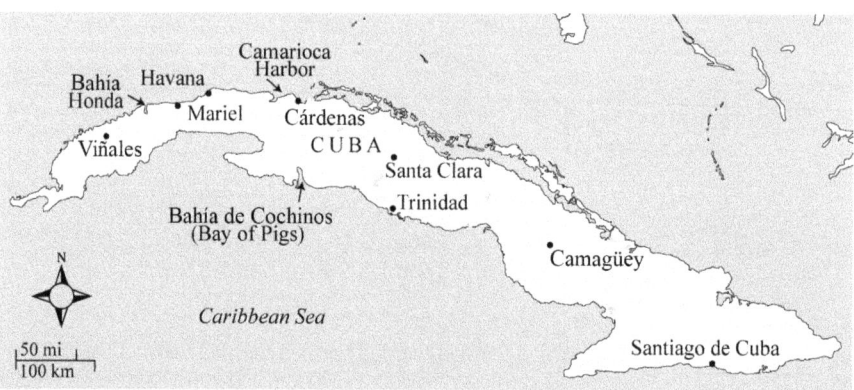

Map of Cuba with some of the locations visited by the author. (Map by Tracy Ellen Smith.)

Scattered throughout the various walks in Old Havana, the searcher will notice what appears to be cannon balls across certain streets; they designate the boundaries of a historic area where no automobiles are allowed. Continue on Obispo, and be sure to stop at a circular wooden barricade erected around a deep excavation in the street. This is not construction, but an archaeological site to illustrate the many layers of this city, founded in 1519.

Continue walking eastward on Obispo Street to the cobblestoned pavement of the Plaza de Armas (Army Square, or as it was known in early Cuba, the parade ground of the army), one of the major plazas in Old Havana that Hemingway knew very well and included in *Islands in the Stream* (**2**). Entering the plaza, the Palacio de los Capitanes Generales (Palace of the Captains General, now the Museo de la Ciudad (Museum of the City of Havana) dominates the left side of the square. The palace was occupied first by the governors from 1791 until Cuba gained independence in 1898 and, since then, has served variously as offices for United States military governors, the presidential palace for the president of the Cuban Republic, the city council and, finally in 1968, it became the City Museum. Notice that immediately in front of the building are wooden paving blocks, the type originally found in front of the palace.

This thick-walled building has columns that support an arched arcade. Upon entering, the visitor views a leafy courtyard with a statue of Christopher Columbus, surrounded by galleries on all sides containing paintings and artifacts. Just before entering the courtyard there

2. Walking in Hemingway's Old Havana   21

is a large staircase leading to the floor above that contains the ornate Salón de los Espejos (Hall of Mirrors), where the end of Spanish rule was declared in 1899. Should this be the first cultural establishment in Havana the walker visits, especially if not traveling in a tour group, there is an "interesting" feature in most, if not all, museums in the city. If you take a photograph, you are expected to give a gratuity to the nearby guard if that person is in it, with many of the guards expecting the money if you simply snap a photograph of the surroundings. Some even become very bold and upon seeing a visitor with a camera will actually approach, take your camera without asking and beckon you to a good display to pose for a picture, then indicate for you to pose in front the object, take the picture and, of course, expect the gratuity. Most take very good digital photographs.[1]

Upon leaving the palace, continue eastward down the Obispo Street side of the square toward the harbor and stop about halfway down the length of the plaza and view the large building to the right that once held the United States Embassy and Consulate. In *Islands in the Stream*, Hemingway's protagonist, Thomas Hudson, travels from his home outside of the city and checks into the embassy. (Hemingway might well approve that the building is now used as a library and also a natural history museum.) Across from this building and in the middle of the square is a well-tended garden, containing palm trees, tropical plants, a fountain, and a statue of Carlos Manuel de Céspedes (1819– 1874) who, in 1868, was elected head of the revolutionary government and later executed by the Spanish. The statue is by the Cuban sculptor Sergio López-Mesa. This green spot in the middle of so many buildings is a perfect place to take a break from the sun while looking out from the small park across Obispo Street. It is easy to imagine Thomas Hudson directing his chauffeur to pull up to the front of the embassy. Hurrying inside, Hudson signs in under the view of a "sad clerk with plucked eyebrows and a moustache across the extreme lower part of his upper lip" and then takes the elevator to the fourth floor trying to meet with the United States Marine Corps colonel attached to the embassy. It may be somewhat difficult to get an unobstructed view during the daytime, as almost all of the streets encompassing the plaza are taken up with individual used book sellers plying their wares, including other items such as former Soviet army military medals. This is yet another reason one should visit the sites at various times.[2]

After some rest and contemplation, continue on Obispo until near the eastern end of the plaza and note that the cobblestone paving now turns to flat stone pavers. Continuing onward, the street narrows and passes between two buildings, emerging onto the Avenue del Puerto (Port Avenue). From here the visitor can turn right and follow the highway that runs along the harbor until coming upon Plaza de San Francisco, another major Hemingway location. For now, the visitor will leave this for another walk, however, if one wishes to later walk along the Malacón (more on this later); it is suggested to cross Avenue del Puerto here, where there are only a few lanes of traffic than to try farther on, across multi-lanes of heavy and fast-moving traffic. When walking in Cuba do not expect drivers to give pedestrians the right of way, and keep in mind that Habaneros are much nimbler at dodging traffic than Norte Americanos.

The hiker who decides to concentrate on the Plaza de Armas should turn left where the street runs between the two buildings and begin on this side of the plaza and will pass on the right, first, the twenty-seven-room Hotel Isabel, the former 19th century home of the count of Santovenia; the ground floor has graceful windows, lined in blue. Upon entering the establishment, visitors are struck by the beauty of a formal sitting room with chandeliers. Passing the reception area, they enter a Spanish-style patio filled with plants and a fountain. Chairs and tables are scattered around the area along with a small bar, a perfect place to sit and relax after a day's walking in the heat of Havana. Just off this area is a restaurant, where one can dine inside or al fresco.

After again escaping the heat for a short period of time, travelers might exit the hotel, turn right, and continue onward and just beyond the hotel is El Templete, enclosed with a fence, where the people of Havana celebrated the first Mass in the city in the early 1500s. A ceiba tree grows near this neoclassical Doric temple and each year on the anniversary of the founding of Havana, November 16, many of the inhabitants of the city, along with visitors, walk around the tree three times, throwing coins at its roots after each turn and making a wish. It is possible that Hemingway, who harbored a number of superstitions, might at some time during his long stay in Cuba have taken part in the tradition.[3]

Near El Templete, early-morning risers enjoy ambling around the plaza and seeing the used booksellers struggling with their carts full of their wares over the cobblestones. (There is a large parking area just beyond El Templete, one of the best places to catch a taxi especially for tourists staying in this area of Old Havana.) Tourists are also likely to see a dog or two lying in the street that may, or may not, deign to lift their heads at a passerby; canines, much loved by the Habaneros, can be seen roaming freely throughout the city.

Shortly after passing the temple, turn left, away from the harbor, and continue up the last side of the Plaza de Armas, passing by the Castillo de la Real Fuerza, the "oldest extant colonial fortress in the Americas." It is from this fortress that the army troops came out to drill in what is now the plaza. A replica of the 1632 weather vane, in the shape of a woman, sits atop the west tower and is named La Giraldilla, representing Doña Inés de Bobadilla. The legend proclaims she patiently awaits her husband, Hernando de Soto, who died in his futile search in Florida for the fountain of youth.[4]

At the end of the Castillo, turn right onto Calle Tacón. This will bring travelers to the next square of interest. Depending on the time of day tourists decide to take the stroll down Tacón Street they may see men sitting around a make-shift table and hear clacking sounds. The clacking comes from players slapping down their domino tiles. Prior to 2011, nearby was a large open-air market displaying arts and crafts, but this has since been relocated to one of the large terminals along the harbor near the Plaza de San Francisco.

Now, turn left off Tacón onto Empedrado Street. A short two-block walk brings strollers out onto a plaza that has three sides containing the former homes of the upper class, now converted into museums. One of the structures has a statue of Wifredo Lam leaning against a pillar (**3**).

Wifredo Óscar de la Concepción Lam y Castilla, better known as Wifredo Lam, son of a Chinese father and a mother of mixed African-Indian-European descent, was born in 1902 in Sagua La Grande, Cuba, on December 8, 1902. The family moved to Havana in 1916, where they expected Wilfredo to study law. Instead, he chose to study at Havana's Escuela Nacional de Bellas Artes "San Alejandro" and by the early 1920s he exhibited in Havana and then moved to Madrid in 1923. There, Lam studied under Fernando Álvarez de Sotomayor y Zaragoza, the director of the Museo del Prado, who also taught Salvador Dalí.

In 1929, Lam married Eva Piriz, and the couple had one son. Tragically, Eva and the boy died of tuberculosis two years later.

By the 1930s, Lam's work showed the evidence of surrealism, inspired by the works of Henri Matisse. After viewing an exhibition of

Pablo Picasso in Madrid, he moved to Paris in 1938, and the painter encouraged him. Eventually, Lam returned to Cuba in 1941 and began to work toward preserving the African-Cuban heritage and the common man of his native land.

Lam married Helena Holzer in 1944, which ended in divorce in 1950. Ten years later he married the Swedish painter Lou Laurin; they had three sons.

Lam continued his fusing of Surrealism and Cubism, combining the spirit and forms of the Caribbean. In 1950, Lam worked with Cuban artist René Portocarrero and others in the village of Santiago de Las Vegas, some twelve miles south of Havana and near the José International Airport. Portocarrero is credited with introducing him to working in ceramics and eventually sculpture.

In 1952 Lam, who had divided his time between Cuba, New York, and France, settled in Paris. He also spent time in Italy. In 1964 he received the Guggenheim International Award. Wifredo Lam died in Paris on September 11, 1982.[5]

On the north side of the plaza is the dominating feature, a baroque cathedral known as La Catedral de la Virgen María de la Concepción Inmaculada de La Habana (Cathedral of the Virgin Mary of the Immaculate Conception of Havana). It is also known as La Catedral de San Cristóbal (The Cathedral of Saint Christopher). Work began on the church under Jesuits in 1748; the work was brought to a halt in 1767, started again in 1777, and finally consecrated in 1789.

The 18th century location was noted for its swampy condition that influenced the baroque architecture, with the cathedral asymmetric to allow the flow of water accumulating in the plaza. A light-colored façade has two towers, with the largest on the right-hand side having two levels. Bells are within each level, with the largest on the highest tower. There is a set of high, wide wooden doors at the main entrance, with two smaller doors on each side of the main entryway. A cobalt blue and red stained-glass window is above the main entry, with smaller stained-glass windows above the other doors. Noted Cuban novelist Alejo Carpentier (1904–1980) described the cathedral as "music set in stone." Unlike many cathedrals, the interior is not ornate, almost austere, but well worth a visit. Supposedly, the bones of Christopher Columbus rested within the cathedral from 1795 to 1898, when they were moved to Seville, Spain, after the Spanish–American War and Cuba's independence from Spain.[6]

For an evening stroll, whether interested in Hemingway or just wishing to take in Old Havana, tourists are encouraged to visit the Cathedral Plaza when the lights are focused on the bell towers, giving out the almost golden aura that seems to envelop the old buildings. There are some people moving through this light trying to capture the glow with their cameras, while others come and go from the Patio Restaurant, near the cathedral. The illuminated towers of the cathedral can also be viewed from the roof observation area of the Ambos Mundos. Again, early-morning risers are rewarded with the plaza all but deserted—except for the occasional policeman who sometimes talks to a sweeper, along with the ubiquitous sleeping dog nearby—that allows more time to take in the beauty of the cathedral without the crowds. With luck, guests who choose to remain longer can watch as activity in the square begins. Some Cubans start setting up tables within the paved area of the square for the nearby restaurant. A few other Cubans, both men and women, dressed in period costumes, begin their preparations for the appearance of a tourist with a camera so they can earn money for having their picture taken. (One early morning I kept my small camera out of sight and watched as two women in traditional garb, after observing El Norte Americano without a camera, turning away while discussing whether they would have better luck later in the day.)

Nearby the cathedral is the Colegio y Seminario de San Carlos (College and Seminary of San Carlos), founded by Jesuits in 1689 as a place of learning and then as a seminary in 1768. There are still students at the seminary. Another reward for early-morning risers is watching a door open in the rather austere and imposing façade of the seminary to admit a student. The outside of the building belies its interior with a cloister leading to graceful colonnaded passages on the main floors, with detailed carvings around the wooden doors and windows.[7]

When finished with visiting this plaza, return to where Empedrado Street meets the plaza, turn left, and continue a half block to La Bodeguita del Medio. This is a restaurant/bar where Hemingway supposedly commented, "My mojito in La Bodeguita; my daiquiri *in El Floridita*," with this saying, again supposedly, has his autograph on a wall in the establishment. Whether Hemingway actually said and wrote his name on the wall is almost immaterial now, for the comment has made La Bodeguita del Medio a mecca for tourist and media stars. Once finished with a mojito, or two, strollers can continue westward a half block, turn left onto Cuba Street and start southward to Obispo Street. On this route and along the right-hand side of the street is a pleasant private courtyard, full of large leafy tropical plants, a few stone benches and perhaps one can observe a cat dozing on one of the benches. Intersect Obispo, turn left and continue on to the Ambos Mundos, ending this slice of Hemingway's presence in Old Havana.

Another important plaza for Hemingway trackers begin, again, at the Ambos Mundos. This time visitors should come out of the hotel at the Obispo and Mercaderes entrance, immediately turn right onto Mercaderes, and walk a few blocks to the Plaza San Francisco (**4**). Depending on the weather, Hemingway sometimes kept his boat, *Pilar*, near the Plaza. He used this route either coming or going from the craft. Alternatively, Hemingway took Obispo through the Plaza de Armas to the Avenue del Puerto and then turned right to reach the area of the Plaza de San Francisco. No matter which route he took, the plaza was important to the writer, so much so he used it in the opening eight lines of *To Have and to Have Not*:

> You know how it is there early morning in Havana with the bums still asleep against the walls of the buildings; before even the ice wagons come by with ice for the bars? Well, we came across the square from the dock to the Pearl of San Francisco Café to get coffee and there was only one beggar awake in the square and he was getting a drink out of the fountain.

Things have changed in the more than seven decades after *To Have and to Have Not* first appeared in bookstores: the fishing docks have been replaced by a terminal for cruise ships, the Pearl of San Francisco is no longer in operation, but the main buildings around the square are still there, although used differently.[8]

This plaza, the second-oldest in Old Havana, faces the harbor and has buildings on three sides, with the fourth along the Avandia del Puerto and the ship terminal that proclaims "Terminal San Maestra San Francisco." Facing the terminal, on the right-hand side of the square, is the 16th century Basílica Menor de San Francisco de Asís. This is now used as a museum for religious objects and, because of its acoustics, is the site for classical music concerts. Next to the church is the attractive *Fuente de los Leones* (Fountain of Lions, or Lion Fountain), carved in 1836 by Italian sculptor Giuseppe Gaggini (1791–1867), who modeled it after the one in the Alhambra, in Granada, Spain, and is the fountain mentioned in the opening of *To Have and to Have Not*.

2. Walking in Hemingway's Old Havana 27

Turning right after the church, visitors can take note that the upper portion of the square is taken up largely with a hotel and the remaining side of the plaza dominated by the Lonja del Comercio, or the former stock exchange, with its statue of Mercury, the Roman god of commerce, at the top. As mentioned, the statue and part of the Lonja del Comercio are visible from the viewing terrace of the Ambos Mundos. There is an excellent restaurant, El Mercurio Café, on the ground floor of the Lonja del Comercio. It was the practice as recently as 2010–11 that female guests be given flowers by the management. There is a section for dining outside and, after finishing lunch or dinner, tourists can retrace Mercadores Street back to the Ambos Mundos.[9]

The third walk was the one most used by Hemingway. Beginning once again at the Ambos Mundos, turn left immediately upon leaving the hotel, which places visitors on the left-hand side of Obispo, walking away from the harbor. Directly across Obispo from the Ambos Mundos is one of the strangest buildings in Old Havana: someone made the decision to erect or remodel the building into a modern, glass-covered structure. The structure amid the classic architecture looks completely out of place in this barrio.

In the 1930s, Obispo Street, with its narrow sidewalks and roadway, was the shopping mecca for Habaneros; at 103, stood the Dubic Beauty Parlor, claiming the title of "the largest and oldest in Cuba." Some of the strollers along the street, however, came just to be seen in such surroundings. A 1930s travel film clearly illustrates the street crowded with many well-dressed tourists. To protect the pedestrians from the sun, canvases were stretched from the roofs of buildings across to buildings on the other side of the narrow street, providing awnings for those in the street below. In *Islands in the Stream*, Thomas Hudson recalls that this was the "street he walked down a thousand times," but he disliked riding in a car down Obispo "because it was over so quickly." Normally, Hemingway did not care to be in a car on many of the streets in Old Havana because of their narrow roadways and "because the sidewalks were too narrow" for the sheer number of people, forcing pedestrians out onto the street. Traffic is now banned from much of the roadway on Obispo and this, too, would probably please Hemingway. (I learned why Hemingway did not care to be driven in Havana's narrow streets. As a passenger in Víctor's Volkswagen "bug," and traveling nearby Neptuno Street, the crowded narrow sidewalks still force people to spill out onto the roadway. Even though Víctor drove slowly, the dodging in and out of the other fast-moving cars—there is some question as to whether most of the other Cuban drivers in Havana know what "slow" means—made the combination of the fast cars and pedestrians an "interesting" ride.)[10]

Continuing on Obispo and after crossing Cuba Street, on the right hand side of Obispo is the Florida Hotel, once a 17th century mansion. If the sun becomes too much and amblers again wish to escape the heat and noise of the street, a good diversion is to go into the hotel. Upon entering, there is a checkerboard-designed marble floor, a small statue, and, beyond the reception desk, a quiet patio surrounded with large stone columns and arches. Taken all together, the ground floor of the hotel offers a cool, tranquil respite from the hustle and bustle of the road. Rested, searchers for Hemingway sites can now return to busy Obispo Street.

During Ernest Hemingway's period of off-and-on living in the Ambos Mundos, from 1932 to 1940, well-dressed Cubans shoppers along Obispo Street beheld a strange sight: a tall well-built Norte Americano departing the Ambos Mundos, usually with newspapers (obtained from the front desk) tucked under his arm, strolling westward along the left-hand side of the street. Unlike most people ambling along the popular shopping way, Hemingway wore a cotton shirt, usually untucked, and moccasins with no socks; dapper Cubans also noted his well-worn khaki shorts. The American writer's destination was the seafood restaurant and bar, Floridita. It would take approximately fifteen minutes to arrive at his destination, unless one block prior to entering the Floridita he stopped at a large Art Deco building whose carved stone sign above the entrance proclaimed La Moderna Poesía (Modern Poetry). The bookstore had window displays of volumes allowing shoppers on Obispo and Bernaza streets to think about the many books awaiting them within the large shop. The shop is still in its location with the same sign. Inside, the shelves no longer have the large volume of books they had in Hemingway's days, but the modern visitor can see why Papa would want to come inside and browse.[11]

Hemingway continued his walk over the cross street of Bernaza and, within a few strides, entered the Floridita at the corner of Obispo and Monserrate streets. The seafood restaurant-bar opened in 1817 under the name La Piña de Plata (The Silver Pineapple). In the years from 1898–1902, the name changed to La Floridita, to reflect the number and influence of Americans, but by the time Hemingway sat at the far left-hand side of the bar, the name had changed to simply Floridita. In the 1930s, like many establishments in Old Havana, the bar had large doors with metal shutters on them that were rolled up each morning, allowing the patrons in the bar to feel as if they were sitting out in the street. A nearby bar, the Pan American, opened either in 1948 or 1949 and had air-conditioning installed, causing many customers to leave the Floridita for the coolness of the Pan American. Hemingway, however, remained loyal to the Floridita, which eventually did install air-conditioning. The coolness, however, brought with it regular walls around the bar and it no longer feels as if one is in the street. With the press of modern-day tourists in the Floridita's bar (5), however, it is sometimes difficult to notice the air-conditioning.[12]

Constantino Ribalaigua began as the Floridita's barman in 1914 and became a master of his trade. He is credited with inventing at least 150 drinks, although he laid claim to the Daiquiri; the Floridita nevertheless is called La Cuna del Daiquiri (the cradle of the Daiquiri). Hemingway is credited with inventing the Daiquiri Special, also known as the Papa Double or Hemingway Special. The difference being it contains no sugar and is usually served as a double; his drinking of these is legendary. A Cuban writer once observed when Hemingway and Ribalaigua died, the Floridita was never the same.[13]

Drinking was not the only reason the Floridita was Hemingway's favorite watering hole. Over the years, the bar became a gathering place for politicians, merchants, and others of the leading people in Cuban society. Though the management did not care to mention this, it also had among its clientele prostitutes. Hemingway, as was his wont, continued gathering material for his writing and learning about Cuba and the Cubans by closely observing the people within the Floridita. The best example of how the writer's time in the Floridita helped him is the story of Leopoldina Rodríguez, who became Hemingway's "longtime friend, confidante and, in all likelihood, his lover." In addition, she became a model for Lucky Lil in *Islands in the Stream*. She frequented the Floridita for over twenty years and, because of her relationship with Hemingway, was "the only woman allowed to enter the Floridita without an escort." Prof. Andrew Feldman, in his study of Rodríguez, writes that this made her "neither a Floridita barfly nor Hemingway's would-be mistress." Instead, she proved to be a "complex woman with her own history and desires."[14]

Leopoldina Rodríguez was the daughter of a maid to the prosperous Pedrosos family who lived near Havana's Plaza de la Catedral. Known to some as "Leo," she had olive-colored skin, dark hair, and did not care for unkind words or actions. One Cuban man said it was "difficult to take one's eyes off of her." Her mother's position allowed her to know and understand the social ways of the upper class of Cuba, which gave her entry into the mores of this class at the turn of the 20th century. Leo's greatest disadvantage was her race; she was of mixed Asian-African heritage. The only chance for a young woman of beauty from the lower class was to "try her luck" with a wealthy man. She succeeded and soon had a son by Alberto Barraque who, perhaps because of her race, did not marry her. He did take her to Europe with him and, while there, the two had a falling out and went their separate ways. But she kept the Barraque name to help her son in Cuban society.[15]

Rodríguez did not immediately return to Cuba. She developed a relationship with José Antonio Primo de Rivera, a Falangist leader executed by Franco in 1936 as a traitor to the Spanish republic. Rivera left Rodríguez enough money to return to Cuba and, with the remaining funds, opened a dress boutique. Like many other small businesses during the depression, the boutique failed. This caused her to start frequenting the Floridita, where she met Hemingway. Feldman, however, writes that there is some evidence that Hemingway may have met Leopoldina in Spain before Rivera's execution and also some evidence she may well have been in Paris as Mary Hemingway (the fourth wife); in her memoir, *How It Was*, Mary mentions that she and Leopoldina had a conversation about the City of Light while in Paris. In any case, Leopoldina Rodríguez and Ernest Hemingway entered into a long friendship.[16]

No matter when Hemingway met Rodríguez, there is no question of his more than two decades of relationship with her, as she is mentioned in his letters. In October 4, 1949, Hemingway wrote to Charles Scribner, his publisher, that Rodríguez was his age and he had known her since she "was a kid" in Spain. Hemingway told Scribner he received the Cuban "local gossip" from her. The few Cubans who have been interviewed about Hemingway have spoken about Leo. Most importantly, however, Rodríguez's niece, the Cuban writer Ilse Bulit, lived in an apartment with her aunt from the 1940s to the 1950s. She informed Feldman that Hemingway gave Rodríguez an allowance and paid for the apartment. By the mid–1950s Leopoldina Rodríguez was diagnosed with terminal cancer and died in 1956 in the apartment Hemingway had rented for her. Hemingway paid her hospital bills during her long illness; he later paid for her funeral, which he personally attended.

One of the most important features of the Leopoldina Rodríguez and Ernest Hemingway relationship is not necessarily whether they were intimate, but, as Feldman writes, "Leopoldina was a resource concerning all things Cuban." She introduced him to Santería, an African-Cuban religion and informed Hemingway of the political and business people she knew and the customs of Cuba. Ernest Hemingway used all this in his writing.[17]

By the 1940s, because of Hemingway's fame, many celebrities visiting Havana made the Floridita a must-see, and a be-seen-at, stopping point. Into the 21st century, the bar continues as a major stop for tourists in Havana. (I visited the Floridita only once because of the crowds. However, my visit was shortly after noon and I decided to try the restaurant located to the right of the bar area. I asked to be seated away from the bar and found it much quieter. There were few patrons dining, the food was good, and although the prices were what one would expect from any major tourist location, the service was outstanding.)

Hemingway, still on Obispo, at times followed a walk that takes in some other places close to Old Havana. One block past the Floridita, still moving away from the harbor, places the walker at Agramonte Street, bordering Parque Central (Central Park). The park was begun in 1836 and finished in 1877; the trees and palm trees provide a restful place amid the cityscape.

Turn left at Agramonte Street, walk one block and then turn right onto Obrapia Street and then in another block once again turn right onto Paso de Martí. Stop here and observe to the left El Capitolio (the Capitol) building. First opened in 1929, it is the result of various Cuban architects and a close replica of the United States Capitol building in Washington, D.C. After the 1959 revolution, it became the headquarters of the Cuban Academy of Science. The building and grounds are well preserved and tended, while the ornate interior is well worth a visit. The entire area surrounding El Capitolio is usually crowded with tourists from other countries and with Cubans from the provinces. For the visitor who is interested in Hemingway, but who is also anxiously looking for the vintage cars for which Cuba is noted, the area around the capital is a very good location to see various makes and models, with many of these immaculate automobiles used to squire tourists around the city.[18]

Travelers should be aware that photographs of fine-looking 1950s cars may not be authentic. One of the things many Cubans who own such vehicles do is put in a diesel engine. Because of the difficulty of obtaining parts, Víctor once said you almost had to "pass a special training course to understand the cars in Cuba." He said a friend of his had a fuel pump in his car modified from an MiG-15 Soviet jet. (Víctor's field of study is in aviation.) Víctor's own car is a 1959 Volkswagen "bug" body that has been changed at least three times, once as a convertible, but then a regular top from another Volkswagen replaced it.

After viewing the Capitol and the vintage cars, cross over Paso de Martí, turn right, and start down this block. On the left is the Gran Teatro de la Habana (Great Theater of Havana). When built in 1917 as the Central Gallego it was considered the most expensive building ever constructed in Cuba. Today, the "neo-Baroque design has decorative touches to its balconies, windows, cornices, and even on the towers" and is the home of the Cuban National Ballet, whose theater sees many performances and with some of the company's dancers performing in "prestigious European and American companies."[19]

Continuing on, within a short distance the walker will see two short statues of lions marking the entry onto a broad marble walkway, known either as the *Prado* or *Paseo*. Trees and stone benches are at regular intervals and give much appreciated shade and rest in the urban environment (**6**). If the stroller wishes short trips away from the Prado, within a block or two off to the right of the walk are a number of sights, including the Museo Nacional de Bellas Artes (National Museum of Fine Art). There is no doubt Hemingway found this marble walkway a pleasant place, as there is a photograph in the Hemingway Collection at the John F. Kennedy Library showing a young Hemingway and his second wife, Paula, at an outdoor café on the Prado. The pleasant walkway continues until it intersects with a multi-lane highway. At this juncture, the person interested in Hemingway can view, across the traffic to the Castillo de San Salvador de Punta and across the entrance to Havana's harbor, the Castillo de los Tres Santos Reyes del Morro, better known as El Morro, and, for those who love lighthouses, the light at the entrance to the harbor is clearly seen. (The Prado is this writer's favorite walk in Old Havana as one sees as many Cubans strolling it as tourists. It is a fine way to have a leisurely walk, even on a hot day.)

This concludes the third important walk in Old Havana for those who wish to track Hemingway. However, if the walker wishes a good side trip, *carefully* cross the highway, keeping in mind all the while that pedestrians do not have the right of way. For the wary visitor, an easier way across this multi-lane highway of fast-moving cars is, as mentioned earlier, to retrace Obispo Street back to where it crosses the Avenue Del Puerto by the Plaza de Armas; there, the roadway narrows to just a few lanes and is not as hectic. No matter which way one negotiates to the other side of the roadway, the walker is now on a broad walkway that begins near the entrance to Havana's harbor and then along the Straits of Florida for a total distance of approximately seven kilometers (4¼ miles) and is known as El Malecón. It is a favorite gathering place of Habaneros and tourists.[20]

Near the mouth of the harbor is a huge statue of General Máximo Gómez (1836–1905). Born November 18, 1836, in the Dominican Republic, he trained as a Spanish cavalry officer and, after retiring from the Spanish Army, moved his family to Cuba. Gómez then took up the cause of the Cubans who wished to throw off the rule of Spain and helped form the Cuban army, eventually becoming its general. After Cuban independence in 1898, General Gómez retired, refusing to accept the presidential nomination in 1901, and died at his villa in Cuba four years later. The statue dates from 1935 and is the work of the Italian sculptor Aldo Gamba. Many visitors who venture to the famous Havana Tropicana cabaret in Havana will notice a large fountain, also by Gamba, entitled *La Fuente de las Musas* (Muses' Fountain), also known as *La Danza de las Horas* (The Dance of the Hours). The large fountain has the statues of eight nude women, holding hands and gracefully dancing along the rim. It was formerly located outside the National Casino, but by 1953 was purchased by the owner of the Tropicana. Unfortunately, the sculptor's history once he returned to Italy is unknown.[21]

Once past the statue of General Gómez, El Malecón stretches westward. The U.S. Army began building a seawall in 1901 and the Cubans finished it in 1952; upon this structure is the Malecón that Habaneros flock to at all times of the day to fish, swim, dance, and enjoy romantic evenings in the cooling breezes. Across the roadway, prior to the 1959 revolution, many wealthy Cubans had large homes facing the Malecón, some approaching mansions, that have fallen into disrepair (7).

The years have taken their toll on Obispo Street. In recent years, however, it has again become crowded, mostly with tourists. Many of the former shops along Obispo now sell trinkets or have restaurants with bands that seem to be constantly sending out the loud strains of "Guantanamera." For those who love the rhythms of Cuban music, the loudness is a free way of hearing it while strolling along the streets throughout the city, but in my travels within Havana I met some Cubans who complained about always hearing the loud tunes and who much preferred classical music, preferably enjoying it within the good acoustics of the Basílica Menor de San Francisco de Asís in the Plaza de San Francisco, or at least hearing a CD containing Cuban pianist Enrique Chia playing the work of Cuban composer Ernesto Lecuona (1895–1963). As of 2011 there were still three large establishments on Obispo Street in operation from Hemingway's day, the Ambos Mundos, the Floridita and La Moderna Poesía.

Habaneros do live in the area of Obispo Street. I once observed children playing and had a soccer ball fly past me as I walked down the crowded street, followed closely by a small boy running in pursuit of the ball, with his mother shouting, no doubt for my benefit, "You almost hit that tourist."

The years also have not been kind to O'Reilly Street, one block from Obispo. Prior to 1959 it also had a good reputation for shopping that changed until it became the street to search for used books. Even that reputation is now a thing of the past and, compared to Obispo, seems almost deserted. This lack of traffic makes it a relatively quick passage by car through Old Havana.

Even if visitors' time is limited when searching out Hemingway's haunts, it is vital that they have access to a guide with a proficiency for Spanish and a knowledge of the area. Such a guide can offer unique opportunities to individually sample Cuba without being part of a large group. Ideally, a schedule can include a walking tour in the morning, then after lunch, a change of pace. Hemingway did appreciate the culture and people of Cuba and the guide can help glimpse this aspect of the country by introducing some of the writers and artists who congregate in the afternoon.

How I usually spend afternoons in Habana with Víctor is an example of what can be accomplished. Víctor knew Pablo Armándo Fernández, the "premier poet of Cuba," and arranged for a meeting. Fernández

2. Walking in Hemingway's Old Havana

Major Cuban poet Pablo Armando Fernández at his home in Havana signing a book for a visitor. A very small portion of his art collection is shown on walls in the left background. (Photograph by Yvonne Love.)

was born in 1929 or 1930 in Central Delicias, Oriente Province, in the eastern portion of Cuba and lived in the United States from 1945 to 1959 and while there attended Columbia University. Upon his return to his native country, Fernández held a number of literary positions and eventually served as the Cultural Attaché in the Cuban Embassy in London. He has received the National Prize for Literature, Cuba's literary award. Fernández is also an essayist, novelist and playwright.[22]

Upon entering Fernández's home, one is offered the inevitably strong Cuban coffee and the talk soon turns to poetry and Hemingway. Despite the interesting conversation, any visitor's eyes will be averted by the modern art collection adorning the walls of Pablo's home. Yvonne Love, Assistant Professor of Art at Penn State Abington College, remarked that the art "rivaled the breadth of the collection of contemporary art" at the Museo Nacional de Bellas Artes. Love also "likened the space to that of the Barnes Foundation in Philadelphia."

Some of the works on display are by such renowned Cuban artists as Wifredo Lam, Manuel Mendive, and Roberto Fabelo.[23]

On another afternoon visit, Víctor drove to the Jaimanitas section of Havana. The first thing I noticed is what appear to be Picasso-type of ceramic standing above the rooftops. As Víctor's Volkswagen drew closer, I got the distinct impression that most of the houses along the street seemed to have been decorated by Picasso. This was a signal that we would soon be arriving at the home of José Rodríguez Fuster, known to his fellow Cubans simply as "Fuster." Born in Villa Clara in 1946, he studied at the Art Instructors School from 1963 to 1965 and began working as a ceramist at the Cubanacan Ceramics Workshop in Havana in 1966. After decorating his own house, he began working on his neighbor's homes and expanded from there. Fuster has been dubbed the "Picasso of the Caribbean." As will be shown in Chapter 3, Hemingway also enjoyed and collected art; whereas the majority of his collection was European in nature, he did have at least one piece representing Cuba.[24]

Víctor introduced me to other interesting artists as well, including Jacqueline and Yamilys Brito, sisters whose homes are near each other in the Vedado section of Havana. Jacqueline paints and works in mixed media while Yamilys works in prints, mostly monotypes and collages, along with pen and ink drawings. Both sisters have been artists since childhood, graduating from the San Alejandro Art Academy and from the Instituto Superior de Art in Havana (ISA); both now teach at the ISA. Their works are exhibited in museums in Europe and the United States. Víctor arranged for me to visit with Jacqueline, whose home has a hallway decorated with wonderful tiles rescued from crumbling buildings.

Víctor later arranged for me to view the work of Sandra Dooley. Approaching her home in the Santa Fe section of Havana—bordered on the north by the Florida Strait—I was immediately struck by the works of art decorating the house's entranceway. Sandra Dooley was born in Havana in 1964; at the age of thirty-six she taught herself to paint by studying the works of Picasso, Chagall, and Matisse. She began working with oils and now incorporates oil pastels and uses fabrics in her mixed-media works. She has said that she would be lost were it not for her painting. Sandra enjoys her dogs and cats and images of them are in some of her works, such as *Sombrero Mel* (Mel as a Hat), Mel being her cat.

2. Walking in Hemingway's Old Havana

With another friend in Cuba I located a painter, Maria Del Rosario Rodríguez, known as "Charo," whose mixed media of acrylics and pastels are combined with native plants of Cuba, producing striking results. I visited her home, where I also met her husband, who doubles as her agent. When I asked permission to photograph the couple, Charo insisted that their small dog also appear in the shot.

On another occasion, Víctor took me to the home of Marta Ximeno, an ethnologist who has done in-depth research about Afro-Cuban religions. She also worked for the National Library and writes children's books; at one time she even had a radio program geared for children. During our conversation, she suggested that I study the sugar cane mills of Cuba and their impact on Afro-Cuban culture. I recall how small she seemed when she introduced me to her husband, Reinaldo López, an artist who was then preparing his work for a show. Reinaldo admitted that it was difficult at first to make a living with his art, so he became an interior designer to make ends meet. After 1959, Fidel Castro's executive secretary grew to love Reinaldo's work and asked that he undertake some important projects, one being the design for the national zoo's lion sanctuary; this closely resembles their habitat without having to put the animals in a cage. Reinaldo and a group of others were sent to different countries to see how they achieved various techniques for housing zoo animals. Their son, David, is a lawyer who enjoys poetry and jazz; he is the author of a book of poetry entitled *New York Jazz*. Sadly, Reinaldo passed away in 2014.[25]

Víctor arranged a luncheon for me to meet Marta Rojas, a journalist and novelist described as a "living legend" in Cuba. Rojas, with her large, captivating smile and sparkling eyes, spoke eloquently of Hemingway and her own career. Born in Santiago de Cuba, Marta, a tailor's daughter, at first wanted to study medicine. After traveling to Havana, she changed her major and obtained a degree in journalism. On July 23, 1953, Rojas arrived in her hometown to cover a carnival. Events of the following day were to change her life.

On July 24, Castro and his followers attacked Moncada Barracks in Santiago, beginning the revolution. Marta Rojas proved to be the right person, in the right place at the right time, to document the events. Her fame grew as she covered the Vietnam War, spending the years 1965–1975 interviewing people on the conflict. The petite Marta smiled when she related having to delay traveling into Hanoi because of heavy bombing by United States aircraft. She eventually switched to writing historical fiction and enjoys the research required in this endeavor. The long lunch went well, and the conversation continued back at her apartment, where I was fortunate enough to obtain a signed copy of two of her works, *El Equipaje Amarillo* (The Yellow Suitcase) and *Holy Lust*, the latter an English translation.[26]

One of the more interesting interviews Víctor arranged was with Guy Marinez García. Although neither an artist nor a writer, García had held a number of important positions over the years, including being head of the Central Metrology Labs (science of measurement) of the Armed Forces. After recovering from a stroke, he attended Havana University and became an attorney. Guy had also worked in the tourist trade along the North Shore and at the Cayo Santa María and might have known something about Hemingway in that area. (More on traveling to the north coast in Chapter 5.) I visited with Guy and his wife, Judith, at their home. As it turned out, Guy said he had no information regarding Hemingway, although he and his family were fascinating nevertheless. During our conversation, Guy and Judith tried to get their very young daughter, Camila, to introduce herself to me. Quite naturally, she was shy at approaching a stranger who had a beard and did not even speak her language. She kept very close to her mother and father, all the while eyeing me with suspicion. Guy, Judith, and Víctor all tried telling her I came from far away and lived on the West Coast, in the United States. This American connection, for some reason, made the girl think I was acquainted with Mickey Mouse. I could mark just when she hit upon this notion, for she began bringing all her toys from another room for me to examine. Camila had a small toy telephone and wanted me to call Mickey Mouse and talk to him. I did this and told Mickey about my new friend and how Camila was a good girl. Her parents and Víctor translated all this to Camila and she stood next to me until I departed. Later, I managed to have Víctor present her with a Minnie Mouse doll; a photograph was taken, documenting the moment for me. I later learned she entered a dance school.

After our visit, Guy, Víctor, and I went to lunch at a paladar located in the Jaimanitas neighborhood of Havana. The dining area is at the end of a long backyard of a private home and the area overlooks one of the waterways entering the Hemingway Marina. I recall Guy's large smile and he seemed to be a person who loved a good joke. Although I gained no new information on Hemingway, I came to the important conclusion that one of the reasons Hemingway loved Cuba was because of such families. I was saddened to learn of Guy's passing in 2014.[27]

After spending an afternoon with Cubans who work in the arts or might know about Hemingway, the traveler can have a leisurely dinner and then experience any of the earlier Hemingway walks in the evening's light. Or, rest up a bit from the morning and afternoon pursuits, then take the walk as the evening approaches and have dinner much later. All of this will make for a full and pleasant day while learning more about Hemingway in Cuba.

While in Old Havana the visitor should also make some time away from pursuing Hemingway, plus meeting artists and writers and randomly pick a street and see where it leads. One may come upon a block in sad shape. In Central Havana, for example, the fourth edition of *Frommer's Cuba* goes so far as to state, "I cannot stress enough the level of decay and decomposition here. Balconies, crown molding, and other large chunks of brick, mortar, and stone regularly drop off buildings here, sometime injuring passersby below." However, the next street might reveal an excellent example of colonial architecture which has been well maintained. By taking the time to leave the heavy tourist areas of the city, the experience can reinforce UNESCO's report when it discusses Old Havana as retaining "an interesting mix of Baroque and neoclassical monuments, and a homogeneous ensemble of private houses with arcades, balconies, wrought-iron gates and internal courtyards." One of the easiest recognizable features of Cuban architecture are the many buildings with colonnades that support a covered walkway for protection from both the sun and rain, leading Alejo Carpentier to dub Havana the "city of columns."[28]

There are also hidden gems of historic interest to discover. After exploring Plaza de San Francisco, for instance, walk a few blocks south on Oficios Street to the Casa Alejandro de Humboldt (House of Alexander von Humboldt) at 254 Oficios and Muralla streets. The early 19th century home was used by the Prussian Friedrich Wilhelm Heinrich Alexander von Humboldt (1769–1859), better known in the United States as Alexander von Humboldt or Baron von Humboldt. Humboldt was a naturalist, astronomer, geographer, geologist, botanist, linguist, artist, and authority on Indian antiquities. He is noted for his travels in Latin American between 1799–1804 that led to the first modern scientific description of the region. The polymath's work resulted in twenty-nine "lavish folio editions" that took from 1805–1834 to complete. Humboldt stopped in Cuba both to and from South America for several months and proclaimed Havana "one of the most pleasant and picturesque ports in tropical America." The house in which Humboldt resided during his Cuban days is now a museum in his honor, featuring exhibits of natural history and the environment. I was lucky that my visit corresponded with a class being held in an upper room in the museum, and watched as a group of Cuban children had a hands-on experience in one of the natural sciences.[29]

While a visitor—unlike Hemingway—may not have years in which to learn about Cuba and its citizens, there are some additional opportunities to gain a glimpse of those residing on this island country. One way, as mentioned earlier, is to employ a good guide for introductions to people in the arts. Another excellent method is to live with a Cuban family. The visitor interested in tracking Hemingway should spend one to two days at the Ambos Mundos, but then move to a casa particulare. The State allows some Cubans to rent out rooms to tourists, not unlike the U.S.'s bed and breakfast inns. A guide can recommend a suitable location; in the absence of a guide there are a number of reputable establishments listed in any good guidebook to Cuba; the Internet, too, advertises numerous listings. Casa particulares range from a simple room in a small apartment to a room in a large colonial building. A good example is Casa Particulare Ana Morales on busy Neptuno Street in Central Havana, the home of Ana and Idalberto. Idalberto, a retired air-traffic controller, has an excellent command of English, and Ana keeps the casa spotless and provides huge breakfasts. The establishment is on the second floor, which dictates that the visitor arrives at a locked door on the street, rings a buzzer next to the address, steps back, turns to the right and looks up at a balcony overlooking the street. Soon the guest sees either Ana or Idalberto, who, with welcoming smiles, look downward and lower a long twine with the key to the door. There is a short entranceway, and the visitor must negotiate a narrow stairway to reach their destination. If there are problems with bringing up luggage, Idalberto will find someone to help.

The casa has two bedrooms, the largest having a balcony overlooking the street. There is a common room with a checkered floor and a shuttered door leading to another balcony. This provides a fine vantage spot from which to observe busy Neptuno Street as Cubans

2. Walking in Hemingway's Old Havana

go about the bustle of their everyday life. The location of the casa is close to the Prada, the Floridita, and within reasonable walking distance to all the routes taken by Hemingway in Old Havana.

Busy Neptuno Street illustrates one of the problems for Cubans not only in Havana, but also throughout Cuba, especially in the rural areas. The researcher in Cuba who arranges to meet a Cuban in Havana will usually eventually hear something like "transportation is the name of the game" for those who do not have cars, which is the majority of people. If a visitor has a guide with a car to see all sections of the city, the passenger quickly observes long lines of people waiting for buses already crammed to beyond capacity. At most bus stops there are some people standing on line with their arms extended, signaling that they would be willing to pay for a ride with a car-owning local. One time, Víctor and I were returning from a location on the far side of Havana. We saw two police officers in their car stopped at a light; they were observing a woman wearing a hospital's nurse uniform. One of the officers left the squad car to approach. After a brief conversation with her, the officer directed his attention to the cars waiting in line. The officer stopped for a brief time at one car and then turned to the nurse and waved her over to the car, where she got into the automobile. The officer then waved traffic onward and returned to his car. Víctor said, "Let me explain what just happened." As Víctor related, transportation is so difficult in Cuba that, many times, when a traffic cop spots hospital workers on foot, they are stopped and asked which hospital they are on their way to. The officer will then go to the line of cars and see if there is anyone driving in that direction. Once finding someone who is, providing there is room in the vehicle, the officer "suggests" the driver take the hospital worker along.

Visitors to Cuba encounter some of the friendliest people in the Caribbean region. After more than a half-century of the United States' embargo of Cuba, the few American tourists might expect to be met with resentment by the locals. In my own experience, the first reaction I received when mentioning my home country was a large smile. In almost every line I stood in, whether in Havana or surrounding cities, locals insisted that I—El Norte Americano—move to the front. While there are undoubtedly Cubans who harbor resentment toward Americans, it is a rare experience to meet one.

One of the best examples of how Cubans have managed to accom-

A self-help project with scrap lumber, labor, and funds provided by the residents in one of the areas of Havana to help the children of the barrio appreciate art. The children painted the outside of the building. Their sign says, "Community workshop / coloring my neighborhood." (Photograph by the author.)

plish much with little involves an accomplished artist by the name of Jorge Jorge. It was his desire to teach children in his barrio to learn something about art. Much of the neighborhood in question contains many dreary looking Soviet-style cement apartment buildings. Jorge found an unused plot of land used as a public dumping place and began cleaning it up. Soon neighbors started helping. The artist and his neighbors found lumber and other building materials and on their own constructed a building. From other materials, they handcrafted desks and tables. Jorge then began to instill in the barrio's children an appreciation of art. He had the children decorate the outside of the structure in the colorful Cuban style with the words: "*Taller Comunitario/Coloreando Mi Barrio.*" ("Community Workshop/Coloring My Neighborhood.")[30]

If trackers of Hemingway have only a week or so to spend in Cuba, they would be well served to pay a visit to the Sierra del Rosario, outside of Havana, in the western province of Pinar del Río. The area is noted for its beautiful natural surroundings that provide a glimpse of the grandeur of some of Cuba's countryside. With the proper guide, one can gain a greater appreciation of the artistic culture of the island. The drive to this scenic spot is approximately an hour from Havana on a good motorway. There is another route nearer the water, but it is a slow, two-lane road used mostly for locals and the transporting of agricultural products.

The first location on this trip outside of Havana should be to the area of the Reserva de la Biosfera Sierra del Rosario (The Biosphere Reserve of the Sierra del Rosario) that UNESCO entered onto their listings in 1985. The biosphere covers 26,686 hectares (65,942 acres), with heights between 50 to 550 meters (164 to 1,804 feet). Avid bird watchers will note there are ninety-eight species of birds, including eleven of Cuba's twenty-four endemic species. At a higher elevation is one of the few places you can view both the north and south coasts of Cuba. When this tracker visited the area, there were few trails available for individual hiking, but some may be available to reserved groups. Within this same general area, ecotourism has been developed with the focus on two locations: Soroa and Las Terrazas.

Víctor told me when he was young his parents and uncle toured Soroa. Within the area, they visited a small waterfall after climbing "400 meters of stairs (1,312 feet)" to reach the *Cascadas El Salto* (the jump waterfall), with the waters having "medicinal properties." If you climb to the top of the falls you may see a rainbow in the mists, thus giving the area its name, the "rainbow of Cuba."

There are approximately six thousand Cubans who live within the biosphere that work with handicrafts, agriculture, raising cattle, and reforestation. Another interesting aspect of the area of the preserve centers on coffee. It was the site of the first major coffee plantation in the New World. There are still some ruins and some restored 19th century machinery for coffee making. A few small farms still produce shade-grown coffee.

Soroa is named for a Frenchman, Jean Paul Soroa, who established "a coffee plantation two centuries ago" in the area. For those with more time, an ecotourism hotel and a restaurant are within this area of the preserve.

Again, if on a tight schedule it is highly recommended the tracker go directly to the orchid garden of Soroa. Look for the sign reading

"Orquideario de Soroa." Developed by a Spaniard, Tomás Felipe Camacho, who built a house on the nearby hill and wanted an orchid garden to have flowers alongside the hillside. In 1943, he created the garden area covering three hectares (seven acres). The garden thrives in the humid climate and contains over 700 species, with 250 of them indigenous to Cuba. A trail allows hikers to pass through large leafy plants, all the while looking for many of the elegant yet delicate orchids. One native to Cuba is the little *Bletia purpurea*, the symbol of the preserve. There is an entry fee and guided tours are available. There is a breathtaking view of the garden and the heavily forested mountains, with the occasional trunk of a Royal Palm tree adding touches of white to the greenery. When Víctor and I toured the area, there was only one other couple in sight. Since then, there is evidence that regular bus tours now visit the garden.

Located close to the orchid garden is Las Terrazas (The Terraces), which should be on any tracker's itinerary. Arriving near a lake, one need only look upward from this entranceway to see the terraces on a nearby hill with houses built in a 1971 social project. These white, tile-roofed homes are tucked in among tropical plants and a smattering of magnificent Royal Palm trees towering over everything. The residents have sensational views of the water and the forested mountains, with many of the people living in Las Terrazas and working within the preserve. There are also some noted artists in the vicinity, including Jorge Pérez Duporte, who is known for doing detailed paintings of Cuba's flora and has also worked in stained glass. Víctor arranged for me to meet Jorge at his studio-home, high on a hill. I still recall being drawn to a very large window where a drafting table and the materials for Jorge's work stood nearby. Jorge is probably used to people admiring the vista. In the background was the distinctive sound of Louis Armstrong's singing. The song being played, if memory serves, was Steve Goodman's "City of New Orleans." I told Jorge that while I like this version I thought Judy Collins's was the one I enjoyed more. I am not sure if he had heard of Collins, so I recommended a CD to him.

Once through taking in the view and discussing music, Jorge showed me some of his detailed paintings. I am not sure his depictions of Cuba's flora are well known in the United States, but they should be. His works are in a number of other countries and "in 1998, he painted 'Flos Passionis' for Pope John Paul II." Just before our departure, he offered to autograph one of the books featuring his art, *La Flora de Este Reino*

2. Walking in Hemingway's Old Havana 45

(The Flora of This Kingdom). Jorge seemed to take a little extra time with inscribing the book to me. When he handed it to me, I was delighted (and grateful) to see that he had made a quick sketch of some nearby flowering plants. Before departing, I once again looked out at that view and thought how wonderful it would be to have a writing studio and home here, but I wondered if I would get any work done with such a landscape spread out before me.

Víctor then took me to La Casa del Campesino (The House of the Farmer), a restaurant in Las Terrazas, not far from Jorge Duporte's home. The establishment, which was open on both sides, had a long traditional thatched roof made of Royal Palm fronds. A band and two older male singers were belting out traditional Cuban folk songs. Víctor pointed out a man from the United States who was the scion of a family who had a very large cattle business in Cuba before the Revolution that, along with other businesses, was nationalized after the new government was established. This man was now looking into the possibility of establishing a cattle business in Cuba, but was finding problems with the restrictions imposed by the embargo. After lunch, we departed for Havana.[31]

If the Hemingway tracker leaves Havana early in the morning, this is the ideal time to see the Orchid Garden and perhaps the waterfall, plus a trip to Las Terrazas and, if you have a guide, arrange a meeting with Jorge Pérez Duporte. Returning to Havana at a reasonable hour, one can enjoy lunch while reflecting on the memories of the beauty of one area of Cuba.

Ernest Hemingway's great love of Cuba, according to Gabriel García Márquez, the Colombian Nobel Prize winner for Literature in 1982, did not spring into existence at first sight but evolved as "a slow, arduous process." This "process" began taking place as Hemingway strolled down Obispo and O'Reilly streets, along the Prado, that marbled, tree-lined walkway near the Floridita, plus the other streets and plazas in Havana. Hemingway absorbed the sights, the smells, and the sounds of the city. While the years have not been kind to Obispo and O'Reilly streets, one can still feel the life and vitality in the crowded streets of Havana that make it a living, breathing siren. Havana's siren song: come, enjoy, and stay. Ernest Hemingway responded.[32]

◆ 3 ◆

Finca Vigía

After spending three or four days tracking Ernest Hemingway in Havana, the tracker should now travel to the next must-see site on anyone's time in Cuba. This entails an excursion outside the core of Havana to San Francisco de Paula. Within the confines of this village is located the second of the three most important Hemingway sites: Finca Vigía, the writer's home. The easiest way to make the short jaunt is by having the tour services of a major hotel arrange for the transportation, or enlist a guide who has a car. There is a possibility of hiring a taxi to and from the location or with public transportation, but, as previously mentioned, the latter method is a difficult means of travel in Havana.

In 1936, while Ernest Hemingway's home was still in Key West, one of the reasons for him to take up permanent residence in Cuba came about when a very attractive woman wearing a "one-piece black dress and high heels; her golden hair [hanging] to her shoulders, and her shapely legs and long arms were almost snow white," sat down next to him in Sloppy Joe's. Hemingway, his skin very dark from fishing, was barefoot, wearing a dirty T-shirt and shorts held up by a hemp rope. The bartender remembered it was like observing "beauty and the beast."[1]

The beauty in question was Martha Gellhorn. Her father, George Gellhorn, the son of a cigar maker, was born in Ohlau, near Breslau, in East Prussia (now Poland). He completed his medical studies at Wurzburg, and then went to Vienna and Berlin. Interestingly, he became president of his university's Jewish fraternity dueling club. At this time in Germany, dueling meant honorable scars on the face and head. Completing his studies, he signed on as a ship's surgeon to see the world.

In 1900, George Gellhorn decided to settle down and chose St. Louis, Missouri. The city boasted a population of a half-million people, at least 100,000 of whom were German. Another strong reason for George to settle in this city by the Mississippi River was that he hoped Dr. Washington Fischel, a local physician, would help set him up in practice. At the time, George Gellhorn was thirty-one, stood six feet tall, wore high collars, round-rimmed glasses, and sported his dueling scars on his bald head. He eventually married Fischel's daughter, Edna.

Edna, also Jewish, graduated from Bryn Mawr and, like her husband, held strong views on liberal politics and equality for everyone. If any club excluded anyone because of their race, religion, nationality or gender, they either refused to join, or they established alternative organizations. Edna spoke out forcefully on suffrage for women, with George beaming in the audience. "He took pride in everything she did." By all accounts it was a happy marriage. George eventually became a noted gynecologist and held professorships of obstetrics and gynecology at both Washington University and St. Louis University.[2]

Martha, the third of four children, was born in 1906. According to her own accounts, she had a well-to-do happy childhood. She later remarked that it was "her good fortune to have been brought up with her three brothers in a 'loving, merry, stimulating' home."[3]

Like her mother, Martha attended Bryn Mawr, but left after two years. In 1929, she held two brief jobs, one with the *New Republic* in New York City, and the Hearst-owned *Times Union* newspaper in Albany, New York. She earned her passage to Europe by writing an article for the North German Lloyd shipping line. Martha traveled throughout Europe, supporting herself by writing. Her first goal was fiction, with journalism helping to pay for her travels. In 1933, she began her first novel, *What Mad Pursuit*.[4]

Martha returned to the United States in 1934 and obtained a position as a relief-investigator for the Federal Emergency Relief Administration (FERA). Her reports to her boss, Harry Hopkins, led to an introduction to the first lady, Eleanor Roosevelt, who introduced her to President Franklin D. Roosevelt. For the rest of their lives, the Roosevelts made time to see her.[5]

Her work at the FERA also led to her next novel, *The Trouble I've Seen*. Mrs. Roosevelt was so taken with the book that she mentioned it three times in her column "My Day." Martha returned to Europe in 1936 and again journeyed back to the United States that same year. In

December, she suggested to her family a Christmas trip to Key West, where she met Hemingway.[6]

Most Hemingway biographers point out the traits that made Martha Gellhorn so different from any of the women in his life. Foremost was her great writing talent. One of the reviews of her book *The Trouble I've Seen* said, "Her writing burns.... Hemingway does not write more authentic American speech. Nor can Ernest Hemingway teach Martha Gellhorn anything about the economy of language." Hemingway had an intense sense of competition and did not care about most writers with talent. He had, to say at the least, a strong ego. Lastly, all of Hemingway's other wives put him as their main focus in their lives; Martha did not. Out of all of his wives, she spent the shortest amount of time with him, and was the only wife to initiate divorce proceedings. It seems inevitable that two such strong personalities would clash. After four contentious years of marriage, Martha divorced Hemingway on December 21, 1945. She married Thomas Stanley Matthews, an editor at *Time* magazine and divorced him in 1963.[7]

It is Martha's bad luck to have married Ernest Hemingway, as it seems she is remembered only as being the writer's third wife. She was much more than that. She had proven to be an excellent writer as well as a "gutsy reporter." She was one of the first female war correspondents of the 20th century. Gellhorn began her reporting with the Spanish Civil War and then reported on the Sino-Japanese War before the United States' entry into World War II. Martha stowed away on a hospital ship and sneaked ashore on D–Day as a stretcher-bearer; accompanied a night bombing run over Germany; and was one of the first to report from the Nazi concentration camp at Dachau after it had been liberated by the Allied Forces. At the age of fifty-eight she covered the Vietnam War and, amazingly at the age of eighty-one, reported on the United States invasion of Panama. Finally, when "war came to Bosnia," Martha felt she was not "'nimble' enough for war anymore." Nevertheless, she continued to travel and was passionately dedicated to a variety of causes.

In the 1960s, Gellhorn made London her base of operations. Battling cancer and near blindness, Martha Gellhorn committed suicide by an overdose of drugs in London, on February 14, 1998.[8]

After Hemingway separated from his second wife, Paula, he moved from Key West to Havana and permanently into the hotel Ambos Mundos

3. Finca Vigía

in 1939. Hemingway had already been living off-and-on in Room 511 in the hotel since 1932. Earlier, Hemingway wrote to Max Perkins, the legendary editor at Scribner's, that he wanted to go back to Cuba to do a few articles. Shortly after this, however, he wrote Perkins that he had begun a manuscript on the Spanish Civil War and it was taking all his time. Hemingway even opted out of a fishing tournament as the manuscript evolved into *For Whom the Bell Tolls*.[9]

In February or April, of 1939, Martha Gellhorn joined Hemingway in Havana, as he had promised her he would find a house for them to live in before she arrived. Upon Gellhorn's arrival, however, she found him still in the Ambos Mundos with fishing gear scattered around the small chamber. The writing had put an end to any effort on Hemingway's

In Hemingway's time, the visitor who came to the main entrance of his home, Finca Vigía (Lookout or Watchtower Farm), first beheld a beautiful ceiba tree. Today, another ceiba still graces the entrance. (Drawing by Bergen Spring.)

part to find a place to live. Martha found living in the hotel unacceptable and pointed out she had lived in bad conditions in many places, but did not see the need for it in Cuba. Furthermore, Hemingway, she said, was "one of the most unfastidious men I've ever known" and, besides, Martha wanted a room for herself to begin work on her own novel.

Gellhorn began looking for a place to rent. While searching a newspaper, she found a fifteen-acre farm known as the Finca Vigía in the village of San Francisco de Paula, approximately sixteen miles outside of Havana, and owned by a Frenchman named Joseph D'Orn Ducamp. This was the farm that eventually became Hemingway's sanctuary and refuge. It allowed him to live in the village area, mixing with the people of his own neighborhood and learning about the customs of his adopted country.[10]

The chapel established in 1775 at San Francisco de Paula became the center of the village. By 1886, the settlement consisted of the chapel and twenty-six houses. Later, the Spaniards built a small tower on what would become Hemingway's farm and equipped the tower with a heliographic signaling device, hence its name, Lookout, or Watch Tower Farm.

While Hemingway lived at the finca, his immediate neighbors included a tinsmith, a streetcar mechanic, a laborer in a brewery, an office worker, a weaver, a cigar maker, a night watchman, a tractor driver, a widow, and a pensioner. The Modelo Brewery that produced Hatuey beer in nearby Cotorro, a textile factory and the Antillana Steel Plant were the mainstays of employment for the villagers.[11] The dirt road remained unchanged for a number of years before it was finally paved. The modest homes in the area provide a striking contrast with the farm. The Cuban houses and the grounds of the museum still provide a large contrast.

Hemingway did have one affluent neighbor: Frank Steinhart, Jr., the son of the former owner of the Havana Railway, the company that operated the streetcars of Havana. For some reason, Hemingway delighted in conducting a feud against Steinhart at the boundary lines between the two properties. Dr. José Luis Herrera Sotolongo, a frequent visitor to the finca, recalled he and his brother, Roberto, being enlisted to join in the "operations" of some of the raids. The "attacks" usually happened when Steinhart gave one of his lavish parties. Ideally, the

3. Finca Vigía

raids took place around midnight. The "attackers," carrying firecrackers and "stink bombs," armed themselves with hollowed bamboo stalks to launch the "ordnance." According to Dr. Herrera, Hemingway covered their retreat so he could see the results of the "raid." Usually, Steinhart would turn loose his dogs, and once he became so frustrated he started to shoot a gun at the Hemingway house. Lying low on the ground, the raiders escaped injury. A truce was finally arranged between the two men by Hemingway's fourth wife, Mary Welsh.[12]

The "house was almost invisible," Martha Gellhorn remembered, because of the rundown nature of the grounds. The untended grass contained "caches of empty gin bottles, and rusty tins, and trees." She remembered the house itself as "a pleasant old one-storey affair of no special style; the six rooms ... large and well proportioned, full of light." At first, Hemingway did not like the finca and left Martha to undertake the necessary work. She used her own money to hire a painter, a carpenter, two gardeners, and a cook. The end result pleased Hemingway. Still married to Pauline, Hemingway decided to split the household expenses with Martha. He continued to use the address of the Ambos Mundos for his correspondence with Pauline. Ernest Hemingway divorced Pauline on November 4, 1940, and married Martha on November 21.[13]

Finca Vigía sits on a hill and, on some nights, the elevation allows its residents to see the twinkling lights of Havana. During Hemingway's residency, bougainvillea hung from a trellis, but the yellow color of the house proved "unappetizing" to Martha and she ordered painters to cover it with a "dusty pale pink." The grounds had a tennis court, swimming pool, and garden area, all of which had been left to ruin. Gellhorn felt the rent of $100 per month reasonable.

A giant ceiba tree stood near the front steps of the house and this, above all else, sold Martha on the finca. "Any house with such a tree," she recalled, "was perfect in my eyes. I never saw a ceiba like it, anywhere." The large trunk of a ceiba, the color and "texture of elephant hide," normally dwarfs the branches of this type of tree. This ceiba, however, had "branches thick as other tree trunks, spreading in wide graceful loops; it was probably several hundred years old." Gellhorn also observed flowering vines climbing "up the wall behind the ceiba; orchids grew from its trunk." René Villarreal, the Cuban majordomo at the finca, recalled that in the 1940s he spoke to some locals in their seventies who remembered seeing the ceiba tree when they were young. In the story of Hemingway in Cuba, the ceiba tree has gained a legend of its own. It also illustrates how the Hemingway legend is portrayed in parts of Cuba.[14]

Hemingway forbade pruning of all bushes and trees on the finca, feeling they should be allowed to grow in any way they wished. This applied especially to the magnificent ceiba. Furthermore, Hemingway knew many Cubans believed the ceiba to be a sacred tree and any cutting, he felt, would be "sacrilegious." Sometimes when Hemingway walked by it he "tapped the trunk" for luck. One of the roots of the ceiba tree had worked its way under the foundation of the house and started lifting tiles in the floor. In some of the rooms this could be hidden, but the damage in the dining room was most noticeable. Hemingway felt that once the root found no water it would recede and the tiles easily repaired. Hemingway's fourth wife, Mary Welsh, disagreed. Villarreal recalled that Mary "secretly" planned on repairing the tiles, which meant the offending root had to be cut off. She shopped for the right type of flooring replacements, plus arranged for workers to accomplish the task and waited for the right moment.[15]

On a scheduled fishing trip, Mary begged off, saying she did not feel well. Once Hemingway departed, she called the workers and they quickly began digging and cutting off the root and laying the new tiles. Just as the workers finished, Mary heard a car coming up the driveway. The weather being too inclement for fishing, Hemingway had returned early. Mary rushed to the dining room to hurry the workers in their cleaning up and getting out of the house. In their haste, they left a shovel in the dining room and did not get the dust cleaned up around the new tiles.

Hemingway quickly took in what had happened and "turned red with rage." He turned his fury on Mary and demanded to know who cut the root. She confessed it was under her supervision. Hemingway grabbed the shovel, opened a window in the dining room and threw the shovel out of the house. Mary had, by this time, retreated to her bedroom. Hemingway went in after her and Villarreal heard the two arguing. Hemingway reentered the dining room and demanded that the severed root be found and kept in the room. He continued his rage for days, refusing to talk to Mary. He also used the ceiba incident to go off a strict diet that limited his intake of alcohol. Eventually, the two made up.[16]

3. Finca Vigía

In 1984, Cuban writer Norberto Fuentes published *Hemingway in Cuba*. This was written almost two and a-half decades after Hemingway's death and long after Mary and Villarreal had departed from Cuba. It appears that Fuentes based much of his material on memories of the staff, or those who merely wished to enlarge the legend of Hemingway. In any case, what follows is the ceiba tree incident according to Fuentes's book.

Mary wanted to cut the root of the ceiba tree and do the repairs to the floor of the house. She went to a gardener that none of the staff knew, as they would have informed Hemingway of her plan. She told the gardener that her bad-tempered husband did not want the root cut, but *she* did. One day when Hemingway went into Havana, Mary contacted the gardener, who soon arrived at the finca and quickly went to work. Just after he cut off the offending root, Hemingway stood in the doorway silently observing his wife, the gardener, and the severed root. He was absent for a brief time before returning with a shotgun. The gardener beat a hasty retreat out the window, the root in his hand. Hemingway pursued him, firing his shotgun into the air. The gardener dropped the ceiba root and made his escape from the finca. According to Fuentes, Mary, for a long period afterward, had to kneel in front of the ceiba tree and ask its forgiveness.[17]

Fuentes states that his informant, the gardener, Pichilo, identifies the wife as Martha Gellhorn, but Fuentes rightly cannot see Martha putting up with such a sentence. Martha herself confirms Fuentes's observation. Sometime after Fidel Castro's revolution and the changing of Finca Vigía into the Hemingway Museum, the ceiba was cut down because the roots were "pulling up the floor." When Gellhorn learned this she indignantly replied, "They should have pulled down the house instead."[18]

Hemingway, with money from the royalties and movie rights to *For Whom the Bell Tolls*, purchased the farm in December 1940. He then bought a nearby dairy farm so that he owned most of the hill upon which the farm rested. By this time, Hemingway knew this was where he wished to live. It satisfied him in two ways: it was far enough from Havana to afford some privacy, and it had areas for lush gardens. As one who loved the forests of Michigan, Hemingway appreciated the number and variety of trees—including mango—on the finca.[19]

Even as Gellhorn started making Finca Vigía a pleasant place to live, she quickly lost interest in actually living there. Years later some of the former staff of the house recalled she had little patience for running a household and delegated the tasks to the Cuban staff. Martha preferred tennis and visiting with friends in Havana's wealthy Miramar neighborhood. After a return visit to Cuba in 1986, Martha recalled that while the finca took up her time, it nevertheless was enjoyable "because of the beauty." Cuba itself, however, lost its attraction and "became nothing, a waste of time." Gellhorn felt the country (or perhaps she meant Hemingway) was "no place for a self-willed, opinionated loner, which is what I suppose I am." In any case, according to Dr. Herrera, by the end of 1943, Gellhorn decided to leave Finca Vigía, never to return. Probably the strongest reason for her departure was clash of egos between the strong-willed husband and wife.[20]

In 1944, while covering World War II in Europe, Hemingway met Mary Welsh Monks in England. Mary was born in 1908 in the small village of Walker, Minnesota, but grew up in the nearby town of Bemidji. She was the only child of Tom and Adeline Welsh. Unlike Hemingway's other wives, Mary's family lived, as the writer Bernice Kert nicely put it, on "limited means." Her father worked as a logger, and supplemented his income in the summer by operating the Mississippi riverboat *Northland*, taking tourists on day trips. Mary's father took her aboard for three months in the summer. Her mother had no interest in these voyages and remained at home.[21]

Upon graduation from high school, Mary Welsh announced that in the fall she would travel to Evanston, Illinois, to attend Northwestern University, where she planned to major in journalism. She supported herself throughout her studies by working part-time. She met and married a drama student from Ohio during her junior year. Mary then dropped out of college and took a job with a trade magazine, *The American Florist*. Her unemployed husband preferred to live off her salary and a small income from his family. After two years, they quietly divorced.[22]

Mary then worked for small publishing businesses and eventually landed a position as society editor for the *Chicago Daily News*. Paul Mowrer became managing editor of the paper and Mary sometimes attended parties at the Mowrer's residence. As fate would have it, Hemingway's first wife, Hadley, was now Paul Mowrer's wife.[23] Mary continued to work for the newspaper, but on a visit to England, Ireland, and Paris in 1937, she met the bureau chief of the *London Daily Express*.

He convinced her to call his publisher, Lord Beaverbrook, in London, about a position. An unenthused Beaverbrook arranged an interview for Mary with the London editor, but this never led to a position.

Upon her return to Chicago, Mary continued her efforts to land a spot on a foreign desk. Beaverbrook came to Chicago and eventually asked her to accompany him on a voyage up the Nile River. Mary refused. Eventually, Beaverbrook said if she came to London, he would find a job for her. On July 2, 1937, Mary began work on the *London Daily Mail*. In the summer of 1938, she married Noel Monks, an Australian who also worked at the *Daily Mail*. Her assignments grew and she covered a variety of events on the continent. Mary and Noel barely managed to flee France when the Germans began their invasion of that country in June 1940. That same year she obtained a position with *Time* magazine.[24]

Mary returned to the United States after the attack on Pearl Harbor in December 1941. By 1943, she was working within an inner circle of friends in London, consisting of the photographer Robert Capa and writers William Saroyan and Irwin Shaw, among others. Her marriage to Noel began to cool. In June of 1944, Mary heard that Ernest Hemingway had been in a car accident and was in a London hospital and decided to pay him a visit. This eventually led to their keeping "steady company," continuing their relationship in Paris after the liberation of the "City of Light." In 1945, she divorced Noel Monks. The next year, on March 14, 1946, Mary and Hemingway were married in Cuba; the couple would remain together until his death on July 2, 1961.[25]

It is Mary Welsh, Hemingway's fourth wife, who made the house a refuge for Ernest Hemingway. Here, for the first time, he could work without being disturbed in an ideal, beautiful setting and where he could also go to relax and enjoy life. As an added bonus, it was only a short drive to the fishing village of Cojímar, one of the places where he moored his fishing craft *Pilar*. Mary quickly took over the task of running the household by supervising and doing the actual hands-on labor. The gardener José Herrero, nicknamed "Pichilo" by the residents of San Francisco de Paula, remembered watching Mary emerging from the rose garden, her skin glistening with perspiration. The people of San Francisco de Paula appreciated Mary's efforts to learn Spanish. Sometime after the departure of Martha Gellhorn, the house was painted white.[26]

In the story of Ernest Hemingway in Cuba, many researchers

rightfully concentrate on his role as a pioneer in big game fishing. Unbeknown to many, Mary Welsh Hemingway also proved to be adept at the sport. Part of Mary's youth was spent on her father's cruise boat; she also enjoyed fishing in some of the many lakes of Minnesota.[27]

Ernest bought a twenty-foot launch with a half deck for Mary and called it the *Tin Kid*. Hemingway's second son, Patrick, had called Mary "Tin Kid" in a delirious moment during a long illness in 1947. The craft, built of Cuban cedar, had an open, five-by-seven-foot cockpit, a four-cylinder gasoline engine, a bilge pump, and small outriggers stabilized by a short mast. *Tin Kid* contained an ice chest and a box to stow needed gear, and were covered with cushions to double as seats. Much to the consternation of some passengers, there were no toilet facilities. With a freeboard of one to three feet, it proved a wet ride in most seas. *Tin Kid* brought people and supplies aboard *Pilar*, and Ernest and Mary often fished from the craft.[28]

Mary Hemingway and Taylor Williams, a friend from Ketchum, Idaho, entered the Marlin Fishing Tournament with the *Tin Kid* going against big craft especially suited for both pleasure and big game fishing. Another friend, who was a mate on a merchant vessel, implored her not to undertake the venture; he insisted that not only did she lack the stamina to handle a marlin, nor could she take being out in the *Tin Kid* for any length of time. He bet Mary ten dollars that she would not last to noon. Mary took the bet. A kibitzer agreed with Williams, stating with certainty that marlin fishing was too arduous a sport for women. The onlooker upped the ante by saying he would bet five to one that Mary would not last the first day. Ernest shouted out he would cover that bet.[29]

At the beginning of the tournament, Mary and Taylor hoisted the flag of the Ketchum, Idaho, Rod and Gun Club in the *Tin Kid*. On the second day of the tournament, Williams hooked onto a fighting fish. Mary recalled the marlin jumping more than thirty times. Unlike the larger fishing craft in the tournament, the *Tin Kid* had no fighting chair and Williams had to use Mary's boat's gunwale to brace against the fish's fight. His catch proved the largest single fish in any class taken during the tournament.[30]

The third day of the tournament it was Mary's turn to take on a marlin. Along with her in the boat were Williams and a Cuban boat boy. Mary admitted she had never actually hooked a marlin. While she had fought and landed a number of marlin, Ernest or someone else in

Pilar had actually set the hook and then given her the rod to fight and land them. As the time neared for her turn, Mary began to wonder if she did have the strength to securely set the hook. Furthermore, she knew that no other woman had participated in the tournament. These two items began to erode her confidence. All of this evaporated when a marlin struck. Mary let the fish run and then, bracing one foot on the gunwale, she pulled on the rod a number of times to set the hook until she felt the heavy pull of the marlin. Even though the species of fish is noted for its ability to either break the line or throw off the hook, Mary landed her seventy-nine-pound marlin within seven minutes.

Later, with three fish aboard, Mary headed *Tin Kid* farther off shore. They soon found themselves caught up in a sudden squall as rain pelted them and the seas rose. As *Tin Kid* approached Cojímar, Mary estimated the waves had increased to twenty feet in height. Fortunately, Ernest had been searching for the boat. Spotting them, he took them in tow, after first bringing the three people aboard *Pilar*.

At the final judging, Mary and Williams placed sixth among forty-seven boats. The Havana Yacht Club's commodore gave a special award to Mary "for valiance." No one recorded how much money Ernest made on his confidence in Mary's abilities.[31]

After Ernest Hemingway's death, Mary managed the Hemingway estate and continued to protect her late husband's image. She published her autobiography, *How It Was*, in 1976. Mary Welsh Hemingway died on November 26, 1986, and is buried next to her husband in Ketchum, Idaho, their last home.[32]

My first trip into Cuba was primarily to research locations used for human smuggling. While discussing the areas to examine, I told Víctor of my interest in Hemingway and wondered if we could work at least a trip to Finca Vigía into my tight schedule. As is his wont, Víctor smiled and said, "Let me see." Not only did he make time for the trip to the finca, he also surprised me with a short visit to Cojímar. Víctor said we would follow the old Carretera Central (Central Highway) that links Havana to San Francisco de Paula. As the Volkswagen "bug" passed from the urban to suburban scene, the route entered a large traffic circle where, at one time, stood a shrine for long-distance travelers to stop and perhaps leave an offering. Shortly after leaving the traffic circle, I saw again the long lines of people waiting at bus stops, along with crowded streets, as we made our way into San Francisco de Paula.

Prior to visiting the finca, Víctor suggested we visit with Prof. Elisa Serrano as she did the art restoration of the house, and eventually the *Pilar*. I visited with Elisa and her husband, Pablo Jane, at their home. Sitting in a room where the walls held a wide range of Elisa's art, I explained my desire to track Hemingway in Cuba in order to see a human side of the writer. Prof. Serrano is a great admirer of Hemingway—she had not only painted a portrait of the writer (which is displayed in her home), but she designed a memorial to him in her backyard; it is a bust she sculpted of Hemingway that sits atop a plinth. I told her that her work reminded me favorably of a Hemingway memorial in Sun Valley, Idaho. Elisa commented about how a woman artist in Cuba could make a similar piece of art without knowing of the Sun Valley monument.

Prof. Elisa Serrano is a talented artist, and her husband, Pablo Jane, is a well-known writer in Cuba. When Víctor introduced me to anyone in Cuba he always liked to point out that I had been to the Arctic and Antarctic. Upon hearing this, Pablo became very animated, and, through Víctor's translation, I learned that Pablo had edited a book of Cuba's involvement with the polar regions. He quickly left the room, returning with the book, *Cuba en el Ártico y la Antártida* (*Cuba in the Arctic and Antarctica*). He wanted me to have his last copy. I respectfully tried to decline the generous offer, saying he should have it for his own collection. Pablo said he would rather the work be in a collection of someone who had been to the north and south extremes of the earth. On each of my subsequent visits to Cuba, I always made sure I had time to visit with Elisa and Pablo.

Prior to 2011, there was no sign directing visitors to the Ernest Hemingway Museum and one needed a good guide, or driver, to find it; however, there is now a sign clearly marking the location. Coming from Havana on the Central Highway, Víctor turned right and entered the street leading up to the museum's entrance gates. Upon entering, I paid an admittance fee as well as a fee to obtain permission to take photographs. On the way up the hill to the parking area, the first thing that struck me was the abundance of lush tropical plants and trees on the grounds that provides a feeling of cool restfulness (Hemingway would no doubt approve, given his disdain for cutting back the greenery on the property). An area designated for parking is near where the farm's original garage was located. Originally, the upper floor of the structure was used as a guest bedroom, especially for Hemingway's visiting sons. The building, in 2011, was used as offices for the museum's staff. Víctor informed me that he knew the museum's director, Ada Rosa Alfonso Rosales, but as she was away on business, Isabel I. Ferreiro, the assistant director, was our tour guide. Ms. Ferreiro told me that the planning committee's goal is to present the house as it was in 1959. In order to protect the home, visitors do not actually enter the building, but view it through the many windows and open doors, with staff members carefully monitoring their assigned areas. With my history publications, interest in Hemingway, and, most importantly, Víctor's and Prof. Elisa Serrano's recommendations, Ms. Ferrierro gave us a guided tour inside of the home.

The first item of interest as we approached the main entrance is the newer ceiba tree. Walking up a few steps and passing through the doorway and making a quick turn to the right brought us into what had been Mary's bedroom. The room has turquoise-colored walls, with a white ceiling. A two-shelf bookcase sits at the head of the bed, which is covered with a blue duvet. Visitors who have already toured the Hemingway home in Key West will be familiar with Hemingway's love of cats, so it is not surprising to find two volumes on felines: *The Care and Handling of Cats*, plus *The Care, Feeding and Training of Cats* on one of the two bedside tables.

We next visited the kitchen, which featured a dining table laid as it would have been for the household staff. A television set is located in the room, as Hemingway wanted the staff to see the unfolding events of the revolution; it also served as a gathering place to watch televised boxing matches.

The next stop was the dining room that has a set of French doors opening out onto a view of the landscaped surroundings, allowing for cooling breezes. The head of the table sits close to these doors and a wall, which holds big game trophies largely from Africa. Also on display is Joan Miró's painting *The Farm* (more on this later). The table is set with custom-made dishes and flatware, on which are inscribed symbols representing the three hills of Paris and Cuba, and an arrowhead, representing the Native Americans near Walloon Lake in Michigan where Hemingway summered every year from early childhood until he left home. The final symbol represents the ranks Ernest and Mary Hemingway held during World War II. The three symbols are also in the formal cloth napkins.

Ms. Ferreiro next led us to what is likely the most photographed

The living room of Ernest Hemingway's home. As with most of the rooms in the house, the walls hold a combination of art and animal trophies. There are also bookcases crammed to capacity throughout the house. In the right background is Karsh's famous photograph of Hemingway. The chair on the right in the immediate foreground is Hemingway's favored spot in the living room. Note a drinks tray immediately to the left. (Photograph by Víctor Pina Tabío.)

area inside the house, a living room that is long and wide with the usual animal trophies on the wall, and low bookcases jammed with books. While most rooms have game trophies on the walls, almost every room, except the kitchen, has books. Entering the living room from the dining area there is a framed picture of Hemingway in a bulky sweater, taken by the noted photographer Yousuf Karsh, a photograph frequently used in illustrated accounts of the writer in his later years. Above the photograph is a *cesta*, a long, curved, wicker scoop attached to the arm used to catch and throw the ball in the game of jai alai. On the same wall there is also a large bullfighting poster done by Roberto Domingo and, in the same area, is a wooden magazine holder made in Cuba. Moving to the other end of the room, along the right side, is yet another low bookcase crammed with books. On the bookcase is a 1950s radio that still works—Ms. Ferriro pointed out the radio is turned on for a short period during the day to give the feeling that the master of the house may be arriving at any time.

At the far end of the room, directly opposite the iconic Karsh photograph, are two low, comfortable chairs covered in a floral pattern, the chair on the right having been Hemingway's. On the left of his chair is a table holding many bottles of liquor. Immediately behind the chairs, and to Hemingway's right, is another set of French doors, allowing the breezes to enter the room. The chair is positioned in such a way that Hemingway could have accessed any book easily with his right hand. A short distance behind Hemingway's chair is a large record player with a nearby cabinet containing at least ten shelves of vinyl record albums. The writer had a deep appreciation for music and art, instilled in him by his mother, Grace Hall Hemingway. This, despite the fact that American writer Dos Passos once described Hemingway as "the only man he ever knew who really hated his mother." There is also a footstool in the living room, in the shape of a rocking chair; on its back are the embroidered words, "Poor Old Papa."

The tour next moved to an office and the library. The library contains densely packed bookcases on both sides of the room reaching to near the ceiling. (A photograph in the John F. Kennedy Library shows Hemingway on a library ladder examining one of his many volumes.) In the office area there are a number of odds and ends, including a stamp pad and stamp that says, "I do not answer letters." A clipboard has a sheet of paper held by two swords (bills) from a marlin. One of the rooms holds the head of an African Cape Buffalo; another wall holds an original work of Picasso, and yet another wall has additional art.

Hemingway's bedroom, the room in which he wrote, contains a low bookcase. On this is a thick book and upon the book is his typewriter. Because he wrote standing up and the bookcase was not tall enough for him to comfortably type, he placed the typewriter on the book to give it the proper height. On the wall above where he typed is the inevitable head of an animal from Africa. Seeing all the game trophies in the house, the English writer Graham Greene is said to have remarked he didn't "know how a writer could write surrounded by so many dead animal heads." Hemingway placed magazines and other material on his bed for ready reference, but the reference matter is not shown in the museum, as the Cuban climate is not kind to paper.[33]

Hemingway preferred to write in his bedroom while standing, with his typewriter on a large book. The English writer Graham Green once remarked he did not know how anyone could write with so many dead animals staring at you. (Photograph by Víctor Pina Tabío.)

Hemingway had a continual battle with his weight, so, not surprisingly, there is a scale in the bathroom. Prof. Elisa Serrano, the art restorer for the museum and an artist herself, uncovered on the wall nearest the scale columns of writing in Hemingway's hand that was his record of his daily weigh-ins. An entry records: "212 [pounds] after trip drinking lots of beer."

The last room of the Hemingway house we were shown on the tour is the guest room. Originally used as a haven for his many cats, as Hemingway's fame grew it also meant a growing list of people who wished to visit the writer, so the felines were relegated to another room. Among the art in the guest room is a painting of Hemingway by one of his former Cuban employees.

Those touring the house may not realize the writer had a very good eye for art, especially the modern art of the period. The story of why there are few such works adorning the walls of his Cuban home is yet another factor in learning about Ernest Hemingway.

Hemingway's interest in art stems, as was previously noted, from his mother, Grace Hemingway, who raised her children in an artistic household. She did become a "painter of regional reputation," but, as the writer Anthony Burgess pointed out, Ernest's taste "was to outclass" his mother's.[34]

This appreciation surfaced as early as the 1920s when Hemingway talked to the American expatriate writer Gertrude Stein in her Paris salon about collecting art. Stein said to forget buying expensive fashionable clothes and concentrate on purchasing pictures. Hemingway demurred, saying he did not have the money to buy a Picasso, which he liked. Stein conceded he could not do that, but he should learn who were the young serious painters of the day and buy their works. Hemingway apparently took Stein's advice, as many of his friends were painters from whom he learned a great deal.[35]

René Villarreal's memoir, published years after he left Finca Vigía, takes readers room-by-room, describing the art on display; only the kitchen and the bathrooms are bare. Most scholars who have focused on Hemingway's passion for art believe the work he admired most was Joan Miró's *The Farm*, now in the collection of the National Museum of Art in Washington, D.C., which was donated to the museum by Mary after her husband's death.[36] Sean O'Rourke, of Mount Ida College, writes that the story behind Hemingway and the Miró painting is an example of how Hemingway could "transform the events of daily life into a well-constructed story." It also illustrates Hemingway's ability to recognize quality art.[37]

Hemingway himself began the accepted story, published in *Cahiers d'art* in 1934. In 1925, prior to his fame, Miró kept the work near him. Eventually, he had to sell the picture, along with others he had painted. Evan Shipman, an American painter and a friend of Hemingway's, learned of Miró's need to sell his works, and found a dealer, the owner of the Galerie Pierre in Paris, to display *The Farm*. However, Shipman made the owner put a price on it, and he purchased it from him.

Shipman, however, changed his mind the same day the owner of the gallery wanted to sell it to him. The painter felt Hemingway should have it, pointing out that Ernest loved it more than he did and therefore it should be his. Hemingway argued that Shipman did not realize the potential worth of the painting and insisted that Shipman should make the purchase. Declining any further arguments, Shipman suggested rolling dice for the painting. Hemingway won. He purchased the work on installments. The price: five thousand francs, which, Hemingway recalled, was "four thousand two hundred and fifty francs more" than he had ever paid for any picture.

As the time for the last payment came due, the gallery owner insisted that Hemingway make the payment immediately, or forfeit the work. Later, it turned out that the owner had received an offer much higher than the price Hemingway would pay for the painting. Hemingway, Shipman, and Dos Passos made the rounds of various cafés and bars frequented by their friends and asked them to contribute in order to make the last payment. They did and, to the gallery owner's disgust, Hemingway took possession of Miró's work.

Hemingway felt the painting made "you feel about Spain when you are there and all that you feel when you are away and cannot go there." He felt "no one else has been able to paint these two very opposing things."[38]

O'Rourke, using material from various sources, the most important being a letter from Shipman, tells a different story. This account begins in the winter of 1922–23 when Gertrude Stein took Hemingway to the painter André Masson's studio in "a decrepit building at 45 rue Bloment in the fifteenth arrondissement of Paris." Hemingway bought four paintings from the artist. From 1920 to 1925 Miró intermittently worked in a studio next to Masson.[39] Among Masson's many friends was Evan Shipman. Shipman, whose father had graduated from Harvard, expected his son to follow in his footsteps. Evan Shipman passed all the tests for entry, except French. His father then sent him to study at the University of Louvain in Belgium during late winter and spring of 1924. In the fall, he traveled to Paris to study at the Sorbonne. During this period, he met Hemingway and Stein. Stein introduced Shipman to Masson and Miró.

Miró, as in Hemingway's story, did have problems selling the painting. The poet Ezra Pound noticed the painting in Miró's studio and devoted an issue of the literary magazine *Little Review* to the artist, reproducing several examples of his work, including *The Farm*. He also brought along Hemingway to see the painting.

Meanwhile, Shipman met Jacques Viot, who worked as an assistant in the Galerie Pierre and wanted to go into business for himself. Shipman took Viot to see Miró's work and he immediately saw the artist's value. Viot arranged a one-man show at the Galerie Pierre in the spring of 1925. For helping him, Viot offered Shipman any one of Miró's works at a very low price. Shipman chose *The Farm* and placed a deposit on it. When Shipman told Hemingway of his good fortune, he noticed how badly the writer wanted the painting. Shipman then offered to toss a coin for it; Shipman won the toss. Sensing the writer's disappointment, Shipman gave the painting to Hemingway. Neither Shipman nor Hemingway, at the time, had the money to pay the complete price, which is why the painting stayed at the gallery until Hemingway paid it off. Shipman then departed for his home in New Hampshire, and Hemingway went off to the festival of San Fermín in Pamplona, Spain. By the end of September both men were back in Paris. Hemingway did not have the two thousand francs to finish his payments. He then announced the picture was a birthday present for his first wife, Hadley, and he, Shipman, and Dos Passos made the rounds of the bars to collect the money. Successful in their mission, they delivered the painting to the Hemingway's apartment.

In Hemingway's story, he rolled the dice and won—instead of losing at a coin toss. According to O'Rourke what likely happened is Hemingway had purchased Masson's *The Throw of the Dice* and "seeing the painting every day in his home, he probably misremembered the toss of a coin as a roll of dice." Hemingway, according to receipts in the Hemingway Collection at the John F. Kennedy Library in Boston, paid thirty-five hundred francs instead of his remembered five thousand. O'Rourke also points out Miró believed Hemingway earned the money by serving as a sparring partner for French heavyweight boxing professionals. According to Hemingway's friend Gerald Murphy, however, he earned it from a part-time job delivering produce. Murphy later told the story, calling *The Farm* "the picture Hemingway bought by 'carrying vegetables.'" After Ernest and his first wife, Hadley, divorced, she got custody of the painting. Hemingway later borrowed *The Farm* and never returned it. That one picture speaks well not only of his eye for art, but also for his ability to recognize a work that would rise in value with the passing of time. Hemingway loaned *The Farm* to the Pierre Matisse Gallery in New York City. When asked to place an insurance value on it, he estimated $10,000 (almost $175,000 in 2016 dollars).[40]

In another room of Hemingway's house hung the painting *El Guitarrista*, by Juan Gris, along with *The Jungle*, by André Masson, while other rooms held another of Gris's works, plus *A Monument in Arbeit*, by Paul Klee, and another by Masson. The unfired ceramic plate of a bull's head by Pablo Picasso is displayed on one of the library's walls. Today, the guest room has a watercolor by a French painter that lived in Havana. On another wall in the same room is a Chinese tempera, a gift to Hemingway from Winston Guest when Hemingway bought the finca. Also in the same room is a painting of Hemingway by Oscar Villarreal, René's brother. A wall of Mary's bedroom held a large painting of the young Ernest Hemingway by the American painter and friend Waldo Pierce.

In *Islands in the Stream*, Hemingway has his protagonist, Thomas Hudson, describe some of the paintings in the house. Hudson remarks about how he loved Masson's forest, the Ville d'Avray, "He loved it the way he loved the *Guitar Player* (*El Guitarrista*). That was the great thing about pictures; you could love them with no hopelessness at all."[41] Hemingway did not limit his interest to European artists and in 1934 wrote he had found a good Cuban painter: Antonio Gattorno.[42]

Antonio Gattorno was born in Havana on March 15, 1904. At the tender age of twelve, he began studies in Havana's Academia de San Alejandro, the oldest art school in Hispanic America. In Gattorno's third year of study at this prestigious school, he received a five-year scholarship to study in Europe. He eventually spent seven years on the continent visiting Italy, Spain, France, Belgium, and Germany, all the while studying with other artists.[43]

Returning to Cuba in 1927, Gattorno spent the next twelve years playing an important part in developing a national identity in Cuban painting. His works depicting Cuban *guajiros*—country workers—"convey the power of simple human dignity set against a background of poverty." During this same period, Gattorno taught at the Academia de San Alejandro, and accepted commissions for murals in public buildings in Havana and theatrical décor throughout Cuba.

Hemingway sponsored Gattorno's first solo exhibition in the United States at the Georgette Passedoit Gallery in New York City, from January 12 through February 2, 1936. He wrote a short article for the May 1936 issue of *Esquire* based upon a catalogue he wrote for the exhibition. In the article, he called Gattorno a "Cuban painter who is also a painter for the world." At the time the artist was the youngest person Hemingway knew, "although there is no youth in his painting." Hemingway wrote of the artist's skill in painting the people of Cuba and that he "was made for painting and for nothing else."[44]

Gattorno moved to New York City, married Isabel do Carmo Moura Cabral on September 30, 1940, and lived for thirty years in Greenwich Village at an arresting address: 10 Downing Street. He did not return to Cuba until 1946. Once a Cuban child prodigy and the leader of avant-garde art in Cuba, the Cuban intelligentsia felt he had abandoned his place as an artistic leader. The intelligentsia also claimed Gattorno betrayed his Cuban heritage by exploring themes less concerned with establishing some sort of national identity for Cuba than his earlier work. He never overcame this stigma. Despite the condemnation, however, Gattorno garnered numerous prizes and presented many solo shows, principally in New York City. His final exhibit, a retrospective covering sixty years of his works, was held at the University of Massachusetts, Dartmouth, in October 1978. He died in Acushnet, Massachusetts, in 1980.

A biography of Gattorno mentions that he "is the type of obscure yet important painter that art professionals dream of discovering: a hidden master with an impressive provenance." Hemingway could recognize Gattorono's work at least by 1935, if not before, as he had the Cuban artist do a portrait of John, his oldest son, in that year. In 2011, the Prado Fine Art Gallery in Miami offered one of Gattorno's works from 1927, *Emance*, for $80,000.[45]

Ernest Hemingway not only collected art, but also helped artists he admired, including Spanish artist Luis Quintanilla. Years later, Quintanilla admitted that neither of "the two of us remembers how we happened to meet." Quintanilla, however, appears in the last chapter of Hemingway's 1932 book *Death in the Afternoon*. Most Hemingway biographers note that before the writer's first African safari in 1933 and while visiting in Spain, Hemingway met Quintanilla. Ernest appreciated the artist's "Goyaesque etchings and radical politics." Hemingway scholar Lawrence H. Martin writes, "Hemingway saw in Qunitanilla, as well as himself, a man of art and a man of action." Quintanilla, born in 1893, started as a Cubist, influenced by his friend Juan Gris. Quintanilla became "a prominent Spanish draftsman and muralist." Despite caring greatly for his art, like many during the turbulent 1930s in Spain he became enmeshed in the events leading up to the Spanish Civil War, ultimately taking an active role in the fighting.[46]

In the fall of 1934, Quintanilla was imprisoned in Madrid for being a member of a revolt in October. Many artists and writers came to his defense. Ernest Hemingway arranged and financed an exhibition of his drawings at the Pierre Matisse Gallery in New York City. Hemingway financed the undertaking and approached friends, trying to get them to purchase what he called "the finest drypoints I've ever seen by anyone alive." He and John Dos Passos also wrote prefaces to the catalogue of the exhibition. Hemingway pointed out to friends the cost for an etching was twenty dollars. Proceeds, except for a 20 percent commission to Pierre Matisse Gallery, went to help Quintanilla. Hemingway also wrote a short article for *Esquire* in which he said the etchings "gives us the first true Madrid that we have seen since Goya." The writer also signed a petition to free the artist.[47]

Quintanilla's son, Paul, noted that, despite the efforts of his father's friends, the artist was not immediately set free, but that they "did result in his receiving a 'highly luxurious' cell'" in the Madrid prison. Quintanilla was released after serving a little over eight months.

The next year, 1936, the Spanish Civil War began and Quintanilla led troops during the conflict. During Quintanilla's active service, a bomb struck his studio, destroying all the frescos stored there. He was released from the fighting in the spring of 1937 to do drawings of the war. These were first shown in Barcelona in 1938 and at the Museum of Modern Art, with a catalogue essay by Hemingway.[48]

With the victory of Generalissimo Francisco Franco and the fall of the Spanish Republic in 1939, Quintanilla went into exile in New York and Paris until Franco's death in 1975. He finally returned to Madrid, living there until his death at the age of eighty-five, on October 16, 1978.[49]

Given Hemingway's love of art and the fact that he displayed much of it on his walls at Finca Vigía, why do present-day visitors see few examples of his collection? As the revolution began to take hold in Cuba in the late 1950s, impacting the quality of living and working at the finca, Hemingway began to worry about the safety of the Miró. Should the revolution encompass his area, he planned on leaving, but did not think he would remain away permanently, but he knew the first stages in war always brings out the worst in most combatants and civilians. The world-famous Metropolitan Museum of Modern Art in New York City had asked for a loan of *The Farm*, and just before the revolution swept Fidel Castro into power, Hemingway loaned it to the museum. It remained there until Mary Hemingway donated the painting to the National Gallery of Art in 1987.[50]

In 1961, shortly after Ernest Hemingway's funeral, Mary received a call from Cuba's Minister of Foreign Affairs informing her that Cuba wished to acquire Finca Vigía and make it a monument to Hemingway. Would she be willing to sign a contract deeding over the property to the government? Mary replied they had left the house with the intention of returning and pointed out that the house contained many things belonging to her that had "no significance" to the Cuban government or people. She then asked if the Cuban government would approve of her and another person, Valerie Danby-Smith, who had been Hemingway's secretary, traveling to Cuba to remove those personal items. By this time, the U.S. embargo was in place. The minister said he would return the call the following day.[51]

Mary immediately telephoned a person she knew to ask his friend, President John F. Kennedy, or perhaps someone on his staff, to grant permission for two passages to Cuba. Within a few hours, the authorization arrived and the next day the Cuban government agreed to allow the two women entry. This request from the Cuban government is a good indication of how Cubans felt about Hemingway, for Mary realized the government could have "appropriated it ... as they had done to so much U.S. property there."[52]

In her memoir, *How It Was*, Mary said she found Hemingway's unpublished manuscripts in a secure place and had no trouble retrieving them. Some of the artwork had been taken out of the house by Cuban friends and kept in their residences until they felt it was safe enough to return them. Only one painting went missing. When she told the Ministry of Culture that she wished to take the paintings, someone within the ministry told her they would not allow the paintings to leave Cuba. She contacted their Cuban doctor, José Luis Herrera, now the medical director of Fidel's army, about the problem. The doctor contacted one of Fidel's aides, who soon afterwards called Mary and said Fidel would visit the finca to discuss the situation. After a tour of the house, Castro told Mary, "I will help with your pictures." Two days later the aide contacted Mary and said to have the material crated and on the pier in Havana the next morning. A fishing vessel from Tampa, Florida, lay at the pier. It was the last ship from the U.S. to have clearance papers to leave the harbor.[53]

Fifty-three years after Mary Hemingway's book was published, Valerie Hemingway published her memoirs, which gives another view of what took place. (Valerie had married Hemingway's youngest son, Gregory.) In Valerie's account, Mary did not know how she would get the material they had already boxed up out of the country. Fidel did come to the house and, after the tour, Mary said she wanted to bring back the unpublished manuscripts, personal papers, and a few of her possession that "include[ed] a couple of the paintings." Mary then said she was having difficulty in bringing out the material.

Castro said, "Yes, that presents a problem." He then nodded thoughtfully as a smile crept over his face. "You have my permission, but there's a little law we'll have to break." Valerie recalls she and Mary laughing "uneasily with him." Before Castro left the house, he promised to help with her departure and to let him know if Mary needed anything. "I am at your service," he said.[54]

A few days later, a black car pulled up to the house. It brought a Russian woman from the Ministry of Culture, who informed Mary of her expertise in art and that she had worked for many years in the world-class museum The Hermitage, in what is now St. Petersburg. "She was training the Cubans in the art of appropriation," Valerie recalled. The Soviet bureaucrat felt the Hemingway material suitable for a great public art collection. She set about cataloging everything. Mary informed the Soviet woman she would be taking some paintings and offered to point out which ones so as to avoid the unnecessary work of cataloging them.

> "Everything in this house belongs to the Cuban government. Nothing will leave the country," the Soviet woman icily replied.
> Mary pointed out that Fidel Castro had already given her permission to take whatever personal possessions she wished back to the United States.
> "This is a communist country," retorted the Soviet woman. "Personal possessions do not exist. Señor Castro knows this better than anyone. He has neither the authority nor the power to change the law. Cuba's paintings will stay in Cuba."

3. *Finca Vigía*

Mary then left the finca. Upon her return, she told the Russian art cataloger that Hemingway was always forgetting her birthday. Mary went throughout the house with the art expert. Stopping in front of each painting she wished to take back, Mary said, "Yes, Papa gave me that for my birthday. I'm sure I could recall which year it was if I put my mind to it." Thus, under the agreement with Castro, she could remove the paintings as her personal possessions.[55]

Valerie's account in how the paintings left Cuba differs only in a few details. The upshot is that all of the boxes left in a shrimp boat. Despite the complications, it illustrates once again just how much Cubans—including Fidel Castro—admired Hemingway.[56]

Collette Hemingway, the wife of one of the writer's grandsons, observed that Ernest Hemingway usually "acquired the works of artists he knew personally." In doing so, he gathered together "some key paintings by some of the finest artists of the 20th century."[57]

Once Víctor and I finished with touring the interior of the finca, we decided to stroll around the grounds. A short distance from the house Mary had a tower constructed early in the writer's ownership to give Hemingway a room to write that afforded a good view. Even without the tower on a clear night one can see the lights of Havana, and the tower enhances the vista. Hemingway, however, preferred working within the house in his bedroom and the cats took over the structure. The tower is now used for displays concerning the writer.

We next moved to the former tennis court that now has Hemingway's fishing craft, *Pilar*. The boat is under a roof to ward off the rain and visitors walk up onto an elevated wooden walkway to obtain a better view of the craft, especially the chair where Hemingway fought marlin. By 2010 the *Pilar* was showing its age, but by 2011, with work accomplished by people such as art restorer Prof. Elisa Serrano, the craft looks as good as when it came out of the Wheeler Boatyard in Brooklyn, New York.

Near the pool area are the grave markers for the dogs and cats that died on the property: Black, Negrita, and Linda. There are numerous photographs of Hemingway with his dog, Black, sometimes called Black Dog. One of the stories of why Hemingway left Cuba was that either the rebels or the Cuban army killed Black Dog. Realizing that even a dog could be a target, Hemingway decided to leave the country until things settled down in Cuba.

On one visit to the finca and while photographing the pet markers, a young Japanese tourist approached me and asked if I spoke English. After receiving a "yes," she pointed out, "You look like Ernest Hemingway." The young woman then asked if her friend could take our picture together. As her friend directed us how he wanted the photograph, I glanced at Víctor who, though laughing, managed to also take a shot of the woman and "Hemingway" together.

The visitor who also takes the time to explore the grounds of the finca is amply rewarded by walking from the house's entrance to a path—probably at one time a primitive road—from the building down the hill to near the entrance gate of the finca. Tropical tree branches overhang parts of the pathway with fern-like plants on each side of the trail, making a tunnel-like effect with the dappled light changing constantly along the track. It is easy to see why Hemingway sometimes had his driver drop him off at the gated entrance so that he could walk this trail to the house.

A Journey into Havana with Hemingway

When finished visiting the finca, I wanted to return to Havana along one route Hemingway used to travel from his home into the city that is described in *Islands in the Stream* and see if we could find any of the sights he observed. With a copy of the novel close at hand, we started off. While not necessary, I was lucky enough that Víctor found in his father's papers an old Standard Oil Company of Cuba road map, *Habana y sus Alrededores* (Havana and Its Environs) that proved helpful to both the trip and Tracy Ellen Smith, who did the maps for this book.

In *Islands in the Stream*, Hudson (Hemingway) departs the finca, turns left onto the Carretera Central and follows it to near Luyano, where he thinks the view off to the left reminds him "for just a moment" of "Toledo [Spain] seen from a side hill." However, forty-one years after *Islands in the Stream* was published, the vista was blocked by foliage and the incursion of urban surroundings. Hudson followed the Carretera Central until he turned right at Fabrica Street and entered the poorer section of Havana with the "poverty, dirt, four-hundred-year-old dust ... cracked palm fronds, roofs made from hammered tins ... and the full-blast radio." Hudson then crossed under a viaduct of rail tracks, saw the smoke from the chimneys of the Havana Electric

3. Finca Vigía   73

Company and dodged heavy traffic before arriving on the avenue that borders the harbor. The modern-day visitor can still see the large old building of the electric company, plus wonder about the ability of Cuban drivers to navigate the roadway under the viaduct with cars seemingly coming from all directions and merging at one narrow location. (This is yet another reason for a tracker to hire a Cuban driver.)[58]

Shortly after Hudson's driver negotiated the traffic bottleneck he entered the street bordering the harbor and observed on the left-hand side perched atop a hill the Castillo de Atarés (Castle Atarés) "where they shot Colonel Crittenden and the others."[59]

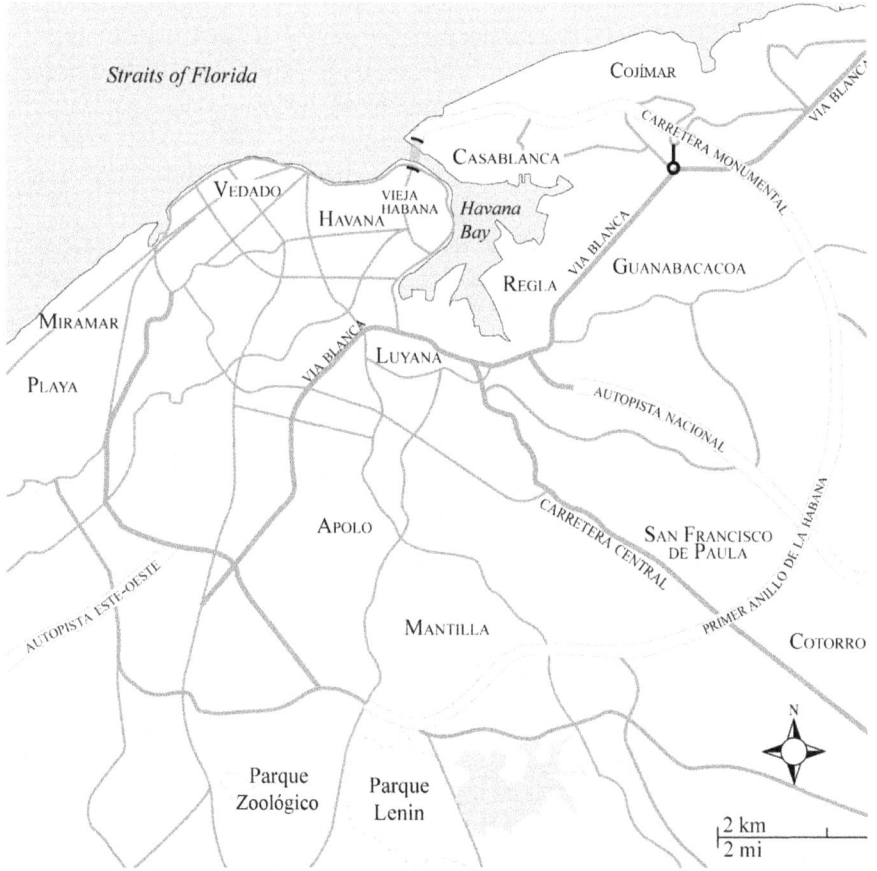

Havana: showing the location of the Museo de Ernest Hemingway at San Francisco de Paula, and the village of Cojímar. (Map by Tracy Ellen Smith.)

The events leading up to Crittenden's death occurred within the 19th century in what is known in United States history as "filibustering." Briefly, it covers the many attempts to recruit private armies in the United States and lead them to capture territory in Latin America. William L. Crittenden was born in 1820; he entered and graduated from the United States Military Academy at West Point in 1845, and later served in various locations and fought in the Mexican War. He resigned his commission in 1849. Crittenden was a nephew of United States Attorney General John J. Crittenden, of Kentucky.

In May 1850, Venezuelan native Narciso López, using hundreds of troops recruited in the United States, landed in Cuba near Cárdenas, capturing the local military garrison and the railroad station. Heavy casualties in the one-day battle, plus the arrival of Spanish army reinforcements, caused López to order a quick retreat with his battered army back to the United States. Undaunted, he again raised a number of troops in the United States and again struck Cuba the next year in August. Among the many United States citizens in the second invasion was Crittenden, now a colonel in López's army.

This second armed force landed at Bahía Honda to the west of Havana but, within three weeks, Spanish troops had completely routed the attackers. Many of the invaders were shot near the battlefield, but Crittenden and fifty of his troops were brought to Castillo de Atarés and shot by firing squads on August 16, 1851; López was garroted by the Spanish at Cárdenas on September 1, 1851.[60] (More on López in Chapter 5.)

As we were on the highway next to the harbor, I looked at the wooded hills on the left and there near the top of one hill is Castillo de Atarés. It is one of the few remaining sights that Hemingway would have viewed on his journey into Havana. By 2011, the castle was used by the police and a visitor should only photograph the castle from a long distance, using a telephoto lens.

Beyond the castillo, proceeding on Port Avenue, Hemingway could look across a bay in the harbor and see Regla, where he sometimes kept *Pilar*. Hemingway could observe the "ancient yellow church and sprawl of the houses of Regla, pink, green, and yellow houses, and the storage tanks and the refinery chimneys of Belot and behind them the gray hills toward Cojímar." He also noted the "calm of the bay that lay in the lee of the hills above Casablanca," yet another location he sometimes kept *Pilar*. From Old Havana, the easiest way to reach both

Casablanca and Regla was by ferry across the harbor. An automobile tunnel now connects Old Havana with Casablanca and Regla.[61]

In 2010, instead of completely following the directions in *Islands in the Stream* to Casablanca, I took the easier journey through the tunnel and shortly came upon Casablanca. As is true with much of the environs of Havana, the years have not been kind to this area. Driving down to the waterfront one sees the abandoned ships and terminal for the former cross bay ferries. What is well worth the excursion to Casablanca is finding and resting on a bench on the waterfront underneath a palm tree while taking in the view south, across the harbor. On a hazy day, one can dimly see the Lonja de Comercio and other parts of Plaza de San Francisco through the mist. Víctor turned the rental car to the west—we would be traveling a good deal outside of Havana and it was best to have a new car—and we eventually arrived near the harbor. Before the 1959 revolution, an unknown Cuban photographer probably made a good living by snapping photographs of ships, especially ships of the United States Navy, entering the harbor. Indeed, such a photograph would be dramatic with Old Havana on the ship's starboard side and the harbor's old fortifications on the port side.

Moving from the waterfront to the more settled portion of Casablanca on the way to Regla, I found an interesting mixture of well-preserved old buildings and those completely fallen into decay. As in Old Havana, residents walk on the roadway and along the way I noticed a young family out for a stroll, with the father carrying a young daughter on his shoulders; they were delighted when we asked if we could take a photo of them. Unlike working with museum staff members, it is not necessary to tip residents in exchange for taking their pictures, but it doesn't hurt to make the offer.

Anyone who spends any amount of time in Cuba will quickly learn that one never knows what new sight awaits around the next corner. After leaving Casablanca's harbor area, I asked Víctor to stop the car so I could get out to take a photograph of a church. Trying to frame the picture without putting too many of the overhead power wires in it, I noticed a person in the distance trying to control what seemed to be a large white dog on a leash. This seemed strange, as all of the many dogs I had seen in Cuba were never on a leash. I continued, without much success, to frame the shot before giving up and just began snapping away. At that moment, the piercing sound of a loud animal's squeal caused me to turn around. Rapidly approaching was a local man leading a grown pig on a leash. The sow, in the manner of all pigs, had its mind made up as to which route it would take—and it was not the one the man had planned. The pig was extremely vocal in its protests, while the man no doubt had his own complaints, although his were drowned out by the overgrown porker's sounds. As the two passed by me, man and pig were now at a trot as the Cuban gave a what-am-I-going-to-do? look as they passed the laughing *Norte Americano* trying unsuccessfully to focus his camera. When last seen, the two were running full out as they continued their loud argument. Leaving Casablanca with a smile on our faces, we approach Regla, the final location on the Hemingway tour.

Hemingway, at times, kept *Pilar* docked in Regla, and mentioned the city's colorful houses in *Islands in the Stream*. Time, once again, had taken its toll on the buildings of the area. After Víctor drove through many streets, trying (unsuccessfully) to find a home bearing the hues described in the novel, I eventually spotted a house located at the intersection of two streets that stood out from its neighbors. Víctor stopped the car a short distance away and I walked closer to obtain a good view for a photograph. As with many homes in Cuba, it had a cement wall encircling the house and the wall was painted gray about a quarter of the distance up, and then white to the top. A series of spindle-like shapes graced the area between the main part of the encircling wall and its roof, making it one of the more decorative locations in the surrounding barrio. Halfway along the front wall there was another nice decorative touch to the entrance: a structure of perhaps eight to ten feet in height that carried on the color scheme of the lower wall and a small roof containing traditional roofing tiles. The structure housed a gate made up of vertical and horizontal twisted iron work painted black with decorative representations of fleur-de-lis painted in blue, all in all a gate, no doubt the work of a very good blacksmith.

The wall prevented seeing much of the patio between the street entrance and the actual door to the house. What *could* be glimpsed on the right side was a raised bed containing what appeared to be banana plants, plus other smaller unidentified tropical foliage; the left side had a smaller amount of large-leafed plants and, apparently, as will be seen, a deck leading off the front of the house to the wall. A single large bush, or small tree, sat on each side of the house.

The house itself was two stories, showing a newly painted white façade gleaming in the direct sunlight. Viewing the structure from the front, I could see the spindle-like forms in the property's wall worked into the balustrades surrounding two balconies. All of the observable windows had traditional wooden shutters, giving the home a pleasing, inviting appearance.

As I busily snapped digital pictures and moved to various spots to obtain different angles, a woman appeared from the house and stood on the deck, leaning on the wall, closely watching me. This seemed like a fortunate opportunity to place a Cuban in the photograph, and with some luck, the opportunity to meet this person and be allowed inside the wall to better photograph the home. This did not seem an unreasonable thought, as most Cubans seemed to enjoy having their pictures taken. I noticed, however, that the woman's increasingly dour countenance suggested otherwise. The next photograph captured a passerby with his head turned toward the woman as she pointed toward the photographer. With an invitation to photograph the home's interior seeming less and less a possibility, I retreated to the car, in case the woman decided to confront me.

Which she did.

She went straight to Víctor and, in Spanish, they had a brief communication. The woman seemed to accept his explanation for the presence of the American photographer and—with only a quick glance back at me—she made her way back to the house. Víctor placed the car in gear and pulled away, a large grin brightening his face.

"The woman wanted to know what you were doing," he explained. "I told her you were tracking the locations Ernest Hemingway knew in Cuba. She then said, 'No one takes a photograph of this house.' Guess why."

"I have no idea," I replied.

"This is the house of the Chief of Police."

We continued Thomas Hudson's drive into Havana by following San Isidero Street—in Hemingway's day the red light district near the water—then past the train station and back out onto the harbor avenue, ending the trip. Hemingway, however, would have continued on to Obispo and the Plaza de Armas, described previously in Chapter 2, but the modern traveler cannot drive in these areas as they are in historical zones that ban automobile traffic.

Earl Wilson, a former columnist for the *New York Post*, once wrote a piece on someone questioning why Hemingway preferred living in

Cuba to the United States. Hemingway replied that he had always worked well in Cuba. The finca put distance between him and the distractions of the city, and its hilltop location made for cool nights. He worked early in the morning, then swam in the pool, reading afterwards. Or he could go fishing or shooting. Both he and Mary could listen to the extensive record collection at the finca or they could attend the occasional concert in Havana. Mary enjoyed gardening and the finca again proved ideal.

Hemingway closed by saying if someone could find a place on a hill in Ohio where he could be very close to "the Gulf Stream and have my own fruit and vegetables the year around and raise and fight game chickens without breaking the law" he would go live there, "if Miss Mary and my cats and dogs agree."[62]

Anyone interested in Ernest Hemingway and his years in Cuba should visit his finca. For an even greater understanding of Hemingway's love of Cuba, make more than one visit and spend a great deal of time slowly savoring the house and its surroundings. Go on a hot, cloudless day and seek a chair in the shade of the present ceiba tree. Let your eyes wander over the front of the house and then turn and look down the well-traveled path with its surrounding foliage leading to the entrance of the finca. Sit in the cooling shade long enough and you can almost hear the *clickity-clack* of a manual typewriter sitting on the book atop the bookcase in the bedroom as Hemingway stands there trying once again to write one true sentence.

❖ 4 ❖

Las Estrellas de Gigi

A goal of my visit to Cuba was to see how Ernest Hemingway interacted with Cubans and how they viewed the Norte Americano author. I set out to accomplish this task by learning something of the Cubans who came into contact with Hemingway while he resided at Finca Vigía.

Seventy-eight-year-old Oscar Blas Fernández Mesa recalled an event leading to a magical time for him as a child of ten. Blas lived in a poor neighborhood just off the main road from Havana in one of the larger fincas in the area of San Francisco de Paula. One of Blas's friends, Fico Ramos Enrique, said, "We were very poor. We lived in houses with dirt floors and straw roofs." On this day, Blas and his friends started down the dusty dirt road to find a place to play, or to throw rocks at the mangoes in one of the nearby fincas. Oscar recalled that the owners of the farms did not want small poor boys picking the fruit. Some owners even employed guards to keep unwanted visitors out. However, as children throughout the world have always done, the Cuban boys tried to find a way around the obstacle. They threw rocks at the fruit, hoping to knock some off the tree. Then they would rush in and grab whatever hit the ground and run.[1]

On this day, the group of children started to make their way down the road to a finca. As they neared a place called Finca Vigía they saw a car parked by the gate. A "strong man" stepped out of the car. Blas recalled, "As curious children, we stood close to him." He began asking the children questions. The large man laughed at many of their replies. He asked if they played baseball and the boys replied they did, but they did not have equipment. "They used a flat piece of wood for a bat and

Oscar Blas Fernández Mesa (in 2008), whose nickname was "Cayuco," was a member of the Las Estrellas de Gigi. Cayuco hit the first homerun and thus received the name *Cayuco Jonronero* (Cayuco, the Homerun Kid). (Photograph by the author.)

a rolled up [and taped] wad of cloth for a ball." Eventually, the children started to move off. Asked where they were going, back came the reply: "To another finca." The "strong man" asked the boys if they played inside the walls of the Finca Vigía. One of the boys explained that the owner did not allow them on the grounds. At one point in the conversation the big man said he was going to buy the farm. Then, he would "allow the children to play and eat the fruit from the trees of the finca and the door would be open to all." Out of respect for the "strong" man, they called him *señor* [mister] and later would call him what many adults did, "Papa."[2]

Blas later remembered some of the boys excitedly said if the man bought the finca, "He would allow them to play [on the grounds]." Others said, "You're crazy! He won't allow us inside." The boys making this comment had only to point out the fact that many farms employed guards. Most owners set rules aimed at keeping neighborhood boys off their land, with the Finca Vigía's former owner even keeping "large dogs" to protect his property.[3]

4. *Las Estrellas de Gigi*

Hemingway kept his word to the boys and even employed some of the children to work around the house. Valerie Hemingway, Hemingway's onetime secretary who later married his youngest son, Gregory, thought that the "children came over to steal the mangoes. Instead of shooing them away, Ernest found things for them to do." Hemingway's granddaughter, Hilary, wrote of one incident in particular. Hemingway had removed the dogs of the previous owner and this meant the children did not hesitate to come over the walls to throw rocks at the bright yellow-orange mangoes.[4] Hemingway spied the boys and started down the path toward the trees. "'Hey, knock it off,' he yelled in Spanish. 'Leave the bloody trees alone. You can have the fruit—but don't harm the trees.'"[5]

Papa soon had the boys picking up the mail and feeding the cats. Ramos received the job of holding doors open for wages that amounted to "pocket money" for Hemingway but meant a great deal of money to the boys of San Francisco de Paula.

At this time, the 1940s, Hemingway's two sons from his marriage with Pauline—Patrick and Gregory—planned to visit Cuba in the summer. Blas said that one day "one of the kids [who worked in the house came to us] and said, 'The American [wants] us to meet his sons.'" Blas recalled that they "were happy that we would meet children from another country. The next day in the morning we went to the finca to meet Patrick and Gregory, who were about our ages. [Hemingway] introduced us with our name and nicknames." (Blas's Cuban nickname, for instance, was Cayuco). "[Patrick and Gregory] shook hands and gave us a hug like great friends."

The Cuban boys then received a huge surprise.

After the introductions, "A person came out of the house with all the equipment for baseball," recalled Blas. "I was very happy. I had never had a [baseball] glove and I found one I liked and told [Hemingway]." He said, "This is Cayuco's."

Hemingway set aside a small area where the children could play baseball. There were only two bases, about seventy feet apart. Over sixty years later, Blas still recalled the feeling of the close-clipped grass between his toes, as the children played barefoot. They owned only one pair of shoes, and "their mothers would have been furious had they worn them out playing baseball; so Patrick and Gregory played shoeless, too."[6]

Hemingway sometimes pitched. "He would throw the ball very

softly because he was afraid to hit us," said Cayuco. "When he played, he seemed like our big brother. He had as much fun as we did."

"Sometimes we would be playing, and he would come back from somewhere in his car," said Ramos. "And before going back into the house, he would play with us."

Blas played center field. In one of Hilary Hemingway's accounts, she speculates as to why Cayuco was assigned this position. Ernest caught Blas throwing stones at the mangoes. Cayuco "had let a rock fly that hit its mark, the largest ripest mango, seventy feet into the trees."

"Damn, you've got some arm, kid," Hemingway said admiringly.[7]

Blas said that sometimes five or six of the Cuban children played on the field at night. At times Cayuco came to the finca to just play with Patrick, because he was older. "We used to run inside the mansion," he recalled. They also played at the tennis courts. Hemingway tried to teach the Cuban boys tennis, but the children seemed more interested in baseball. Besides, where in their everyday world would they play tennis?

Hemingway, according to Blas, also tried to teach the boys the fundamentals of boxing. He let the boys hit him, but did not return their blows. "One saw that big, smiling, good-natured man, so strong and healthy, perspiring, encouraging his opponents to jab him hard, telling them he could stand anything." The air rang with boys shouting encouragement to their friends.[8]

Gilberto Enríquez, one of the boys who came to the finca, recalled the time that another boy, Félix Sosa, sparred with Patrick Hemingway. Sosa hit Patrick a number of times below the belt. Hemingway took the gloves away from Patrick and put them on, saying to Sosa, "That's not the way to box. I'm going to teach you how it's done." Sosa, when he saw Hemingway put on the gloves, feared he would really have to fight the big American. He threw off his gloves and ran home. A few days later, Hemingway sent a boy to bring Sosa to the farm so they could make peace and Sosa would not feel hurt. "The truth is," said Gilberto, "that Hemingway did not have a mean bone in his body."[9]

Gilberto also recalled that at Christmas time "Hemingway could be seen surrounded by almost twenty boys, roaming the streets of San Francisco de Paula setting off [firecrackers]." Enríquez remembered that the boys felt that they were part of a "commando team." Firecrackers in hand, they once sneaked up to a barbershop, threw them in the door, and "flung themselves to the floor." Most of the time people believed it was only children playing, but when they saw that Hemingway was responsible, they sometimes became angry and said, "Damn it, that American is too old for this kind of thing," but that is all that happened. Gilberto felt that because of his size and strength no one in the neighborhood wanted to "tangle" with him. But mainly, they did not say anything because he was well liked and "people forgave him his childishness." He "used to run away with the boys as fast as he could, but [you] can imagine what this must have looked like; that big man among fifteen or twenty kids running uphill or downhill through the streets of San Francisco de Paula. People would say, 'Why, it's Hemingway!' and then they heard the explosions: 'Hemingway and his fireworks.'"[10]

Eventually Hemingway established a baseball team. According to some accounts, the writer paid for the uniforms, including hats. Valerie said that "a local seamstress [made the] uniforms from discarded sugar

Ernest Hemingway established and equipped a baseball team for the Cuban children who lived near his home. He also wanted to have boys to play ball with his sons when they visited him. The team was dubbed Las Estrellas de Gigi (the Gigi Stars) after his youngest son, Gregory. Note the boys are playing barefoot, as their mothers would never have allowed them to play in their good shoes. (Photograph courtesy of the Ernest Hemingway Collection, John F. Kennedy Library.)

sacks." The team now needed a name. The boys decided upon Las Estrellas de Gigi (The Gigi Stars) after Hemingway's youngest son, Gregory. "In royal blue letters, the word *Stars* was emblazoned across the chest with a star on the hats." Center fielder Cayuco Blas chose number 5 for his hero Joe DiMaggio of the New York Yankees.[11] Soon, the Stars began playing other Cuban teams. The children piled into Hemingway's car and he drove them to the games, relishing his role as manager.

About this time, two things happened concerning the team. First, Hemingway felt that perhaps the boys would enjoy playing on a well-maintained field. Every Wednesday and Sunday, the boys rode into Havana to the Club de Cazadors (The Hunters' Club). On occasion, Hemingway took his sons to this club for skeet shooting. At the time, the club was restricted to the upper classes only, but with Hemingway as their coach, this did not apply to the dark-skinned Cuban boys.

Hemingway realized there needed to be two teams at the finca, so the boys could remain sharp. He again recruited boys from the neighborhood and equipped them with uniforms. At times he pitched for both teams. "Papa would bat, too," Blas said. "When he got a hit, he would make one of the little kids run for him." It hardly mattered who ran, and where: "No score was ever kept."[12]

Hemingway's love for the children of San Francisco de Paula further showed itself when tragedy struck the neighborhood. Rodolfo Villarreal worked in the Hemingway house with Ramos until the age of ten. One day while Rodolfo rode in a wagon loaded with fruit, he fell underneath the wheel. As Rodolfo writhed and screamed in agony in the dirt street, his older brother, Luis, recalls, "We didn't know what to do." Rodolfo somehow managed to reach their home and his mother sent word to Hemingway that Rodolfo had been hurt in a serious accident. Hemingway quickly sent his car and driver to take mother and boy to the nearest first-aid station. They had to reroute Rodolfo to a hospital, but they could not save the boy. When Hemingway learned of Rodolfo's death he sent word to the family, asking that they allow him to pay for the funeral expenses; he also had two flower arrangements delivered to Rodolfo's home: one on behalf of the Finca Vigía; the other from the employees. Shortly thereafter, Hemingway had René Villarreal take over Rodolfo's duties in the house and also recruited him for the baseball team.[13]

The family of Fico Ramos also learned of Hemingway's compassion.

When Fico's sister died, Hemingway personally delivered a wreath to the Ramos' home and offered his condolences. "For him to come to a house like ours," said Ramos, fighting back tears. "Honestly, I was just an employee, but he always treated us like family." Mary taught Fico to cook and he "helped her make a Chinese luncheon for Ernest's fiftieth birthday."[14]

By 1943, Patrick and Gregory had stopped visiting their father in Cuba. They had grown older and were pursuing other interests. Soon, the children of the neighborhood drifted back to playing in the dusty street, and the ball field fell into disrepair. The children, however, returned once a year at Christmas to wish their former manager a Merry Christmas. He would tell the boys stories of his travels and, as each filed out of the house, he gave them a dollar bill.

Despite the dissolution of Las Estrellas de Gigi, the boys who played never forgot their magical time at the finca. Cayuco Blas said, "Life in the forties was really hard. At that time [Hemingway] was like a father to us."[15]

When Hemingway returned to the farm after one of his journeys, Luis Villarreal said, "I came to welcome him back along with many of his neighbors in San Francisco [de Paula]." In the 1980s Luis, still living close to Finca Vigía, said, "I no longer like [coming to the finca, as it] saddens me—part of my life was spent here, close to a person whom we loved and who loved us so much. And now he is gone."[16]

In 2008, Oscar "Cayuco" Blas recalled that he once hit a home run off of Hemingway's pitch. After he trotted over home plate, Papa came up to him, put his hand on his shoulder, and said, "Cayuco, you are a home runner." This then led to his other nickname, "Jonronero," the Home Run Kid. Blas paused in telling this story and his dark countenance creased into a wide smile. "I have never forgotten him."[17]

If René Villarreal's life had been spent in the United States, it would be labeled a classic Horatio Alger story. René Luis Rosa de La Caridad Villarreal Vergara and his identical twin, Luis René Rosa de La Caridad Villarreal Vergara, entered the world on August 30, 1929, in the Havana suburb of Vedado. His father, Mario, and mother, Felita, had six children—five boys and one girl. Mario worked as a cook in a hospital in Havana, and Felita took in laundry. They lived in a modest home near the gate of the Finca Vigía. Both parents worked hard and, René recalled many years later, the children all went to school fully clothed and with shoes, which many in San Francisco de Paula did not.[18]

By the time of the establishment of the Estrellas de Gigi, the neighborhood and people of San Francisco de Paula had come to like their new resident. Most could not pronounce Hemingway's name and called him Mr. Way, with the boys calling him Papa.[19]

After the death of René's older brother, Hemingway asked his parents' permission if René could take his older brother's place working in the house of the Finca Vigía. He wanted the boy to tend the cats and dogs and run errands after school. The parents consented, and René was told by Papa to look upon the finca as his own home. "La Finca was a paradise to an eleven-year-old boy," René would recall fifty-nine years later. Hemingway approved of René's dedication to the pets of the farm and eventually gave him more duties.

René also recalled that the cook, Maria, always prepared a dinner for the staff in the late afternoon and served it in the pantry. She invited Fico (another boy who worked in the house) and René to join them. Fico never hesitated. René, however, felt guilty about eating such good food while his family at home lived on beans and rice, with no meat. He refused to eat Maria's cooking, but would offer no explanation. She began to make it her duty to get the boy to eat, without success. This struggle kept up until one day Hemingway heard the commotion in the pantry and came in to investigate. He asked René if he did not like Maria's cooking. The boy began crying and refused to answer. Hemingway then told Maria not to force him to eat. Eventually, Maria learned of the reason behind his refusal to eat. When Hemingway was informed, he instructed Maria to make extra food and have René take it home. René's mother at first though the boy had either begged for or had stolen it. He convinced her that Maria said El Americano had asked her to do it. This continued until Hemingway wrote a letter of recommendation for René's father, Mario, to obtain a better-paying job at another hospital that allowed him to bring leftover food from the kitchen. After this, René ate with the staff at the finca.[20]

Hemingway continued to watch René's progress. Villarreal recalled that he did not have much contact with Martha Hemingway. When "Miss Mary" replaced Martha, however, René had more interaction with this wife. Another reason for his having more knowledge of Mary is that, by this time, René had become the assistant to the house's majordomo.

René remembered that Mary spent a great deal of time with the gardeners, learning the Spanish names for all the plants and flowers. She even practiced her Spanish on the staff. Mary also took the time to visit René's home and visited with his family. She enjoyed speaking to his nine-year-old sister, Nilda, and invited her to the finca's house to play with Mary's cat, chat with her, and work in the garden. Afterwards, she walked Nilda home.[21]

As Mary settled in to the house, a series of events took place which led to the dismissal of the majordomo. In her memoir, *How It Was*, Mary recalled that René "looked at me with questions in his eyes" when hearing of the dismissal. Mary had made a favorable impression on René, and vice-versa. She recalled the seventeen-year-old boy as a "quiet, intelligent, well-mannered young man ... he and I were tacit friends."[22]

Mary told Villarreal that even though Papa thought he might be too young for the responsibility of majordomo of the house he shouldn't worry, and she was right. Eventually, everyone on the staff, although older than René, spoke highly of him and had no problems with his assuming the position. Even Gregorio Fuentes (no relation to the writer Norberto Fuentes) the mate of the *Pilar* expressed his belief that René was the perfect candidate for the job. In her memoir, Mary wrote that René learned his responsibilities and worked "with such devotion and goodwill" toward all the staff that he became her "*hijo Cubano*" (Cuban son). He retained his position for all the years the Hemingways continued to live at the Finca Vigía.[23]

Luis Villarreal remembered that the Papa and Mary would sometimes be away from the finca for a year, and "my brother ... was left in charge of the house. When Papa returned, everything was in order." Years later, René would proudly say, "I was the only person allowed to go into his room when he was writing."[24]

Earlier, when Hemingway found that René did not excel at baseball, he began to teach the boy how to box, a sport at which he became highly proficient. Boys from San Francisco de Paula started coming to the finca to box with him. René quickly earned the title of "Kid Vigía." He enjoyed the sport so much that once, while the Hemingways were gone on one of their trips, he went to a gym and trained to box professionally, in the welterweight class. He continued to use his "Kid Vigía" in the ring. Villarreal won five fights, three by knockouts and two by decisions, and lost one, but decided to retire. René felt he did not have the "discipline" to continue onward.[25]

As the years passed, the people of San Francisco de Paula knew that a member of their village, René, had gained Hemingway's trust and respect and, in at least one case, came to Villarreal for help. Villagers began to speak of the improvement of the Carretera Central from Havana past San Francisco de Paula. While this meant more employment and better access to the city, the bad news came from Guanabacoa. The much larger neighboring community had an aqueduct and planned to run its pipes through San Francisco de Paula without giving them access to the water. Years later, René explained that, during the summertime, the residents of San Francisco de Paula suffered from the dry season and often "went a couple of days without water." The previous year, for example, it had gotten so bad that Hemingway had opened a previously sealed well—it had been sealed to prevent anyone from falling into it—and allowed the villagers to come onto the finca for their water. The residents of San Francisco de Paula met to raise money to bribe the people working on the aqueduct to channel some of the water to their village. The efforts to raise the needed money fell short; a delegation then asked Villarreal if he would speak to Hemingway for help on their behalf. René went to Hemingway, who immediately wrote a check for the needed amount.[26]

René had a life-changing event in 1953 when a young woman walked by his family's home. Her name was Elpidia (although she was called "Fanny"). She asked René if he would hold onto the large dog she was walking. Fanny's "long black, wavy hair, her dark eyes, and her shapely figure" quickly attracted the twenty-three-year-old René, and the two were soon dating. They had been engaged for one year before he brought her to the finca and introduced her to Hemingway. At the meeting, Ernest said, "*Cuida bien a mi hijo cubano* ("Take good care of my Cuban son"). The three walked out to the front steps of the house and had their photograph taken. (The photograph is on the dust jacket of René's memoir.) The next day, Hemingway said that René should take the guest bungalow so that he could be near Fanny. So trusted was he that he was given permission to live in the house when the Hemingways were gone for any length of time. René respectfully refused, explaining that he and Fanny had rented a place just outside the grounds of the finca. On March 10, 1957, René and Fanny were married. Their first born, a son, died in infancy. After recovering from this loss, they went on to have three boys and two girls.[27]

To say that René remained loyal to Hemingway is to understate on a grand scale. He took strong exception to the way Papa was portrayed in the Cuban film *Memories of Underdevelopment*, based upon a fictional work by Edmundo Desnoes. The director, Tomás Gutiérrez Alea, said that after viewing the film, René "did not seem to understand the film was a work of fiction.... René got a gun and went looking for Edmundo and me. He wanted to kill us."[28]

A Cuban writer recalled that, while interviewing René, he produced "a letter that looked as if it had been folded and unfolded hundreds of times. He must have known the contents by heart, yet he had tears in his eyes as he read it solemnly." This was Hemingway's last letter to him. His former employer wrote of his illness and that "Old Papa is no longer what he used to be."[29]

René remained at the finca after the Hemingways left Cuba in July 1960, not long after Fidel Castro came into power. He never saw Papa again.

Before Mary returned to Cuba for the last time, Villarreal had a surprise visit from Castro. The prime minister knew of René's closeness to Hemingway and wanted him as a guide to the house. Castro informed him that he wanted to make a museum of Finca Vigía.[30]

Just prior to her departure from Cuba, Mary gave checks to all the household staff, with Villarreal's reflecting the largest amount. She also told him, "Papa and I always thought of leaving this house for you and your family." After leaving the finca, government officials forbade him from entering the grounds. He went three months without employment before finding a position at a steel mill.[31]

In late 1962, Fidel Castro showed a visitor the finca. While this took place, René was visiting a friend who lived near the farm. A short time into René's visit there came a knock on the door. Two armed militiamen wanted Villarreal to accompany them in their Jeep. His friend quite naturally felt very nervous, but René recalled he had a "clear conscience" and went with the two men. Expecting to be taken to a nearby headquarters, Villarreal was surprised when the Jeep turned into the grounds of the finca. The two men took René to a waiting Castro and his guest. Fidel wanted René to lead the tour. After finishing, Castro pointed out the damage to the house and grounds. He wanted Villarreal back in charge of the finca and to restore it so it had the feeling Hemingway still lived there. René accepted the position.

By 1963, some government officials began to cause employment at the new Museo de Ernesto Hemingway difficult for Villarreal. At one point, he had to close the museum while being sent to train to "defend Cuba against foreign invaders." When a delegation of foreign visitors from the Soviet Union came to see the museum and found it closed, it embarrassed several in the government and an order came down that Villarreal "was not to be bothered unless the country was under attack."[32] In spite of this, the situation continued to deteriorate for René. He learned of spies sent to work at the finca to report on his work. In 1968, René decided he could no longer work at the farm and could no longer live in Cuba. He managed to get word to Mary Hemingway to help get him and his family out of the country. Villarreal gave his resignation and a government official again forbade him from entering the finca's grounds. In 1969, Villarreal received a two-year hard labor sentence of cutting sugar cane, a "mandatory service you had to provide for your country if you wanted to leave." The work entailed working twelve hours a day and receiving a single peso for a day's grueling labor. In addition, he was called a *"gusano"* ("worm") for wanting to leave Cuba.[33]

At the end of his sentence, on March 12, 1972, with Mary Hemingway's help, René Villarreal, his wife and five children flew to Spain. In 1974, the family migrated to the United States and found a home in New Jersey. Five years later, when the Cuban government allowed exiles to visit family in Cuba, René returned, but was not allowed to visit the finca. It was not until 1983 that he was allowed to do so. He paid a final visit in 1996. Sadly, René Villarreal passed away in 2014.[34]

◆ 5 ◆

Tracking Hemingway Eastward to Santiago de Cuba

If Hemingway searchers have at least two weeks in Cuba, they should consider driving to the east and west of the capital city, exploring areas that are off the beaten tourist tracks. These lesser-known locations will provide searchers with a greater understanding of why Hemingway loved Cuba, how the citizens viewed him, and how the environment contributed to his writing. Again, it is highly recommended that the inquisitive traveler employ a knowledgeable guide.

In 1978, William Least Heat Moon, after losing his position as a teacher and separating from his wife, set out in an old van on a road trip around the United States that eventually covered approximately 13,000 miles (20,921 kms). He followed only small, out-of-the-way roads, which he named "Blue Highways," based on the color of these roads in an old Rand McNally road atlas. His best-selling book, *Blue Highways*, is an interesting view of rural America. Over three decades later, I wished to copy Least Heat Moon's idea and explore to the east and west of Havana in search of Hemingway by following Cuba's "blue highways," along with some strange byways.

The route for any eastward journey should largely hug the north coast for a great deal of this first aspect of the trek. The north coast was important in Hemingway's time in Cuba, as he perfected his deep-sea fishing in this general area. He actually began his long interest in big-game fishing while living in Key West. In 1932, Hemingway hired Joe Russell as a guide and, aboard Russell's boat *Anita*, sailed into Cuban waters, furthering his passion for the sport. In February 1933,

Hemingway learned that S. Kip Farrington landed a 155-pound blue marlin off Bimini: the first on record ever taken with rod and reel at the eastern edge of the Gulf Stream. Farrington gave up a career on Wall Street to become "one of the world's leading sports fisherman." He wrote prolifically on fishing and other subjects. Farrington also held records of his own in deep-sea fishing and served as saltwater editor of the popular sporting magazine *Field & Stream* from 1937 to 1972. Farmington's feat is one of the reasons Hemingway first entertained the idea of procuring a deep-sea fishing craft of his own.[1]

By this time, Hemingway had read a brochure from the Wheeler Boatyard in Brooklyn, New York. They were noted for building beautiful handcrafted wooden boats. In 1920, one of Wheeler's series of craft, the *Playmate*, measured thirty-eight feet. Hemingway, after doing his normal studying of any subject that interested him, decided the *Playmate* was the type of sea-going boat to pursue his quest for big-game fish. This desire for a fishing craft came about while the writer was in the midst of his preparations for a European trip and an African safari. But, as Pauline's ubiquitous rich uncle Gus had put up the money for the journey—some $25,000 (almost $440,000 in 2016 dollars)—Hemingway was understandably reluctant to approach Uncle Gus again, this time for the $3,500 ($63,000) needed to make the down payment on the boat. Putting his imagination to work, he came up with an alternate plan.[2]

Upon their return to the United States, and before the journey back to Key West, the Hemingways stopped off first in New York City. While there, Hemingway entered into an agreement with Arnold Gingrich, the editor of a new men's magazine, *Esquire*. Gingrich loaned him $3,000 for the down payment and Hemingway agreed to provide the magazine with monthly articles. At $250 for each, this meant a year's worth of pieces. The arrangement proved agreeable to three parties: Hemingway, Gingrich, and the readers of *Esquire*—four, if one wishes to count the many readers since the 1930s who have read the articles. Many of the stories centered on Hemingway's observations on the sport for which he is most noted in Cuba: big game fishing— marlin fishing in particular. Hemingway's gratitude to Gingrich "lingered beyond the contractual obligations." As the agreement was concluded, Hemingway sent the short story "The Snows of Kilimanjaro," which he called "the best story Gingrich ever got" and "more than repaid" the editor for his loan.[3]

5. Tracking Hemingway Eastward to Santiago de Cuba   93

With the cash for the down payment, Hemingway went to the Wheeler Boatyard and ordered the *Playmate* cruiser. He requested some specifications of his own for the craft: larger fuel tanks, the transom lowered twelve inches to help in pulling in large fish, a live fish well, a second deck chair, and an auxiliary motor independent of the main engine. The total cost of the boat: $7,455 (about $135,000 in 2016 dollars).[4]

Wheeler delivered the wooden boat to Miami on Saturday, May 12, 1934. It measured thirty-five feet, five inches, instead of the advertised thirty-eight feet, due to its specified alterations. The craft's beam measured eleven feet, five inches, drew five-and-a-half feet of water and registered at fifteen-and-a-half gross tons. Two gasoline engines, a Chrysler Crown that developed eighty horsepower and a four-cylinder Lycoming motor, produced forty horsepower for trolling. In good seas and with everything working correctly, the boat made sixteen knots. Attached to the bows were the metal U.S. Coast Guard identification numbers K26761 and a round metal plaque with the letter "W," for Wheeler, gracing the point of the bow.

Hemingway christened the craft *Pilar* and painted its name, along with "Key West" on the stern. A number of explanations have been put forth for the name. One such explanation is that it is named for the statue of the Virgin Mary in Zaragoza, Spain; another is that Pilar was said to be one of Pauline's secret nicknames when she first met Hemingway; and, very likely, it was named after the main character, Pilar, in Hemingway's *For Whom the Bell Tolls*. Despite these theories, no one really knows for sure the source for the vessel's moniker.[5] Captain Bra, of Key West, and Hemingway sailed *Pilar* from Miami to Key West, and one can only imagine the joy the new owner felt on the shakedown cruise.[6]

Canadian fir and high-grade Honduras mahogany made up the sides and decks of *Pilar*. The craft could never really be called a yacht: Hemingway meant it for deep-sea fishing, a "fishing machine." Walter Houk, who sailed five times in *Pilar*, recalled "people who expected a pleasure boat often found her uncomfortable." Houk, however, recalled, "In a heaving sea, I found [*Pilar*] felt reassuring underfoot."[7]

Walter Houk was born on June 14, 1925, in Walnut Park, at the eastern edge of Los Angeles. He graduated from the U.S. Naval Academy at Annapolis, Maryland, in 1947, and immediately resigned his commission to enter the Foreign Service. By the end of 1949, Houk arrived at his new post in Cuba. His articles on Hemingway are valuable for many things, not the least of which is the information regarding his time aboard *Pilar*.

The purchasing of *Pilar* is one of the major events in Hemingway's life for, as Houk notes, the craft gave Hemingway access to Havana and the Cuban north coast, locations that would later figure prominently in his writing. He now had the ability to spend more time not only trolling for marlin, but also learning more about the fish. Hemingway, of course, no longer had to depend on chartering a boat and this made it much easier to move to Cuba to continue his marlin observations and to fish. Mark P. Ott, of the English department at Deerfield Academy, compares Hemingway's writing style prior to obtaining *Pilar* to the artist Cézanne—abstract. With Ernest's long years of studying the sea, his style changed to that of the great 19th century American artist Winslow Homer—realistic. *Pilar* is the model for the craft in *Islands in the Stream*, published posthumously.[8] As Hemingway learned about the great fish while in *Pilar*, he grew to love the sea. He says it best in *The Old Man and the Sea* when describing the feelings of his protagonist, Santiago: "He always thought of the sea as *la mar* which is what people call her in Spanish when they love her."[9]

When Hemingway and Pauline first fished in Cuban waters aboard José Russell's boat *Anita* in 1932, they met Carlos Gutiérrez. Carlos began fishing with his father for tuna and marlin at a young age and by the time Gutiérrez met Hemingway he had been fishing for more than fifty years. Throughout his life, Hemingway read as much as he could on any new subject. He also looked for someone who knew the subject very well at the working level rather than someone who only knew theory, or as one would say in colloquial naval language, he wanted someone at the "deck plate level." Gutiérrez became his first Cuban teacher on big game fish, and he stressed that to catch really large marlin one had to learn the habits of these magnificent fish. In the Hemingway Collection at the John F. Kennedy Library in Boston, there is a small "Standard School Series Notebook." In it are Hemingway's notes about what he remembered Gutiérrez telling him about marlin in the Gulf Stream. Some Hemingway scholars believe Gutiérrez is the model for Santiago.[10]

When Hemingway took ownership of *Pilar*, he had also heard of very good fishing off Bimini, but instead of trying out his new craft in

5. Tracking Hemingway Eastward to Santiago de Cuba   95

that island's waters, he shaped a course for Cuban waters on Wednesday, July 18, 1934. He remained there for three months, making it his longest deep-sea extended fishing trip. Why he chose to go to Cuba is unknown, but it may well have been because he felt more comfortable in waters he knew. Eventually, in the summer of 1936, Hemingway did spend a month and a half off Bimini, becoming "something of a legendary figure on the island."[11] For the 1934 Cuban trip, Hemingway wanted José Russell as mate, but with the ending of Prohibition, Russell's legitimate business, Sloppy Joe's Bar, took up most of his time. "Times might be hard, Cap," he told Hemingway, "but ol' Mr. Hoover done put a helluva thirst on all the honest folks." Instead, Hemingway shipped with his Cuban teacher, the now fifty-five-year-old Carlos Gutiérrez, aboard as mate.[12]

One member of Hemingway's 1934 crew, Arnold Samuelson, seems almost like a character in a novel summoned up by the writer. Samuelson, born February 6, 1912, in a sod house in North Dakota, spent a great deal of his early life hunting, riding, fishing, and "avoiding farm labor." His only ambition: to become a writer. Samuelson attended the University of Minnesota, majoring in journalism. Although he passed all the courses he did not graduate because he would not "pay the $5 diploma fee."[13]

Samuelson was tall, liked boxing, and worked as a cub reporter on the *Minneapolis Tribune*. His interest in pugilism and his working as a reporter are much in the vein of Hemingway's early years. In 1932, Samuelson set out to see the country, earning money by cutting hair and playing the violin. He wrote a few articles for the Minneapolis newspaper on his wanderings. In 1934, after reading Hemingway's article "One Trip Across," the young man decided to make his way by hitchhiking and hopping railroad freight cars to Key West to tell Hemingway how much he enjoyed his writing. Samuelson arrived in Key West when he was Depression–era destitute, with only a loaf of bread and no place to stay. His sole means of accommodation, in fact, was the city's jail. It may be difficult for modern readers to imagine a young man doing all this just to walk up to Hemingway's door, knock and then hope the writer would answer so he could tell him how much he enjoyed his article. Yet, that is exactly what Arnold did.

When Hemingway first met Samuelson he brushed the young man aside, but upon learning of Arnold's living conditions he took him into his house and began talking to him. Samuelson professed his desire to write. Hemingway later commented that Samuelson was very serious about writing and that he told the young man seriousness was one of two traits a person should have for writing fiction. The other was talent. Hemingway read some of the articles Samuelson showed him and felt the material very bad, but he realized that an aspiring writer's first efforts are not always the best indicator of talent. In an unusual move, Hemingway offered Samuelson a position as night watchman on *Pilar*.

Arnold Samuelson spent the entire cruise of 1934 on board *Pilar*. As was Hemingway's wont, he at first nicknamed Arnold the "Maestro," because of his abilities with a violin, but eventually shortened it to "Mice." Hemingway has forever captured the young would-be writer in the article "Monologue to the Maestro," published in *Esquire*. Hemingway admitted Samuelson's writing "improved steadily," but as a sailor the young man was "a calamity[:] seeming sometimes to have four feet," with "an incurable tendency toward sea-sickness." Samuelson, however, took dictation from Hemingway every day and placed the transcript in the log. It "was the one thing I could do better than anyone else on board," Samuelson later wrote. He also kept a detailed notebook throughout this period. Samuelson's book *With Hemingway: A Year in Key West and Cuba*, edited by his daughter after his death, contains his observations in the notebook and is a mine of information on Hemingway during this period.[14]

Samuelson never attained his goal of becoming a serious writer. He did, however, publish an article on fishing in the Gulf Stream in *Outdoor Life* after leaving Key West, then an article in *Esquire* in 1937, entitled "Mexico for Tramps." Hemingway sent a telegram of congratulation. Shortly after this, Arnold married, and he and his wife took off on an Indian motorcycle, in search of adventure, including a stint in Alaska working in construction during World War II.

Samuelson finally settled in the small town of Robert Lee, Texas, some 259 miles southwest of Dallas. He rarely left his small town, except for some temporary construction jobs. Arnold and his wife had two children. To feed his growing family, he built prefabricated houses. In 1955, *Esquire* accepted an article by Samuelson, for which he received another telegram from Hemingway. For some reason, however, Gingrich did not publish the piece. Over the years, Samuelson began to become something of a recluse and was looked upon as odd in the town of Robert Lee. One resident summed him up, calling him "a strange man."

Upon learning of Hemingway's death in 1961, Samuelson wrote to Arnold Gingrich, using stationery from Hemingway's house in Key West. Gingrich had only published one work by Samuelson, but had maintained an off-and-on correspondence with the man from Texas. Gingrich let Arnold's comments close out the column on Hemingway's death. Later, the editor sent a note to Arnold saying he was more moved by Samuelson's comments on the Key West paper than "any single thing connected with Ernest's death."

Samuelson's only daughter, Diane Darby, recalled her father's laborious efforts at reworking the manuscript of his time with Hemingway, trying to get it to read the way he wanted it in the hope that "it might be literature." His manuscript lay forgotten until his daughter found it and spent a great deal of time getting it ready for publication, which came out in 1984 entitled *With Hemingway: A Year in Key West and Cuba*.

Samuelson has rated only a few passing sentences in lengthy biographies of Hemingway. Prof. Robert Lacy, in 2003, compared Arnold to Icarus, the boy who flew too close to the sun, the sun in this case being Hemingway. Paul Hendrickson, who has written the most on Arnold Samuelson, thinks the frustrated writer produced something that "wasn't just good; it was fine." Arnold could never complete it to his satisfaction and this caused him to turn upon himself. On September 11, 1981, Arnold Samuelson, "the Maestro," was found dead on his property at the age of sixty-nine.[15]

Upon Hemingway's return from his first African safari, he received a letter from Charles B. Cadwalader, director of the Academy of Natural Sciences in Philadelphia. Cadwalader asked Hemingway if he would be interested in cooperating with the Academy's scientists in researching the large game fish in Cuban waters. Hemingway's reply stated, "It would be interesting to have a complete collection of these fish [Marlins] and determine scientifically which are truly different species and which are merely sexual and age variations of the same fish." The contract with *Esquire* provided Hemingway not only with a means of writing his observations on marlin but also allowed him to write as a natural scientist. Hemingway agreed to take Cadwalader and Henry W. Fowler, the chief ichthyologist of the Academy, on his Cuban trip.[16]

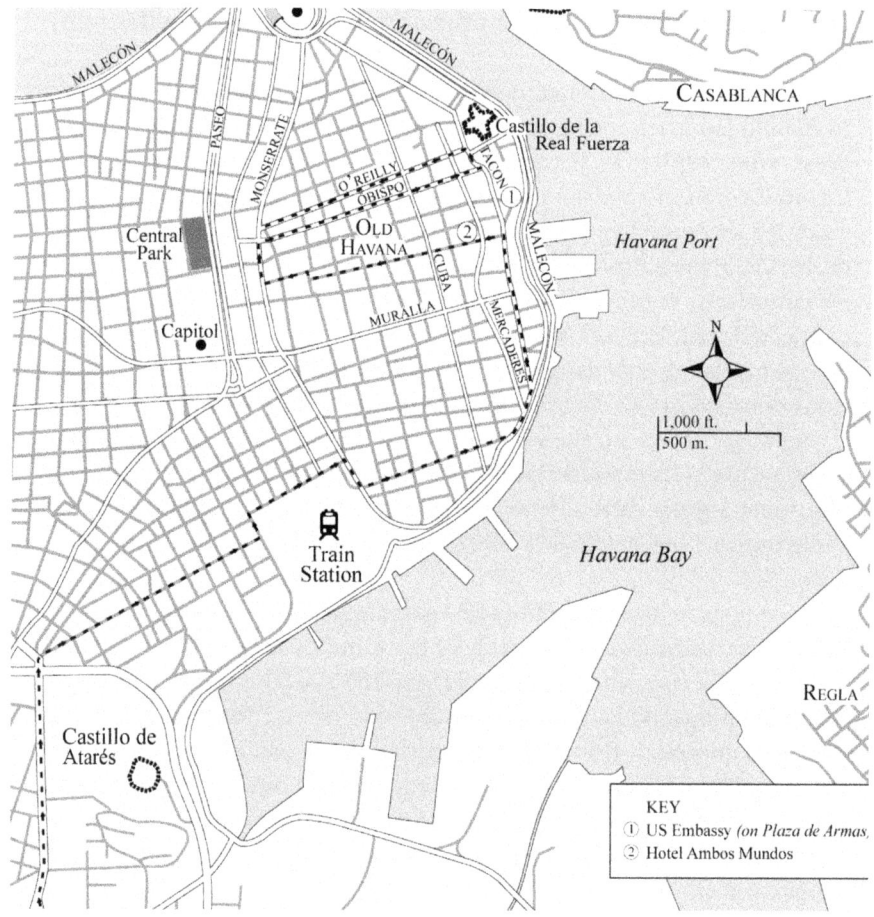

Map showing a drive from the outskirts of Havana into Old Havana as described in Hemingway's posthumously released novel *Islands in the Stream*. (Map by Tracy Ellen Smith.)

Hemingway never described Cadwalader or Fowler. Samuelson, however, called the two men "scientificos" and is unflattering to Cadwalader. The young man pictured Cadwalader as a "short-legged, slightly pot-bellied [man, who] always has the club-room conversationalist expression on his freckled face, and when he talked to one person he spoke as if he were making a speech to a crowd." Samuelson had never met such a wealthy individual and Cadwalader's New England accent did nothing to endear him to the young man. Cadwalader also did not drink wine or whiskey, "but would only drink bottled mineral water."[17]

5. Tracking Hemingway Eastward to Santiago de Cuba

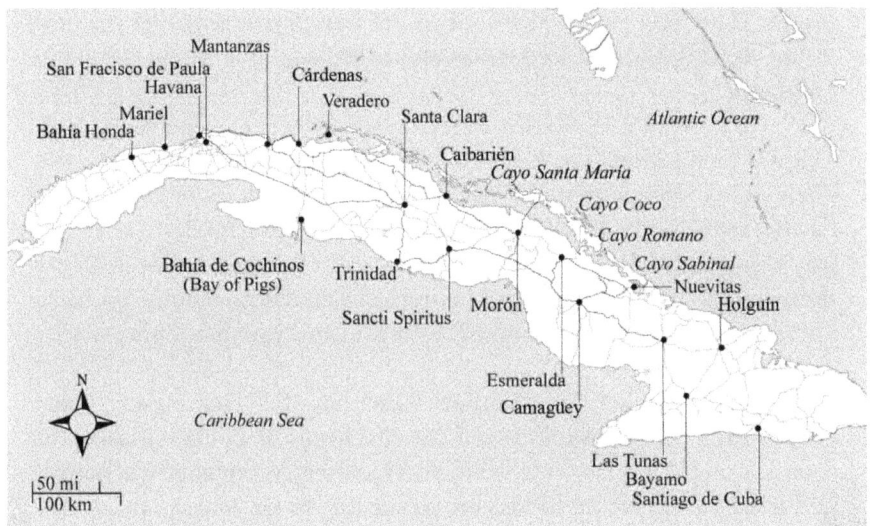

The eastern and western routes the author followed, beginning at Havana. The eastern route generally hugged the north coast, returning along the south, with the western ending at Bahía Honda. (Map by Tracy Ellen Smith.)

According to Samuelson, Cadwalader would say, "I venture to say we will encounter a marlin today," to which Hemingway would reply, "Hell, yes, we'll get one." Samuelson handled Fowler a little more gently: he "had white hair and the stiff-jointed walk of a man beginning to get old." Both Cadwalader and Fowler professed shock at the number of Cuban prostitutes approaching them, so they avoided walking the streets and failed to see much of Havana.[18] Despite Samuelson's poor descriptions of the "scientificos," the cooperation with the Academy of Natural Sciences proved a success. Cadwalader later wrote that because of Hemingway's knowledge of marlin, Fowler obtained enough data so the ichthyologist could "revise the classification" of the fish in the Atlantic Ocean. The director of the Academy further wrote he could not formulate the right words to really express what Hemingway's cooperation meant to him, Fowler and the museum. Hemingway, probably wishing to continue showing he had an affinity for natural science, wrote to Cadwalader saying the director proved a good shipmate. Ernest admitted that when he missed a marlin, he claimed that "the fish jumped off in spite of all that science and skill could accomplish." In closing, he hoped they would meet again and, recognizing Cadwalader's aversion to liquor, said, "We'll split a bottle of scientific water." The 1934 voyage did not end the work, however. Over the next year, Hemingway sent iced specimens to Philadelphia, along with photographs.[19]

Dr. Lawrence H. Martin, of Hampden-Sydney College, feels Hemingway's continued work for the Academy of Natural Sciences also helped his writing about la mar. Hemingway's articles in *Esquire* and a long article, "Marlin Off Cuba," appeared in *American Big Game Fishing* along with articles from other noted sport fishermen. The in-depth research and the "variety and interest of details couched in his lucid prose, make this chapter one of the most satisfying monographs ever written on a fish."

Hemingway's father, Clarence Edmonds "Ed" Hemingway, loved the natural world and followed the teachings of Louis Agassiz, the Swiss-American scientist who taught a hands-on examination of nature. Ed passed this love on to his son. According to Dr. Martin, the article in *American Big Game Fishing* "is Hemingway's most notable offering to the memory of Louis Agassiz and his own naturalist father."[20]

Fowler acknowledged Ernest's work in a paper when he named a new species of fish (*Neomerinthe Hemingwayi*). The ichthyologist wrote, "For Ernest Hemingway, author and angler of great game fishes, in appreciation of his assistance in my work on Gulf Stream fishes."[21]

Most readers know about Hemingway's fishing for marlin, but probably few general readers recognize his World War II exploits along the northern coast of Cuba. Before the United States entered the war against the Axis Powers in 1941, the campaign undertaken by German U-Boats (submarines), under the command of Adm. Karl Dönitz, to cut off supplies to a beleaguered Great Britain exacted a terrible toll. In the North Atlantic shipping lanes between the New World and England, the submarines sank approximately 950 merchant ships, totaling approximately two-and-a-half million tons of shipping. Even at the height of the air raids on London, Prime Minister Winston S. Churchill later wrote, "The only thing that ever really frightened me during the war was the U-Boat peril."[22]

The U-Boats not only prowled the North Atlantic, they also sought out ships in the Caribbean and Gulf of Mexico. In the war years, approximately 95 percent of the oil supplied to the industrial east coast, especially those areas noted for shipbuilding, came from the Gulf ports.

5. Tracking Hemingway Eastward to Santiago de Cuba 101

A prime target for the U-Boats focused on oil tankers sailing through the Gulf and the Florida Straits.

During the early morning hours of February 16, 1942, two U-Boats, *U-156* and *U-67*, brought home the submarine war to the region. Both submarines either slipped into the harbors of Aruba and Curaçao or lay offshore and fired at any ships within the harbors or shelled the refineries.

At one time crews of tankers sailing in the region refused "to go to sea without proper escorts. This virtually stopped England's major supply of oil." By the end of November 1942, U-Boats sank 263 ships in the Caribbean, almost twice as many as on the fiercely contested North Atlantic convoy routes.[23]

Despite the large amount of shipping sunk by the Germans, the U-Boat captains faced three dangerous routes to reach their prey in the Caribbean: the Straits of Florida, the Old Bahama Channel at the northeastern coastal portion of Cuba, and the Yucatan Channel at the southeastern portion of the island. All of these routes put the U-Boats in great danger from aircraft and ships.

Cuba, at first neutral, declared war on the Axis Powers. This meant that air bases and U.S. Navy ships now had permission to operate out of Cuba. The eminent maritime and naval historian Adm. Samuel Eliot Morison points out that of all the Allies in the Caribbean region, Cuba had a fleet of gunboats and patrol craft and proved "the most cooperative" in providing whatever it could to the Allied war effort. Cuba did help the Allies, but it also attracted the attention of the Nazis.[24]

The Cuban government also worried about Nazi agents, but even more worrisome were Falangist sympathizers—the Fascist supporters of Franco's efforts in Spain. Cubans had good reason to be wary of any nation favoring Franco. The Falangist wanted Nazi and Italian Fascist victories in Europe so they might take over Cuba. Martha Gellhorn Hemingway, in July of 1941, wrote to her editor at *Collier's* magazine there were "770 Germans here [in Cuba] ... and 30,000 Spaniards who are organized into the Spanish Fascist secret society, the Falange.... I tell you that the American Ambassador here is constantly and intensely concerned with the local Nazi activities, and the English ambassador is equally so." Although Adolf Hitler gave orders for his U-Boat captains to attack neutral shipping, he forbade actions against ships from Spain.[25]

Cubans, as with many of the people in the United States, saw some of the results of the U-Boat attacks wash upon their beaches, which naturally caused concern. Thus, by 1942, there existed in Cuba a sense of suspicion and unease, just as with their large neighbor to the north. This feeling of unease in the Caribbean country, along with the thought of spies and saboteurs operating on the island, proved irresistible to Hemingway "and he decided to do something about it."[26]

Ernest first responded to this concern by gathering together a group of his friends from all walks of life. He then organized them into an amateur spy ring to gather information on the Falangist. Hemingway dubbed his group the "Crook Factory."[27]

Hemingway took his idea of the Crook Factory to Spruille Brandon, the United States ambassador to Cuba. Brandon, as Martha mentioned in her letter, also felt unease at the situation on the island and agreed to accept Hemingway's idea. He allocated five hundred dollars (about $8,150 in 2016 dollars) in operating funds for the group of spies. Unfortunately, this led to an agency's dogging Hemingway, both in reality and in his mind, for the rest of his life: the Federal Bureau of Investigation (FBI). The local agent in charge considered the gathering of intelligence as FBI turf and resented the embassy establishing a network of agents. The bureau, as is their wont, began a file. Other items about Hemingway helped thicken the file.

One of the items came from Raymond Leddy, the local agent in Havana. Leddy reported Hemingway had written an endorsement against the FBI when they arrested some people in Detroit for violating the Neutrality Act by joining the Spanish Republic Forces in the Spanish Civil War. Further, when Hemingway introduced Special Agent Leddy to a friend, Ernest reportedly said the agent was a member of the "American Gestapo." Continuing to build the file, Ernest had also made a speech before the Writer's Congress, a group with leftist leanings. There was never any love lost between the FBI and the State Department and now the bureau particularly resented Ambassador Braden being friendly with Hemingway and approving of his activities, especially since Ernest did not answer to the FBI, nor did they supervise him. Some agents questioned his motives.[28]

Nevertheless, members of the Crook Factory began circulating throughout Havana. They slipped away to the finca at night to give their reports to Hemingway, accompanied by the inevitable drinking. One can see where FBI agents would shake their collective heads over such an arrangement. Martha not only shook her head, but lashed out against the nightly meetings at the farm. The Office of Strategic Services (OSS), the predecessor of the Central Intelligence Agency (CIA), did not want to use Hemingway as an agent. Although admitting Hemingway had many abilities, officers felt because he was a writer he would probably not work well with military officers telling him what to do.[29]

By April 1943, the Crook Factory ended. Two things brought about the demise: President Franklin D. Roosevelt consolidated counterespionage work under the FBI, and Ambassador Braden changed his mind about the operation and ordered it shut down.[30] Terry Mort, one of the few writers to look more deeply into many of the activities of Hemingway's World War II activities in Cuba, believes the Crook Factory unsuccessful and took on all the "air of comic opera." Conversely, he concedes given the times in Cuba it did "seem like a good idea" at the beginning. Ernest had friends in all walks of life and "assorted Cuban versions of Damon Runyon characters," just the type of people who were most likely to hear things.[31]

Mort also points out that J. Edgar Hoover's action as head of the FBI did not reflect well upon the bureau. He feels the time spent in investigating Hemingway and other writers of the period might have been spent in more important activities during a world war. Mort feels the time spent on this not only unnecessary, but also based upon "an almost comic lack of understanding of [the writers'] political influence, much less their ideas."[32]

Hemingway's next proposal can be traced to Alfred Stanford, commodore of the Cruising Club of America, prior to 1941 suggesting the idea of pleasure boats helping the United States Navy in the upcoming war. The navy rejected the idea, causing intense howls of protest from editorials and strong letters by powerful people decrying the service's rejection. In response, Adm. Ernest J. King, Commander in Chief of the U.S. Fleet and Chief of Naval Operations, did an end run: he detailed the United States Coast Guard to supervise the program.[33] The program became officially known as the Corsair Fleet, but dubbed the "Hooligan Navy" by those who served in the armada of pleasure craft and amateur boat operators.[34] The fleet used the small craft involved as a picket line, or early warning system, to drive down surfaced U-Boats and await aircraft or ships to come into the area. Ideally, they would also sink the submarines.

With the science of over a half century of hindsight, a matchup of a U-Boat against a yacht crewed by amateurs is a losing match for the yachts. Yet, even Adm. Morrison observed that the patrols should have been organized before the United States entered the war. "It ... might have saved many a merchant seaman's life at a time when the survivors from torpedoed freighters and tankers drifted about for days [unseen].... The yachtsmen, or some of them, were eager to stick their necks out; but at the time of the greatest need, the Navy could not see its way to use them. Eventually, the Navy took in the little boats, and yachtsmen found their place in the war effort."[35]

Basically, Hemingway built upon the premise of the Corsair Fleet and proposed using his fishing craft *Pilar* along the north coast of Cuba, much as the Corsair Fleet worked along the coastlines of the United States; that is, he patrolled for hours in a given location. Hemingway's core crew for his sub-hunting consisted of Winston Guest as his executive officer. Guest's nickname, "Wolfie," originated from the Hemingway boys: they thought he looked like Lon Chaney in the movie *The Wolf Man*. Guest was first cousin to Winston Churchill. He was wealthy, thirty-six years old and an internationally recognized champion polo player. Ernest had met Guest during his safari in the thirties.

Another of the crew was Juan Dunabeitia, a Basque seaman, whose abilities as a sailor earned him the nickname "Sinbad the Sailor." Gregorio Fuentes remained the mate of *Pilar*. Recruited to throw the grenades down the U-Boat's conning tower was Paxtchi Ibarlucia, an expert jai-alai player and frequent guest at the Hemingway home. Lieut. Col. John W. Thomason, Jr., U.S. Marine Corps, the United States Naval Attaché in Cuba, recruited Sgt. Don Saxon, U.S. Marine Corps, from the U.S. embassy in Cuba to maintain the weapons and operate the radio. Other members were Hemingway's friends who came and went, such as Fernando Mesa, an exile from Catalonia, and Roberto Herrera, a Cuban whose brother was a doctor and had served as a surgeon for the Loyalists in the Spanish Civil War. The code name for Hemingway's sub-hunting: "Friendless."[36]

Just as with the Hooligan Navy in the United States, *Pilar* really stood no chance of sinking a submarine for a number of reasons, not the least among them was being it did not have sonar to detect a submerged U-Boat. Even if Hemingway's craft had sonar and could locate a U-Boat running beneath the surface, *Pilar* could not attack the U-Boat for it could not mount the needed depth charges to carry out an

5. Tracking Hemingway Eastward to Santiago de Cuba 105

attack. An extreme example of this inability of the craft making up the Hooligan Navy happened in May 1942 when the *Jay-Tee*, a thirty-eight-foot cabin cruiser tried to attack the surfaced *U-333* near Fort Lauderdale, Florida. Recall the length of the *Pilar* measured thirty-eight feet. The *Jay-Tee*'s crew: two elderly fishermen. The U-Boat submerged. *Jay-Tee* pursued. Suddenly, the two fishermen found themselves in a boat being lifted out of the water as the U-Boat surfaced below them. Hearing strange noises as he tried to surface, the U-Boat captain took the prudent course of action and submerged. Apparently, he had no idea that he had tried to surface under the *Jay-Tee*. The crew of the Hooligan craft managed to make it safely to port. As proof of the encounter, the fishermen pointed to some paint scrapings.[37]

Hemingway's plan entailed a U-Boat surfacing and investigating it with *Pilar* had some merit—at this stage of the war, some submarine commanders would surface near fishing boats and obtain fresh supplies. What Hemingway did not mention, however, is the U-Boat captain then had three choices of what to do after taking the supplies: let the fishing craft go without any further action; place the fishing craft crew in a lifeboat and then sink the craft; or sink the fishing vessel and kill its crew.[38] Moreover, the plan centered on convincing a U-Boat captain to come close; this proved one of its weakest points. To survive any length of time in a submarine, no matter from what country, a captain must be very wary. Even presuming a careless captain, once those aboard *Pilar* opened fire, *Pilar* did not have the speed and maneuverability to escape return fire. Furthermore, the machine guns Ernest needed could not be mounted on *Pilar*, leaving the main armament to submachine guns.[39]

As with others in the Corsair Fleet in the United States, Ernest and his crew made their possibly greatest contribution to antisubmarine warfare in locating and then radioing for aircraft and warships to undertake the actual engagement of a U-Boat. At the beginning of the war, however, even this proved difficult: there simply were not enough surface vessels or aircraft to come immediately to the aid of a Hooligan Navy sighting.

All of the pros and cons of the Corsair Fleet aside, in the early summer and autumn of 1942 Hemingway and his crew practiced in a series of informal runs as they awaited the installation of needed electronic equipment. For example, they investigated a suspicious cave near Matanzas, to the east of Havana, in July.

Hemingway and his crew may have sighted one submarine, but like most of the Corsair Fleet Hemingway never engaged in any combat with a U-Boat. As the balance of the Battle of the Atlantic slowly shifted from Axis to Allied forces, the need for the small craft fell off. The ending of the Corsair Fleet along the United States' coastline came on October 1, 1943, and the last U-Boat attack in the Caribbean came in November 1943.

Some have accused Ernest Hemingway's patrols in *Pilar* as being useless and little more than boyish adventure, or he spent the time mainly researching the area for a novel that eventually became *Islands in the Stream*. Terry Mort has written the best-detailed account of Hemingway's patrols along the north coast of Cuba. He feels Hemingway's country was at war, and although he did not love war, Hemingway believed once you are in one, you must win it. "That in itself is enough to legitimize the patrols." Furthermore, the patrols "reflect the complexity of a man who is often oversimplified and dismissed as someone who lived an interesting and exciting life.... But just as his work was complex and often beautiful, so the patrols of *Pilar* were more than they seemed to be—a kind of synecdoche for his life and work.... More was going on than what first appears."[40]

Víctor and I began our eastward trek hugging the north coast to both enjoy the seascape and begin viewing the coastline Hemingway would have seen from the sea. The first stop was at the city of Matanzas, some sixty-two miles (99.7 kms) from Havana. In recent years, the amount of oil derricks, with most flying the flag of the People's Republic of China, have increased. The city of Matanzas had a 2004 population of 132,678 and sits alongside the large Bay of Matanzas. When Hemingway was ready to take *Pilar* into action, hunting submarines, he first brought his craft to the Matanzas area to practice. The city is noted for its poets, culture, and Afro-Cuban folklore. The first of the main reasons the traveler should stop in this city is for a visit to the publisher of *Ediciones Vigía* (Watchtower Editions). *Ediciones Vigía* emerged from the efforts of a group of artists in 1985 that wanted their work in print. The group started with the loan of a typewriter and a mimeograph machine. (These are still in use.) There was and is a shortage of paper and the group used scrap paper, cardboard, leaves, and yarn, producing stunning limited editions of hand-decorated publications of some of Cuba's most important writers and those of other

5. Tracking Hemingway Eastward to Santiago de Cuba 107

countries. They also produce books for children. Readers never know what surprise each page of these works will bring. One book, for example, printed some of the writings of the Cuban national hero and an important figure in Latin American literature, José Martí. The book cover contains a roll-down wrapping made of corn husk. I was warned to make sure there were no bugs in the house who liked corn.[41]

Not only does *Ediciones Vigía* produce these colorful and unusual works, the building they use is a restored colonial house on the Plaza de la Vigía. The house overlooks the San Juan River. *Ediciones Vigía* is one of the best examples of the ability of Cubans to produce something beautiful with whatever limited material is available to them. After the purchase of some books from *Ediciones Vigía*, the traveler should move to the second reason to stop in this city, the restored Hotel Velasco that sits on the Plaza Libertad. The façade of the two-story hotel is painted in colors of cream and white, along with nicely worked white spindles in the balustrades and dark green window frames and entranceway. Though presenting a pleasing exterior, it does not even hint of what the traveler will see upon entering the reception area of the establishment. Once inside the door, a visitor seems to enter a time warp and is now in what the hotel must have looked like in at least the late 19th or early 20th century. The eye is quickly drawn to two very large columns of veined marble with a touch of gold at least two stories high. Chairs with embroidered fabric and framed in dark wood, along with dark wood small tables are arranged in groupings for conversation and tropical plants are scattered about the area. Suspended from the ceiling are old Spanish-type chandeliers in worked iron and painted black. All of this provides an ambience where one can find a comfortable area to meet and visit with friends. Along the right side of this large welcoming room is a long marble-topped bar made up largely of dark wood. To the left, on the wall is a mural-sized painting of Matanzas by the local artist Roberto Braulo. A stairway winds up to the second story, which has seventeen rooms. Walking through the first floor and a short distance from the bar is a very large restaurant.

No matter what time a traveler departs Havana, before departure it is recommended to make arrangements to remain at Hotel Velasco for one night. Use Matanzas as a central point to take in the city and countryside around the city and, again, depending on the time, it is an easy drive to Varadaro, where Cuban tourist agencies try to have tourists visit the peninsula that juts out into the Caribbean and has some of the country's best resorts for those who want time for plenty of sunny beaches. Varadaro can more than provide choices of beach locations for any visitor who loves to loll in a hot sun. The resort areas are divided into Old and New Varadaro, with the old usually frequented by Cubans and the new geared for tourists. Whatever area in Varadaro the traveler chooses, there are numerous beachside restaurants for those who like to dine outside close by the sea. This tracker preferred Old Varadaro and was amazed at the lack of people on the beach. Víctor noted it was still too cool for Cubans, the temperature being at least in the high 70s Fahrenheit.

For the visitor interested in locations concerning Hemingway and who is also interested in history concerning Cuba and the United States, it is a short drive from Matanzas to Cárdenas, one of the invasion points of General López's invasion of Cuba. This is where the general was executed (see Chapter 3) and the historical society supposedly has tucked away in the collections the garrote used to execute him. (This tracker chose not to view the garrote.) A drive to the waterfront area and the view over the bay will remind the historian of the first and second naval Battles of Cárdenas Bay during the Spanish American War of 1898.

The reason for using Matanzas as a central location rather than push onward along the north coast is because, even with a Cuban driver, traveling the "blue highways" of Cuba can at times result in high blood pressure and great stress. (Of course, one can say the same of many highways in the United States.) Most of the roadways, while paved, are narrow two-lane affairs, much like some rural areas of the United States. Cuba has one major motorway stretching almost halfway across the country and is relatively easy to follow. However, on most of the other roads and especially in the rural areas that make up most of the various regions of the country there appears to be no obvious route signage. More importantly, out of a city there are seemingly no other lights and once the tropical night descends it is hard to describe the darkness. But if you can picture the blackness of the most moonless night, place a blanket securely over your head and that will give an idea of traveling at night in rural Cuba. Remember, there are no visible route signs and even if there were, there are no lights to illuminate them. The visitor traveling through this darkness might, at times, see a slight flicker of a television set emanating from a farm, but that will be it. All of this can be somewhat manageable with good headlights, but another factor enters into the calculus of driving at night in Cuba. As mentioned in Chapter 2, in the urban areas of Cuba "transportation is the name of the game." It is doubly so in the rural areas. Cubans use bicycles, horses, and horse-drawn carts for their transportation and, unfortunately, most do not display any type of lights. As if this is not bad enough, as one nears any type of settlement in the countryside, people will be walking along, and many times on the roadway, again, without any illumination. Víctor and I, because of a limited time schedule, decided to press on from Matanzas late in the afternoon and had to travel for some distance at night. At one point, Víctor was traveling about fifty kms an hour (thirty-one mph) with nothing but the Cuban dark enveloping us. Suddenly, two things happened: a man appeared out of the gloom on the roadway pedaling a bicycle with no lights. Víctor quickly swerved in the opposite lane, missing the bicyclist by about a foot, while at the same time, a truck was approaching at high speed in the same lane causing another swerve, putting the car almost on two wheels and missing the truck by no more than three feet. Needless to say, both of our hearts continued beating rapidly for the next few hours, with both of us swearing if we made it to our destination we would never drive in the dark again. While it is somewhat safer on the major motorway, a traveler can still see horse-drawn carts just off the roadway not showing lights. It cannot be repeated enough, those who wish to follow the "blue highways" of Cuba should only do so in daylight. Furthermore, why travel at night and miss some interesting countryside?

Once the traveler departs Matanzas, or if the tracker has decided to stay at Varadaro, the next location along the north coast route to stop for the night is at the town of Caibarién, close to 200 miles (321.8 kms) away. As we traveled over the narrow paved road, I watched sugar cane harvesting in many of the passing fields. At least one to two machines would be cutting the cane and spewing it out into accompanying trucks. The trucks with high stakes to haul as much of the harvest as possible move out of the field and onto the narrow road. In this area of Cuba, and many others, I could quickly recognize the location of a nearby town by observing in the distance a tall chimney, indicating a sugar mill. In earlier years, much of the cane was transported to a mill on narrow-gauge railroads, but now many of the railroads seemed abandoned; trucks now, apparently, carry most of the cane. Some of the field operations are large with other types of machines in the field, some flying Cuban flags, and containing kitchens for the workers. Those who live in large agricultural areas in the western United States and know of the harvesting of the large fields of wheat would quickly recognize the scene. If the Cuban operations are close to a town or a farm, the traveler may see small children catching a few canes and drinking from them.

The problems of transportation in Havana are magnified in the rural areas. Just as large chimneys in the distance herald a town, the problems of getting around also indicate the visitor is approaching a town. Some kilometers from a settlement, an increasing number of people will be seen walking along the roadway, plus the number of horse-drawn carts and bicycles increases. It is not unusual to see an older Cuban grandmother walking toward a town in eighty-degree Fahrenheit heat, carrying her grandchild and holding an umbrella that shields both herself and the child from the baking sun.

The Cuban ability to improvise or find some way to work with what they have helps somewhat with the lack of commuting in the countryside. Someone obtains a very large flatbed truck and then builds wooden sides on the bed and then puts some high hoops connecting the sides. A piece of canvas is placed over the hoops, benches are added along the sides, a steep ladder-like stair is added to the rear of the truck and there is now a bus for service between towns. As in Havana, there are long lines waiting for transportation, with the same hand signs showing willingness to pay for room in a passing car.

Throughout travels away from Havana I caught other glimpses of Cubans coping with what is available for them. At one major intersection near the main motorway approaching a city there stood a large group of people awaiting a ride and a woman wearing a uniform standing near the road with a clipboard. This official's duties were to check a passing vehicle's license plate and if it was state owned, she stopped it and determined where the car was bound to and if there was any extra room in the car. If so, she then consulted her list of the waiting people, their destination. If those standing on line were traveling to the same place as the state owned car, or close to it, she had the traveler(s) ride in the car.

In a small town in eastern Cuba I watched a young family trying to obtain a ride. The father spotted an empty dump truck and apparently the driver had given the father the signal to get aboard while the truck was still moving. The family ran alongside the slow-moving empty truck. Somehow the father managed to get up into the bed of the truck—how he accomplished this feat is unknown—but he next leaned down and hoisted his wife and daughter into the vehicle, just as it started to pick up speed and they vanished down the road.

The city of Caibarién (2004 population, 38,064), is known as *"La Villa Blanca"* (The White Town) for its sandy area and beaches. Founded on October 26, 1832, the economy was based on sugar cane, tobacco, and fruit. In addition, it was the center of sponge fishing. All the sugar mills are now closed, with the exception of the largest that is now a museum. Today tourism is the main economic source for the city with the largest attraction being the beautiful offshore *cayos* (keys). A causeway a few miles to the east of Caibarién travels over the Bahía (Bay) de Buena Vista connecting the mainland to Cayo Santa María. A traveler may wish to visit this cayo to see a different type of beach resort area than the larger developed ones at Varadero. I was there for a different reason. At Caibarién I was introduced to José Armando Ocampo, who worked in the town's library, and a fellow employee, Juan Emerio Sánches Freyre, who wanted to tell me that he recalled seeing Hemingway along the north coast during the writer's submarine hunting with *Pilar*.

The next day's schedule was to the city of Morón and then northward toward Bahía de Perros (Bay of Dogs). After leaving Morón, the road winds through a long stretch of trees, with the surroundings changing to scrubby foliage in a swampy area and, finally, we viewed the bay. Another long causeway stretched across the bay that was absent in Hemingway's day that had allowed *Pilar* to carefully sail in from the Atlantic Ocean. At the beginning of the drive across the bay is a Ministry of the Interior Station with its *Tropas de Guardafronteras* (Border Guard Troops). After showing my passport with the loose paper visa, the officer said, "Don't lose the visa, it's gold!" Interestingly, I did not have to pay a fee to cross over the causeway, but Víctor did, the reason given: El Norte Americano will probably spend money at one of the resorts, while the Cuban will not.

The destination of this particular route along the north coast was Cayo Guillermo, the northwestern tip that reaches out into the Old Bahama Channel and the Atlantic Ocean. After passing by resort after resort, with most saying "members only," the traveler arrives at the parking area of Playa Pilar (Pilar Beach), named after Hemingway's fishing craft, but probably many years after the writer had left Cuba.

In short, marketing to bring in tourist business extends into Cuba. A wooden walkway leading from the parking lot to the beach area offers protection for the sparse vegetation within the sand and passes close by a restaurant where the visitor may take a long leisurely lunch. To say the area is beautiful does not do it justice. The sand is white and the water a light blue and as the sea deepens the color changes into azure and then, in even deeper water, the change is to lapis lazuli. It is hard to picture a more enchanting place: the deep blue colored sea, white, puffy cumulus clouds floating slowly above it. I found it difficult to leave this to again take up the quest of tracking Hemingway. Perhaps the beauty of the area will allow a future visiting Hemingway scholar to forgive giving the beach *Pilar*'s name. There is, however, a strong probability Hemingway did pass nearby this location during his 1930s visits to the north coast and during his time while hunting submarines.

Depending on how much time the Hemingway tracker spends at both *cayos*, the next stop should be the town of Ciego de Ávila, located about 460 kilometers (290 miles) east of Havana, along the Carretera Central, but will be longer in distance and time to travel if following the "blue highways" of the northern route. The town is on a major railroad line and located in an area in eastern Cuba where the land seems to squeeze into a narrower area than the rest of the country. Ciego de Ávila is closer to the Caribbean than the north coast of the country and was founded in 1840 and in 2004 had a population of approximately 135,736. A good location to stay is at the casa particulare Sra. Aleida Castro—one of the homes that the state allows the owner to rent rooms to tourists (the owner's husband was an architect and designed the house). The upper story has a large deck-like arrangement, which the couple's son wanted to use for a restaurant. As with many casa particulares, the son went out to a market and brought in the supplies needed for dinner and breakfast. (If a guest wishes to dine here, order the beef that is prepared in the house.) A one-night stay at the city will provide some rest before continuing east and northeastward back to the north coast to the cayos and the area in the eastern portion of Cuba most noted in Hemingway's life.

Noted Cuban writer Enríque Cirules has examined Hemingway in the Cayo Romano, the largest island in the Archipiélago de Sabana-Camagüey that stretches along the north coast far to the east of Havana and within the boundaries of Camagüey Province. Cirules, a native of

Nuevitas, a major port in the area, has the advantage of knowing the region and its people. According to Cirules, Jane Mason and Hemingway reportedly sailed the entire length of the Romano Archipelago in the 1930s in her boat, making Nuevitas their homeport. They would put into one of the cayos and Hemingway wandered "over its swamps and bogs," taking in all of the wildlife and scenery.[42]

The people Cirules interviewed informed him that Hemingway also explored some of the unusual settlements in the region, such as a French village with the name of Versailles. The main crops the settlers of this town cultivated were bananas and henequen, a plant used in the making of rope, but when Hemingway visited, the settlement had failed and only fishermen's huts dotted the former settlement. However, on a nearby rise "less than a league away, one could still see the ruins of a mansion."[43]

With Nuevitas as Hemingway's main base during his time in the 1930s in the Romano Archipelago, he visited two unusual settlements: Palma (Palm) City, a German settlement, and La Gloria (Glory, or Paradise), a United States settlement. (More on these settlements later.) Despite the scenery and unusual settlements, Hemingway's interest remained focused on the fishermen and turtle hunters of the cayos. Cirules rightfully observed these poor fishermen "possessed an extraordinary marine culture.... They were men who had a profound knowledge of all the secrets of the sea, although they could not read a single line, and had to sign documents with their mark."[44] Most of the Cubans that Cirules interviewed recalled how much time Hemingway spent in talking to these people whose living depended upon the sea. For their part, the Cubans interviewed by the American writer seem to have accepted him not as writer but as one who knew the sea and wanted to learn even more. A consistent theme throughout the story of Ernest Hemingway in Cuba is his desire to know more about everyday Cubans and their lives, especially those who worked on the sea.

The Romano Archipelago is important to the story of Hemingway during his use of *Pilar* to hunt submarines. At first the patrols took him to the cayos of western Cuba. In November 1942, he began patrolling in the vicinity of Bahía Honda, approximately forty-three miles (69 kms) from Havana. In May 1943, Hemingway received orders to operate in another area, the Central North Coast. The base of operations was a small isolated key called Confites, located northeast of Cayo

Cruz. The area had seen U-Boat action: U-176, for example, had sunk two vessels just off Nuevitas, the middle of Hemingway's patrol area. Two days later, on May 15, the Cuban patrol boat CS-13, commanded by Capt. Ramirez Delgado, sank U-176 westward from the earlier attacks and in the Old Bahama Channel. *Pilar*, however, did not arrive in the region until May 20, 1943.[45]

Cayo Confites became Hemingway's main base. From here, Hemingway ran daylight patrols to various cayos, returning late in the evening. The crew would immediately wash down the craft and prepare it for the next patrol. As this work progressed, *Pilar*'s radio operator sent a coded message on the day's events and in return received a coded message outlining the details for the next patrol. Underway, some of the duties of the crew involved landing at one of the small cayos, checking for possible hidden radios or supply dumps. For these missions, a select armed landing party had to take a small boat to the island. Instead of spies or U-Boat crews, what the landing parties usually met in the mangrove swamps, if there was no wind, were hordes of mosquitoes.

The time at Confites was not a lark. Supplies came at intervals from Nuevitas and most of the time while at the cayo was spent in the grinding tedium of keeping up the boat. Of course, that did not stop them from playing cards and drinking. A notebook in the Hemingway Collection at the John F. Kennedy Library has the tallies for how much various crewmembers owed in card games. Likewise, time at sea did not involve a leisurely cruise as a small boat can seem to shrink in size to a crew confined for hours on end in a small craft, along with the fact that *Pilar* was not an easy riding craft. The area's humidity caused clothes to cling to the skin of the crew as the sun beat down mercilessly upon the men. Boredom, the climate, the small boat, plus the uncertainty of not knowing whether a U-Boat might suddenly surface or appear on the horizon, made the time both on patrol and at Confites tedious and stressful in the extreme. After six weeks, Hemingway received orders to return to Havana. *Pilar* arrived on July 18, 1943, and immediately Hemingway had his wooden boat in for repairs while awaiting orders for the next patrol. Even though he did some desultory patrols, this, in effect, ended Hemingway's war patrols in Cuba.[46]

Once rested at Ciego de Ávila, the next stage of the route in tracking Hemingway led toward the city of Camagüey some sixty-six miles (106 kms) away and there we had to do one of two things: head directly to

5. Tracking Hemingway Eastward to Santiago de Cuba

the city and make arrangements for a two-night stay, or start toward the city and at the small town of Crucero de Céspedes turn left and start northward again toward the coast. After our normal consulting over routes and time, Víctor turned toward the coast to see how much we could cram into one day, which included one of the major cayos dealing with Hemingway. Our upcoming experiences should be recalled when any future Hemingway tracker begins making plans to visit this area.

After turning northward, using Víctor's not very detailed map, the plan was to turn right at the village of Esmeralda, then continue eastward until reaching the small settlement of Jaronú, then turning northward until reaching another causeway to a cayo that Hemingway visited. After exploring the area, we would return to the main route and continue on to Camagüey. This route involved a long, rough clockwise circle that encompassed Palma City, La Gloria, Nuevitas, and ending in the city of Camagüey. The area is noted for sugar production and cattle.

All proceeded according to plan and at Jaronú Víctor made the left turn and started toward the coast with the causeway beginning near Playa Jigüey. Once across the Bahía de Jigüey, the map indicated there was one main road to Cayo Cruz and is as close to Cayo Confites as can be managed in a car. Another road branched off the main roadway and headed toward the east and then made a turn to the northwest to a location on the map labeled Punta El Inglés (English Tip or Point). Just before the road turned northwest, the map indicated the position of the former settlement of Versalles.

The road to Playa Jigüey passed through high, dense foliage forming a leafy green tunnel-like passage. Low stratus clouds and cool winds—by Cuban standards—announced the nearness to the bay. Víctor, upon observing an approaching motorcycle coming from the direction of Playa Jigüey, flagged it down to check if he was traveling in the right direction, a not uncommon event because of the poorly marked roads. Visitors to Cuba will notice that in most cases Cubans are very helpful in giving directions. The few times Víctor asked a police officer for directions, the officer always saluted upon Víctor's approach. In this event, when the approaching motorcyclist stopped, it turned out his motorcycle had a sidecar attached. Again, because transportation is so difficult and most cannot afford a car, this was the family's only means of transportation. The father, wearing helmet and goggles, drove and the mother rode on the seat behind him and in the sidecar sat two small girls bundled in layers of blankets against the brisk day. Lifting his goggles, the man listened to Víctor and then replied politely, while just the faces of the children with quizzical expressions peaked out from their wrappings, probably wondering about the two men in a new car and one obviously not a Cuban. Víctor thanked the father and we continued on course, while the sound of the family's motorcycle faded away. The memory of those two small quizzical faces looking out from behind their coverings remains one of the indelible moments of my time in Cuba.

Once again underway, Víctor related that the father of the family said there was a border station near Playa Jigüey and he was not sure we would be allowed to cross the causeway. Víctor and I felt if we were so close to the causeway we might as well continue and see if the information was correct. Arriving at the causeway, there stood a Ministry of the Interior Station with its *Tropas de Guardafronteras*. A border guard said the only way we would be allowed to continue onto the cayo was to go back to a town and find an official guide who would have to accompany us onto the island. The officer had no idea where to obtain a guide or how long it would take to obtain one or how much it would cost. The area, at least in 2011, was being preserved as a natural area. Stymied at this turn of events, and very pressed for time, Víctor and I held another discussion on whether to press on to the next goal, the former German settlement of Palma City. Retracing the route back to Jaronú, Víctor turned the rental car left and said his map indicated a shorter route to Palma City. Another quick consultation came up with the decision the route might save time. The new way started with the normal narrow two-lane paved highway and then turned into a red dirt road, beginning one of the more "interesting" parts of traveling in very rural Cuban in search of Ernest Hemingway.

While the paved roads in rural Cuba generally carry little traffic, the red dirt road seemed completely deserted. There were large potholes, with most of the very deep ones having tracks around them, but at least this indicated some type of traffic had used the route. It proved impossible to make more than thirty kilometers per hour (eighteen mph) and for approximately the first hour there was no sign of any settlement, only stubby trees, shaped by the winds from the bay. Finally, off to the left a clearing appeared and, in it, a farm with pens for pigs. Three men stood by the pen apparently discussing something, perhaps

5. Tracking Hemingway Eastward to Santiago de Cuba

the health of the porkers. Víctor stopped, got out of the car and walked the few feet over to the farmers and began talking to them. The farmers glanced over to the car and smiled, Víctor probably explaining the passenger was a *Norte Americano* seeking areas that Hemingway had visited and why he was taking photographs of the group. The farmers nodded and one began pointing in the direction leading away from the farm. Returning to the car, Víctor said, "We are heading in the right direction to Palma City" and we continued slowly onward.

The low trees remained an on and off feature, but the wooded terrain thinned and gave out onto a rolling countryside. Upon approaching the crest of one small hill, the road led downward with more of the typical large holes in the road—"holes" do not adequately describe the obstacles the red dirt road presented. A number of ruts disguised as tracks went around the holes, apparently made by farm tractors. Unfortunately, the rental car did not have the highest of ground clearance. Picking out one of the shallowest set of ruts, Víctor started down the hill and, after a short distance, both of us got out to check the clearance and found the car was approaching bottoming out. Choosing among the many ruts, Víctor found another set to navigate. Making it finally to the bottom of the hill and starting up the next rise, the tracks became shallower and finally disappeared altogether and became the red dirt road again. About halfway up the hill stood some cattle alongside the road, with the seemingly ever-present white egrets following the animals.

Now the roadside view changed to sugar cane fields, with some of the cane in blossom. Shortly thereafter, another clearing appeared to the right of the road. Within this isolated spot was a small house made of what looked like cement and a tin roof. A farmer was working on shelling corn by hand, but, with a smile, interrupted his work to walk over to the fence and confirmed that Palma City lay ahead.

During all this I thought, This is a great way to really see rural Cuba. I certainly had not seen any tourists and wondered if William Least Heat Moon felt the same when he explored his "blue highways." I did, however, notice that Víctor, between watching for potholes and deep ruts in the road, kept glancing upwards and looking worried. I, on the other hand, was too busy watching the passing scene and taking notes to wonder what was concerning him.

Slowly, more and more houses began to appear and we knew we were approaching a settlement. Stopping a man on a bicycle, Víctor explained he was trying to find the way to the main section of Palma City, plus the reason for our interest in the city. A smile from the Cuban, who then said, "Follow me, I will show you the way and then introduce you to my cousin, who can help you." Off he went on his bicycle.

The fast-pedaling bicyclist led the way into the main section of Palma City. The town center consisted of a very wide red dirt road divided down the center with trees. It appeared the original settlers wanted their main street to remind them of home and did their best to produce a boulevard. While they did not have a paved road, the wooded section in the middle of their thoroughfare made the attempt to provide some beauty in their then-new settlement. Some houses still remained scattered along both sides of the boulevard.

According to the Cuban writer Cirules, Palma City "always aroused Hemingway's interests." Primarily German, with a few U.S. citizens, the settlers "built beautiful houses with gardens and flower-covered fences." The farms "became a true thing of beauty" due to the "native red soil—the most productive in the world." Being German, the people of the settlement also produced "good beer." In short, the homes of Palma City during Hemingway's visit reflected their European heritage.[47]

Víctor and I soon found ourselves in the home of the bicyclist's cousin and being served the inevitable Café Cubano. The cousin said her neighbor was a ninety-year-old woman who would be interested in meeting us and sent someone to invite her to meet the visitors. After a quick period of time, the spry old woman appeared and soon was sitting in a rocking chair explaining she had come to Palma City from Germany and had lived in the settlement most of her life. After a few minutes, the nonagenarian suddenly rose from her rocking chair and said, "Follow me. I will take you to our historian." The woman with her guests in tow walked at an amazingly fast pace for someone her age. She stopped at one of the small one-story Cuban rural houses made of cement with a metal roof and two rooms: a bedroom and the other a combination of a small kitchen and living room.

Ivon Leyva Zaldívar, the city's historian, worked in another city, but when she was at home gathered information on Palma City. She pointed out that the city's homes and some shops were of two stories in the European style. As time went on, however, the buildings did not fare well. A large hurricane in the 1930s finally leveled all but one of the buildings; she offered to take us to the structure. Ivon, along with

5. Tracking Hemingway Eastward to Santiago de Cuba

the ninety-year-old woman, Víctor and I walked along the red dirt street and passed a few styles of rural Cuban houses, some in the manner of bohíos, the traditional rural single-story home made of wood from the palm tree for the sides and with the roof made of thatched palm fronds from the same type of palm tree, and others like Ivon's made of cement and metal roofs. Some of the homes had fences with flowers growing out of the wooden posts as described by Cirules in his book. The dark interiors of some of the dwellings showed the flickering light of television sets. The abandoned remaining two-story European house of the original settlers was boarded up, but it was evident that at one time in the past it would have been much like a home in a town in Germany.

Returning to Ivon's home, she informed us that the city's economy was based upon agriculture. She also mentioned it was difficult for her to find information on the city. I mentioned uncovering a book in my research by James Meade Adams, originally published in 1901, about the early history of their neighboring city of La Gloria. Upon returning to the United States, I obtained a copy and, through a friend returning to Cuba, brought the book to Víctor and he mailed it to Ivon's home. The United States embargo prohibits direct mail service between Cuba and the United States.

After receiving directions for a faster route out of Palma City, Víctor and I departed and once again traveling on pavement, I now had time to think about the red dirt road route. It slowly dawned on me why Víctor kept looking at the sky with a worried look: if it had started to rain hard while on the red dirt road, the dirt would have soon turned to red mud and bogged down the car. It would have been a long walk to the nearest farm, if not all the way to Palma City, to find someone with a tractor to pull the car out and take it to a paved highway. I felt it was good that I had remained ignorant of the possible problem. For future Hemingway trackers, it is suggested the easiest route to Palma City, especially in a rental car without four-wheel drive, after leaving Playa Jigüey is to travel southward until reaching the town of San Francisco, turn left (eastward) and drive to the town of Cubitas and inquire there for the best route to Palma City. It will entail driving on some improved dirt road, but certainly not like the red dirt way Víctor and I traveled.

The drive to and the stop at Palma City took more time than expected and another conference with Víctor and we hammered out a new plan that scrapped the planned circle route to Camagüey because it would entail driving at night. Instead, Víctor would take a shorter route south to Camagüey and then we would continue the next day again northward to the sites having something to do with Hemingway. The city of Camagüey is 344 miles (553 kms) from Havana, but this is a direct route and not the one we followed. A 1922 tour guide of Cuba reads that Camagüey was "very old, and looks its centuries." Eighty-nine years later, with a population in 2004 of more than 321,000, it is Cuba's third-largest urban area. Seeing the narrow sidewalks filled with people spilling out onto busy streets provided a great example of "culture shock" after the recent north coast sojourn. I stayed in Casa Lancara, another of the homes the state allows the homeowners to rent out rooms, very close to the important Church of La Merced and Plaza de los Trabajores (Workers' Square). The owner, Alejandro Sánchez, informed Víctor he had only a room for one person, prompting Víctor to search for another location.[48]

The outside of Casa Lancara, located hard by a very narrow sidewalk, looked like nothing special. Once inside, however, it proved a neoclassical home with very high ceilings and the traditional wooden shutters to keep out the noise of the street. Señor Sánchez, his wife Dinorah, and two young children, made me very welcome. Within the house, there is a restful location with an opening in the roof, and beneath the opening, at the floor level, are many decorative plants. A vine grew, Jack-and-the-Beanstalk fashion, from this location upward and out the opening in the roof that allowed a patio within the house. Orchids steamed downward from the vine. All this provided an enjoyable place to relax and read, with Dinorah seemingly pleased to see someone in the patio engrossed in a book.

Dinner and breakfast were served in a dining room reminiscent of the colonial days with a shuttered window overlooking a long finely carved dark wooden table, lovingly polished to a high sheen, covered with a white lace tablecloth, suitable for seating eight people. A dark sideboard, along with glass and wood cabinets, lined one side of the room. The opposite side of the room had a low table with small rocking chairs arranged around it and a delicate chandelier hanging from the very high ceiling.

Alejandro joined me for breakfast and, upon learning of my reason for visiting Cuba, began animatedly discussing Hemingway. He said many times people visiting Cuba asked him about Hemingway and he had a number of questions to ask about the writer. Guest and Casa Lancara owner had an interesting hour over breakfast discussing Hemingway.

Víctor returned and we were soon heading toward the north coast, arriving first at Nuevitas, where Hemingway reportedly stopped in the 1930s and the port where supplies were landed and shipped to his cayo for his work in hunting submarines during World War II. The city is still an important shipping port for sugar cane from the nearby region, with a population in 2004 of 44,882. Spending only a short time viewing the harbor, Víctor drove southward and then turned westward for the village of Sola, turning again to the right in a northerly direction to the former American settlement of La Gloria. A few miles along this road, Víctor waved down a rider astride a Soviet-made motorcycle and asked if we were heading in the right direction. Receiving a positive reply, Víctor continued to proceed on the way until seeing a sign within a stone foundation alongside the road proclaiming La Gloria, indicating what turned out to be a larger settlement than Palma City.

La Gloria came into being when the Cuban Land and Steamship Company was established in 1899. At that time the United States was struggling to recover from an economic depression, and Paul Van der Voort (1846–1902), an American Civil War veteran, became an officer of the company. The company's promise of a new start in Cuba, where "it is always June," along with fertile soil and a chance for riches, naturally struck a chord with those seeking a place to live and escape the economic conditions in the United States. Some three decades after the American Civil War, a number of the first 211 people to sign up were veterans of that bloody conflict. The company hinted La Gloria was already an established settlement. The first group of new settlers from the United States made their way aboard the steamer *Yarmouth* to the port of Nuevitas. Some of the would-be settlers took one look at Nuevitas and decided they did not want to go any farther and returned to the United States in the same ship.[49]

Those who wished to continue on to La Gloria found that to reach their new home by land from Nuevitas they faced a strenuous forty-mile overland trip on foot or horseback. Instead of this rugged trip, most of the group decided to await a Cuban maritime pilot to guide them on a sixty-mile journey aboard three small schooners to the nearest landing location to La Gloria, with the understanding the port was a developed one. Upon finally arriving at this location, the new settlers to Cuba were greeted with only a makeshift pier and a collection of nearby tents. The land was muddy and the air thick with mosquitoes and sand flies. Once again the group found this was not La Gloria—it lay an additional four miles inland and this caused even more people to give up and return to the United States.

The final group of pioneers, all men, except for the wife of one of the company's employees, set out on a corduroy road (made of logs) which soon fizzled out to a muddy track. Among this group was James Mead Adams, an officer of the company and chronicler of the beginnings of the city. Adams described the trek as a "mixture of water, mud, stumps, roots, logs, briers, and branches" with "times the traveler [finding] himself almost afloat in the forest." James went on to say, "It was hot and hard work, this four-mile walk under a tropical sun" while dragging most of their baggage with them. The long tramp finally brought the 160 remaining settlers to the location of La Gloria, which amounted to only a few tents. From this humble beginning, the group began surveying and building. Additional people arrived, with women among them. After a year of hard work, Adams proclaimed the "enthusiasm of the colonists was unbounded" and "filled and thrilled with delight over their new home in the tropics. The climate was glorious, the air refreshing and soothing, the country picturesque and healthful, the soil fertile and productive. Not for a moment did they doubt that, after a few short years of slight hardship and trifling deprivations, a life of luxurious comfort lay before them." All of which illustrates that fanciful advertising and "spin" is not a 21st century invention.

Despite the hyperbole of Adams, La Gloria did prosper. By 1914, the residents had built wooden houses and the thriving settlement boasted wide streets, along with concrete and wooden bridges and a hotel. La Gloria could also claim electric power and a public lighting system, a sugar mill, a local newspaper, a streetcar, plus entertainment for residents from a twelve-musician orchestra. Population estimates at the height of La Gloria range from 1,000 to 3,000, with other European nationalities taking up residence in the thriving city.

La Gloria was not the only United States colony in Cuba. In 1913 there were thirty-seven, and by the 1920s at least eighty foreign colonies were scattered throughout Cuba. While sugar has always been the largest economic factor for the United States' push into Cuba, colonies such as La Gloria focused on other agriculture and fruit and winter vegetables for the U.S. market. Prof. Carmen Diana Deere, of the University of Florida, points out these communities, which flourished from 1898–1930, were a part of the U.S. effort to annex Cuba. While it is not the purpose of this book to explore this subject, suffice it to say that Prof. Deere details a number of reasons for the decline of the colonies, including the eventual demise of the hoped-for intervention of the United States and the protectionist policies of the United States on fruit grown in Cuba.[50]

"The well-known American colony" of La Gloria clearly shows on a small map in a 1922 tourist guide to Cuba. At the time, the colony, situated some forty road miles west of Nuevitas, could be "reached by steamboat" from the port and probably was still in operation during Hemingway's early years in the archipelago.[51]

Augustus C. Mayhew (1879–1961) is a good example of a United States citizen in La Gloria. Born in South Norwalk, Connecticut, he arrived in Cuba in 1901. Mayhew purchased land and operated an apiary, exporting honey from what he called the "Bee Ranch." A photograph of La Gloria taken in 1914 shows a church and houses that would not be out of place in any small town in the United States. Around 1915, Mayhew married Beulah Nevada McAbee, who was the daughter of a store manager in the colony. They had four children. During the 1930s, Mayhew purchased a hundred-acre orange grove. When Augustus C. Mayhew, Jr., returned from service in the U.S. Navy during World War II, he took over the management of the orange grove. Mayhew, Jr., married, and his family of three children remained in La Gloria until they sold their property in 1953 and returned to the United States.[52]

Beside the reasons given by Prof. Deere for the decline of La Gloria, sugar prices rose and the remaining United States citizens sold their holdings for a good price. Even though the years have, as in many rural areas of Cuba, not been kind to La Gloria, it has not faded away. Many of the buildings of their glory days are gone; however, there remains a smattering of new Cuban style homes and some bohíos, some abandoned but others still in use. There is some evidence of a few paved roads within the confines of the former city, but there are more of the ever-present red dirt streets. One piece of evidence of a relatively modern addition to the city: a baseball field. As in most of this region, agriculture remains the main economic force.

Víctor and I spent a short amount of time in La Gloria and then traced the route southward through Minas to Camagüey for another night in the city. As noted elsewhere, the traveler in Cuba never knows what the next sight will bring, especially while in the rural areas. At one point, we were traveling through open fields interspersed with trees and brush near the road and a scattering of Royal Palms in the background. Rounding a curve and stretched across the highway there appeared cattle being herded by men on horseback and dogs yapping at the animals. The cattle caused Víctor to stop the car, allowing a chance to watch Cuban *vaqueros* in a scene almost out of any picture taken in the western United States. One vaquero, wearing a Stetson-type hat and a yellow rain slicker against any sudden downpour, lassoed a steer and, with a taut rope tied to the pommel of his saddle, guided the animal to the side of the road. After viewing this slice of the "Wild West" in Cuba, the journey continued to Camagüey for another night's stay before setting out the next morning for El Cobre, some eighteen kilometers (eleven miles) from Santiago de Cuba.

This route passes through Bayamo, a small town with great historical interest to Cuba. It is the birthplace of Carlos Manuel de Cespedes, considered the father of the Cuban nation. His statue graces the small and restful park in the center of Plaza de Armas in Havana, not far from the hotel Ambos Mundos. Bayamo is also noted for being the birthplace of the Cuban national anthem, "La Bayamesa." When Fidel Castro returned from exile in Mexico he gathered his followers and went into the nearby rugged mountains of the Sierra Maestra and began operations to overthrow the Batista government.

The city is also noted for its use of horse-drawn carriages and, while passing through the city, the route went by a sculpture of a horse and carriage. This is also a monument to a popular song of traveling through the narrow streets of Bayamo in a horse-drawn carriage. After leaving Bayamo, Víctor and passenger continued eastward until reaching El Cobre, the last destination having anything to do with Ernest Hemingway in the eastern portion of Cuba.

The Spanish established El Cobre in 1550 near a slave-worked copper mine—*cobre* being the Spanish word for copper. An important Cuban legend started in this small town. There are a number of versions, but generally it follows this line. Around 1612, two Indians and a slave boy in a small boat were caught in a gale in the nearby Bay of

Nipe—the bay closest to Cobre—and they feared for their lives. In the storm-tossed waves they spotted something and, upon retrieving the object, they held a wooden Black Madonna with a sign that proclaimed: Yo Soy La Virgen de la Caridad (I am the Virgin of Charity). Miraculously, the young men made it to shore, convinced the statue saved their lives.

At the time, there was a church in Cobre dedicated to Saint James, the patron saint of the Spanish conquest. The Madonna was placed in a small thatched hut located beside the church. The statue twice disappeared from the hut and was found on the hill above the town. There developed small shrines to the Madonna in a number of locations until the mine was closed and the slaves freed in 1630. This statue replaced St. James above the high altar of the church. Since that time, the Madonna has been credited with a number of miracles.

In 1916, Pope Benedict XV visited the shrine and declared her the patron saint of Cuba. Eleven years later a triple-domed church was built on a hill with the long name of El Santuario de Nuestra Señora de Caridad del Cobre (The Sanctuary of Our Lady of Charity of Cobre). The Madonna is now clothed in a golden gown, with a bejeweled crown and dangling earrings. She resides in a clear glass case and is facing the congregation during church services and afterwards the case is turned to face a small chapel. In this chapel are many objects offered from supplicants for their prayers.

In 1954, Ernest Hemingway received the Nobel Prize for literature. The announcement of the prize mentioned his novel *The Old Man and the Sea*. Hemingway dedicated the prize to the Cuban people and had the gold medal accompanying the award given to El Santuario de Nuestra Señora de Caridad del Cobre and for years it was displayed in the chapel with other offerings. Apparently, it was stolen, but recovered, and is no longer on public display.[53]

Approaching El Cobre from the northwest on a narrow, winding, hilly road I caught my first glimpse of El Santuario de Nuestra Señora de Caridad del Cobre on a distant hill that allows one to appreciate the setting. The hill upon which the church rests rises like an island in a sea of trees. The church itself is framed against a background of a mountain of dense foliage and, appropriately, the tailings from the ancient copper mine.

Once Víctor navigated the car through the narrow and crowded streets of El Cobre to the parking area of the church, I viewed a cream-colored basílica with three round, brick red roofs. A series of steps ascends to the entrance of the church. So as not to disturb those worshipping inside the church, I took no photographs of the interior. Coming out of the church, I was struck by the sun peeking in and out of the scattered stratocumulus clouds, putting on a display of crepuscular rays dramatically lighting the surroundings. El Santuario de Nuestra Señora de Caridad del Cobre and its surroundings helps give credence to what some photographers and artists who dub the display "God rays."

We departed from El Cobre late in the afternoon en route to the next destination a short eighteen kilometers (eleven miles) away, Santiago de Cuba. The city marks the end of the quest for sites that have something to do with Ernest Hemingway, eastward from Havana. If we had traveled on a direct route from Havana to Santiago de Cuba it is 534 miles (860 kms). However, Víctor and I had followed anything but a direct route to trace Hemingway along the north coast in the eastern portion of Cuba. With the exception of being denied access to one cayo, thus being unable to reach the isolated Cayo Confites, the goals for this aspect of tracking Ernest Hemingway in Cuba had been met. Chapter 6 continues the quest for Hemingway sites westward to as far as Bahía Honda.

✦ 6 ✦

Tracking Hemingway Westward from Santiago de Cuba to Bahía Honda

Upon arrival in Santiago de Cuba, Víctor found lodgings for us at a casa particulare, in the central section of the city. Cuba's second-largest city had a 2004 population of 494,337. After a leisurely breakfast in a rooftop dining area, during which I marveled at how the breakfast was brought up the many steps of a narrow, circular stairway, plans were made for the long drive westward. Until returning to the area of Havana, there would be no known new areas that had anything to do with Ernest Hemingway. Over the normal morning planning session, taking into account budget and time constraints, we decided the return trek would be largely a chance to see a different view of the countryside and at least a few stops at locations that dealt with Cuban history and culture. The first two sites were in Santiago de Cuba.

The first stop was to photograph the former Cuban Army Moncada Barracks, where, on July 26, 1953, Fidel Castro led the abortive raid that is considered the beginning of the revolution that toppled the Batista government six years later and thus in Cuba it is called the 26th of July Movement. After successfully overthrowing the government, Castro ordered the walls of the barracks demolished and established a school at the location. Later, he ordered some of the walls reconstructed and a museum established at the site.

The next site visited deals with what Theodore Roosevelt has famously labeled "The Splendid Little War," the Spanish–American War of 1898 that was fought both in Cuba and the Philippine Islands. Two battles in that short conflict were fought around the Santiago area. The first, the Battle of Santiago de Cuba—one of the major naval engagements of the war—between the United States Navy and the Spanish Caribbean Squadron, began on July 3, 1898, when Spanish ships, which had been bottled up in Santiago's harbor, began their movement toward the mouth of the bay. The engagement began at approximately 9:45 a.m. In just over an hour, five of the six ships of the Spanish Caribbean Squadron had been destroyed or run aground, with only one armored cruiser remaining. The commander of the cruiser tried to outrun the attacking force, but eventually ran his ship aground and scuttled it to prevent the sure loss of his crew by the pursuing United States battleships.[1]

The bloodiest land battle of the entire Spanish–American War took place in Cuba and is one which many Americans probably have heard something about: the Battle of San Juan Hill—also known as the Battle of San Juan Heights. The reason for the popular knowledge of the battle is largely due to two men, one being a very good artist. One of the United States' military units that made the assault on the hill was Theodore Roosevelt and his 10th Volunteers, forever known as the "Rough Riders." Roosevelt would go on to become vice president, and then president of the United States. "Teddy" Roosevelt seemed naturally to attract attention. Never one to shy away from publicity, he did lead his troops in dislodging Spanish troops from the advantage of a commanding height. What is not so well known is that other troops, notably African American units of the 10th Cavalry—the "Buffalo Soldiers"—and the 24th (Colored) Infantry, engaged in the majority of the heaviest combat. Also rarely remembered in the United States is that in the engagements Cubans also fought against Spain; it was, after all, their bid for freedom from Spanish rule.

In Cuba at the time of the war was the noted United States artist Frederick Remington. An editor for William Randolph Hearst's newspaper the *Chicago Sun-Times* convinced Remington to supply illustrations of the war. The artist's output is probably most noted by two works, *The Scream of Shrapnel at San Juan Hill* (1898) and *The Charge of the Rough Riders at San Juan Hill* (1901), both of which captured the collective imagination of the American public. The latter work has since been used in many books and articles on Theodore Roosevelt.

The successful United States assault was against Spanish troops

6. Tracking Hemingway Westward to Bahía Honda 129

dug in along the crest of a high stretch of ground given the names of San Juan Hill and Kettle Hill by the American forces. The battle casualties illustrate the difficulty of ground troops dislodging soldiers dug in at a commanding height: 205 American soldiers were killed, and 1,180 wounded; 58 Spanish soldiers were killed, with 170 wounded.

The battle's location was outside of Santiago de Cuba, but 103 years later, the site is now inside the sprawling city. Sometime in the past, the battlefield was made into a commemorative area, primarily featuring the efforts of the United States' troops. The site is well maintained and an amusement site is now located next to the battlefield. After Víctor parked the car, as we moved toward the site, a Cuban with an identification badge on his shirt wanted to know if he could guide me around the area. While there were plenty of plaques and it could easily be a self-guided tour, the offer was a way for a Cuban to earn extra money, thus the suggestion was accepted. As in any former battlefield later made into a memorial and historic site, there were cannons, statues, and plaques on display. There is a tower close to the middle of the tour where one can obtain a good view of the course of the battle. Inside the tower there are plaques (all in English) with arrows pointing to the location of certain events.

The small site is enclosed with many trees and, even walking at a slow pace and reading most of the signs, one can easily finish within an hour and a half. One of the aspects of the battle site I noticed was the great efforts of some group, or groups, in the past to record the names on the plaques of people who took part. Another interesting aspect of the battlefield is, at certain spots, when glancing through the trees surrounding the ridge one can glimpse part of the Ferris wheel in the nearby amusement park.[2]

Once back into the car, Víctor set the route westward that would once again pass through Camagüey and arrive back at the city of Ciego de Ávila. At this juncture, Víctor then turned to a southwesterly direction toward Trinidad.

Trinidad is one of the best colonial cities in Cuba to visit. It was founded in 1514 at the site of a native settlement by Diego Velázquez who named it Villa de la Santísima Trinidad. The city grew prosperous largely because of the sugar industry located in the nearby Valle de los Ingenios. When the sugar economy took a downturn in the 1860s, it caused the economy to collapse. From then on the city drifted into obscurity. This has been a boon to 21st century travelers as it left the heart of the city as it was in the colonial era. By 1958, the beauty and historical value of the city had been recognized and the Batista government forbade any modernization. The heart of the old city was made a UNESCO World Heritage Site in 1988. The historic area is relatively small and is centered on the Plaza Mayor and is a pedestrian-only area, with cobblestone streets, pastel-colored houses, with intricate wrought-iron grills, and the commanding Iglesia (church) de la Santísima Trinidad, whose tower can be viewed from some distance away. The heart of the old city has guarded barriers to stop any automobile from entering. However, one of the best locations to stay is the Casa Particulare de Liliana Zerquera, very close to the church. A visitor should make advance reservations and, upon arriving at the barrier to the historic area, tell the guard your destination to gain entry. Be warned, as the traveler approaches the barrier, there will be a number of Cubans whistling or shouting to attract your attention, offering to park your car. *Do not accept these offers*, no matter what they say, for as mentioned, reservations at Liliana Zerquera's home allows the tracker to enter into the historic area, unload baggage and then someone at the casa particulare will either take or direct the guest to a parking location.

Liliana Zerquera, whose father was the historian of the city, lives near the church. The long light blue façade has tall windows, with traditional wooden shutters. Walking directly from the cobblestoned street and through a wooden door that is at least ten feet tall, the guest is transported back to the days of colonial Trinidad. The living areas have the dark furniture of the period, with many of the walls graced with art, some by Liliana herself. As with much of the colonial architecture of the time, the house is arranged around a large center patio. Three sides of the home are living spaces and the fourth is against a city wall. The patio has an old well along with many plants, large and small, with some orchids scattered around the patio. Standing in the center of the patio, I viewed, on one side, three large openings for folding wooden doors that makes the patio and much of the interior living spaces seem as one. When residents are ready for bed, the doors are closed. Above the doors, large fan-shaped stained glass windows allow additional light into the living areas. This arrangement means guests can relax out in the patio and even enjoy dining there, or if it is raining, can have their meal inside and still feel they are dining alfresco. On another side of the square is an alcove entered through two archways interesting for their white-painted filigreed ironwork. Inside the alcove sits an iron table and chairs in the same color scheme.

Should the Hemingway tracker need to convert funds into Cuban Convertible Pesos (CUC), the "hard" currency in the country, Liliana will escort the guest to either a bank or to a money exchange establishment, a CADECA, scattered throughout Cuba. Even if the traveler is familiar with exchanging money, Liliana will make sure everything runs smoothly. Normally, the exchanges have long lines, even in rural areas, but, as mentioned, when residents see visitors to Cuba facing a long wait they will usually insist they go to the head of the line. I entered the CADECA with Liliana and when the Cubans in line saw the Norte Americano was at least number ten to be served, they insisted I go to the head of the line. Through Liliana, I said I did not mind waiting my turn; however, the people insisted and Liliana said it would be impolite to turn down the generous offer, so I was quickly served.

Even if pressed for time, the traveler should explore some of the cobblestone streets and especially the Plaza Mayor. There, the you can sit on a bench and enjoy the many flower garden plots encircled with low fences that create a patchwork of vibrant colors while examining the colonial architecture. I regretted not having more time at Casa Particulare de Liliana Zerquera to learn and see more of this colonial city.

Leaving Trinidad on the main highway and approaching an overlook, Víctor suggested a stop. This proved once again Víctor was a guide who knew how to show a visitor his country. The first thing at the turnout was the inevitable souvenir store, but of far more significance, is the chance to walk to the edges of the area. Stretched out below is scenery that encompasses much of what is known as the Valle de los Ingenios or what some Cubans call the Valley of One Hundred Sugar Mills. From the overlook, the view takes in part of a region that begins about 7.5 miles (12 kms) outside of Trinidad with the vale encompassing three interconnected valleys stretching approximately 140 miles (225 kms). At one time, in the 19th century, more than fifty sugar mills lined the valley, and, in 1827, more than eleven thousand slaves worked the mills, with many more working in the fields. Also enclosed within this long dale were the plantations and summer mansions of the slave owners. Cuba's sugar industry began a slow decline, accelerated in the 1990s when most of the aid from the Soviet Union was withdrawn. UNESCO's declaration of the city of

Trinidad as a World Heritage Site also includes the Valle de los Ingenios, proclaiming it "the best preserved testimony of the Caribbean sugar agro-industrial process of the 18th and 19th centuries, and of the slavery phenomenon associated with it." The UNESCO statement, however, does not mention the verdant beauty of the valley. We arrived at the overlook on a day when the sun peeked out between scattered stratocumulus clouds, revealing breathtaking views of varying shades of green, along with the color of plowed fields and with fields filled with sugar cane along with the presence of stately Royal Palms. Even better is traveling on the road that runs parallel to and within the valley. Note to railroad buffs: in 2011 there was a train for tourists running from Trinidad to one of the old sugar estates in the valley, and back. For those visiting Trinidad, this would be an interesting way to see the beauty of rural Cuba and the Valle de los Ingenios.[3]

We took the route that runs for a number of miles alongside the valley and I watched the play of the shadows of the clouds drifting across the fields, trees, and the Sierra de Sancti Spiritus. This is a vista best captured by the works of great landscape painters. The route continues until turning from the valley to the nearby small settlement of Manaca. After crossing the railroad tracks that cut through the town, there is an unusual sight. Looming over the small settlement towers a pagoda-like structure, which upon first observance seems to be slightly canted to the right. The 142.7 feet (43.5 meters) Manaca-Iznaga tower has inspired legends of why it was built. One states that the Iznaga brothers made a wager on who could gain the most fame. Alejo built the tower, while Pedro constructed a well twenty-eight meters (91.8 feet) deep. Yet another story says Alejo built it to lock in his adulterous wife. More prosaic, however, is that the tower was built by Don Alejo María del Carmen Iznaga y Borrell to oversee the fields to make sure no slave escaped, and to watch for fire. A bell would be rung in either case. The early 19th century structure is made of mud bricks and mortar, has seven levels, with each level having a different geometrical shape, from squares to octagons. From the top, the visitor has a view of the valley for at least five kilometers (three miles).[4]

After leaving Manaca, the route gains elevation. As we entered part of the Sierra del Escambray (Escambray Mountains) range. This part of the range is known as the Sierra de Sancti Spiritus and within this section is the Parque Nacional Topes de Collantes (Collantes' High National Park). Wet winds coming from the Atlantic Ocean make the

6. Tracking Hemingway Westward to Bahía Honda   133

A view of the Valle de los Ingenios, stretching out before the Sierra de Sancti Spiritus near the colonial city of Trinidad. (Photograph by the author.)

north face of the mountains a lush area for plants and animals, while the south side is drier; the Valle de los Ingenios and Trinidad lie in this section. Caves, rivers, canyons, and waterfalls are among the natural wonders of this region. There are abundant bird species, including Cuba's endemic and national bird, the tocororo (*Priotelus temnurus*), with a deep-blue crown, barred wings, and the throat white and shades of light green, becoming dark green near the tail. The bird gets its Cuban name from its call *toco-toco-toco-toco*.

The route is a narrow two-lane road with numerous sharp curves, with many potholes and should be traveled at a slow speed with a good car. All of this should not distract the passenger from the beauty of the region. Turning yet another curve along this stretch of the route, off to the left I beheld a sight probably little changed in Cuba from the 19th century. Some distance from the road sat a farm, with plots of land recently cultivated, awaiting either the planting of crops, or those just planted. Two traditional bohíos, plus a larger modern house made

A farm within the Sierra de Sancti Spiritus near Trinidad. Of the three buildings in the background, the one to the far left and the far right are bohíos, the traditional Cuban rural homes whose sides are made from the lumber of the royal palm tree; the roof is thatched from the fronds from the same type of tree. (Photograph by the author.)

of wood sides and with what appeared to be a modern composition or shingle roof, made up the buildings on the property. Just barely seen on the front porch of the house was a man in a rocking chair. A tall, narrow pole brought one power line to the house. All this is set against a backdrop of lush vegetation, intermixed with stately royal palm trees. In the far distance loomed densely forested mountains set off by white stratocumulus clouds slowly drifting above them. If one wants to see a traditional small Cuban farm in a beautiful setting, this is it. The farm lies within the confines of the Parque Nacional Topes de Collantes, so, one hopes, it may continue to exist without incursions from the nearby city of Trinidad.

Once back onto the flat lands, Víctor set a course northwestward for Havana. The normal route from the mountains would intersect the well-paved and fast motorway that would take us to Havana in the least amount of time. However, a town with the name of George Washington on the slower Carretera Central—the former main highway from Havana to Santiago de Cuba—was too intriguing for me to resist, and I asked Víctor if he knew anything about the settlement. He did not, but guessed a United States sugar company had probably founded the town. Being the exemplary guide he is, he agreed to follow the slower route to see the settlement. To reach George Washington the route intersected the Carretera Central at Santa Clara, known as Che Guevara's City, and made a left turn toward the town with the unusual name, with about 160 miles (270 kms) yet to travel before reaching Havana.

Once again, I never knew what the next stretch of road would bring. At intervals along the way to George Washington there were men standing along the roadway with a large amount of cheese held alongside one arm and the other arm beckoning for cars to stop and buy their products. Víctor explained the men were offering "white cheese" made from cows, as the province had a large number of cattle. There are two types of white cheese in Cuba: those that take some time to ripen, and others called "fast production." The latter seemed to be what was being offered along the roadside. Víctor recalled that anytime his father took him through the province he would stop to buy fast-production cheese.

Even before seeing the well-maintained sign proclaiming the town of George Washington, there was the display of a small steam engine that was once used to haul loads of sugar cane. In the distance, two large chimneys rose high into the sky, one with "George" and the other "Washington," proving Víctor was again correct: the settlement had a major sugar mill complex with many railroad tracks leading to large buildings. Driving around the few streets in town, I spotted a low-walled enclosure with something on each side of the entryway. Víctor stopped the car and I walked over to the enclosed space and found it to be a playground. What adorned each side of the entryway were two cartoon-like characters: on the left a young boy, and on the right, a young girl. Víctor informed me these were two Cuban characters in a popular story to tell school children about their history. It began as an animated audiovisual production and then morphed into a television series entitled *Elpidio Valdés*, with stories about a boy colonel of that name and his girlfriend, María Silvia. Both are "*Mambises*," the Cuban fighters against the Spanish. Each episode is based upon fact, but has comic parts to it, with the children having different adventures, such as "Elpidio Valdés against the armored train." The characters also appeared in a series of comic books. "I can assure you," Víctor said, "those comics are very popular in Cuba, not only with children, but with adults, too."[5]

Departing George Washington, we still had a long trip before reaching Havana. On this afternoon the heat seemed more oppressive than normal, probably because it was nearing the end of a long trip. In any case, in one small town there was an open-air café/bar and Víctor decided to make a rest stop and then buy some bottled water before pressing onward. When Víctor asked the owner of the establishment the location of *el baño*, the man looked at me and immediately knew I was not Cuban and informed Víctor his baño was not very good and directed Víctor to another establishment a few blocks away.

We finally arrived back in Havana late in the afternoon. Víctor had arranged for me to stay at Casa Particular de Ana Morales on busy Neptuno Street in Central Havana (described in Chapter 2). This became the place to rest after the eastward trip and the place to stay while accomplishing the last of the road trip locating areas that had something to do with Hemingway away from the Havana area. After a day's rest, it was now time to travel westward. Unlike the trek to the east, the journey to the Bahía Honda area is much shorter.

There are two routes westward out of Havana. For a number of reasons, we took the route that ran along the sea to La Boca and then turns left to the city of Mariel. The route provides great seascapes and, furthermore, runs along the eastern side of Mariel Bay, which is bottle-shaped, with the mouth relatively narrow. The problem with this route is, as mentioned previously, it is a narrow, two-lane road, with many potholes, and is used for transporting agricultural products. The journey is scenic, but very slow. The wide southern portion of the bay is where the city of Mariel is located. In recent years, there has been a large building project to make Mariel one of the important ports in Cuba and this has caused work on repairing and improving the roads into the city. The city plays a part in the Hemingway story and is also an important part of modern Cuban history.

Hemingway, in the 1950s, sometimes kept *Pilar* farther west, at Cayo Paraíso (Paradise Key). He would invite friends in Havana to meet him at the Port of Mulata before sailing to Cayo Paraíso, and usually this meant a stop at Mariel to pick up ice before proceeding through the rural areas ahead. The route through Mariel took them past a large Catholic church and on one of the hills overlooking the city and harbor stood the Cuban Naval Academy. Originally designed as a gambling casino by American lawyer Horaio Rubins in early 20th century, the building is in the shape of a castle, complete with crenulated turrets. The casino never came into being and, in 1916, it became the site of the naval academy; other buildings were added as well. One of the major features of the academy was a large staircase that ran from the foot of the hill to the entrance of the academy. It became one of the leading institutions in Latin America, with a merchant marine academy, the Academia de la Marina Mercante, nearby. The naval academy changed after the 1959 revolution and, in 1977, was abandoned and a new academy established west of Havana. By 2011, the building has slowly deteriorated, but still shows traces of its former grandeur.[6]

Mariel, in 2010, had a population of 44,786. In 1980, the harbor was the scene of the beginning of the Mariel Boatlift. This took place when at least 125,000 Cubans fled their country, mainly to Florida, in a variety of craft, with an unknown number of refugees perishing in the attempt.[7]

Once clear of Mariel we remained on the same route and toward the village of Cubanas, whose large bay has a naval base located there. The route gains elevation as the traveler continues westward out of the village; the height gives a view of the Bay of Cubanas seen through tropical vegetation. For the rest of the trek to Bahía Honda, the road remained at the higher elevation, so I had views of the shining blue sea on the right, while on the left there were high hills covered with dense vegetation, interspersed with the ubiquitous Royal Palm. In this rural strip between high hills and the sea, I saw a farmer behind a brace of oxen plowing a field, with the inevitable white egrets checking the furrows thrown up by the plow.

Somewhere along this route, Víctor stopped so I could take a photograph. Lining up for a shot, I heard what sounded like whistling. Looking up, a small boy riding bareback on a horse, was indeed whistling some tune as the horse moved by at a fast pace—he was not about to slow down to have his picture taken. Seeing a child made me wonder about the location of schools in these rural areas. I learned that a flagpole and a small statue of José Martí in front of the building usually identifies these single-story structures.

Continuing westward, eventually on the right and through the Royal Palms, I could see the waters of Bahía Honda. In this area, approximately forty-three miles from Havana, Hemingway's World War II first official patrol area of *Pilar* took place in late November of 1942. The patrol area was selected as a good location to spot any U-Boats cruising the Straits of Florida to Gulf of Mexico ports, or the Panama Canal; the reasoning proved correct. During a patrol on December 2, a lookout on *Pilar* spotted a ship hull down on the horizon. Hemingway's craft lay near Cayo Médano de Corigua, to the west of Bahía Honda. As the ship drew nearer, Hemingway identified it as the passenger liner S.S. *Marqués de Comillas*, a 9,922-ton Spanish ocean liner. The *Compañia Transatlántica* had their ship's regular route from Barcelona, Cádiz, New York, Havana, and Vera Cruz. Being Spanish, and a neutral nation, the ship passed along its normal route without problems from U-Boats. Nearing the location of *Pilar*, Hemingway noted that the speed of the passenger liner slowed for at least fifteen to twenty minutes. At this slower speed, and at a distance, the crew of *Pilar* noted farther out to sea yet another vessel, painted gray and towing some type of craft.[8]

Hemingway turned *Pilar* toward the unidentified towing vessel and had the fishing lines deployed to simulate a scientific fishing mission. At a range of three miles, the vessel changed course to present a broadside silhouette of a submarine. As part of the crew prepared for combat on the side of *Pilar* away from the submarine, a large barracuda struck one of the fishing lines. Hemingway kept his boat on its present course, while slacking off the line and continued holding a fast speed, as it would have the appearance of fishing craft fighting a fish. Hemingway tried to get closer to the submarine, but the vessel increased speed and pulled away. Thinking that the submarine's mission might have been to rendezvous with the Spanish liner, Hemingway turned *Pilar* toward the Marqués de Comillas and searched its track line, with no results.

In his log, Hemingway stated that if the submarine in question belonged to the U.S. military, the incident should be forgotten. If, however, it was a German U-Boat then it might have been making its way to a rendezvous with the Spanish ship. As the incident happened during the noon hour, it is probable that most of the passengers would have been eating, and Nazi agents might have put material overboard for the U-Boat to pick up. The most daring guess would be a submarine would quickly come alongside the ship and the agents on the ship would help agents from the U-Boat clamber aboard the Spanish ship.

Hemingway and his crew felt they had spotted a U-Boat, but were uncertain it was connected in any way with the Marqués de Comillas. However, the liner's slowing in the area of the sighting seemed highly suspicious. Acting on their beliefs, Hemingway radioed the embassy in Havana, who then contacted the Key West headquarters of the Gulf Sea Frontier, the command in which the sighting took place, and requested the FBI meet the Spanish liner and inspect its crew and passengers when it arrived in Havana. After interviewing the passengers and crew of the Spanish liner, the special agent in charge discounted the sighting, causing Hemingway to claim the FBI botched the incident.[9]

Did Hemingway and his crew actually see a U-Boat? In the long run, it really does not matter. Hemingway's crew saw what they felt was the enemy, sped toward the it, and started the necessary actions to engage according to their plan. As Lord Horatio Nelson, the British hero of the Battle of Trafalgar, wrote, "No captain can do very wrong if he places his ship alongside that of the enemy."[10]

One generally overlooked personality in the story of Ernest Hemingway's war on submarines is the military attaché assigned to the American embassy, a U.S. Marine Corps officer by the name of John W. Thomason, Jr. Born on February 28, 1893, in Huntsville, Texas, Thomason was the oldest of nine children of Dr. John W. Thomason and Sue Hayes Goree. His childhood years were spent in a house noted for its large library; this exposed him, at an early age, to the classic writers. Despite living in a literate home, however, John proved, at best, a spotty scholar. He excelled in English and history and was talented in sketching, but let other subjects slide.[11]

Thomason eventually tried three colleges, obtained a certificate to teach in rural schools and fell in love with the girl next door, Leda Bass. With his mother's help, he convinced his father to send him for a year to the Art Students League in New York City. By this time, World War I had started in Europe.[12]

Returning home from New York at the age of twenty-two, John went to work as a cub reporter for the *Houston Chronicle*. The paper discovered that Thomason wrote extremely well. With a steady job, John proposed to Leda, and she accepted.[13]

In 1916, answering a call from the U.S. Marine Corps for 150 young men to be commissioned as second lieutenants, John enlisted. After some training, he received his commission, not in the reserves but, surprisingly, in the regular Corps. This meant he had a better chance to remain in the service as a regular. John quickly married Leda between training assignments.[14]

Second Lt. John W. Thomason, Jr., U.S. Marine Corps, arrived in Europe in May 1918. He served with the 49th Company, First Battalion, 5th Marines. While fighting during the Battle of Soissons, from July 18–28, 1918, two German machine gun crews held up his company's advance. Thomason and one of his men charged and took the position, despite withering machine gun fire. For his bravery, John received the Navy Cross, the second-highest award for valor in wartime a marine can receive.[15]

Thomason carried a sketch pad in his pack and took it out at every chance. He eventually became known as the officer who sketched while under fire. Thomason eventually received a promotion to captain.[16] Thomason came home in 1919 after a year of occupation duty, a regular officer and a hero who decided to make a career in the Corps.

Another U.S. Marine Corps officer and hero would play a significant role in Thomason's life: Laurence Stallings, who became a major writer upon his return to civilian life. Stallings wrote the immensely popular play *What Price Glory?* and the novel *Plumes*. He also penned the script for the MGM film *The Big Parade* (1925), directed by King Vidor. The film proved so successful at the box office that it became the most profitable feature of the silent era. Stallings also became the literary editor of *The New York World*, which is how he met Thomason.[17]

Having returned to the United States from Europe, Thomason received orders to Cuba during a period of political unrest in the 1920s. He commanded a company of mounted infantry at the old colonial city of Camagüey. His only son, John W. Thomason, III, was born there. Thomason began doing sketches and short articles. Following the old adage of writing about what you know, he sent pieces concerning the Great War to New York-based magazines. Back came the rejection slips. Thomason next commanded the marine detachment at the Naval Ammunition Depot, near Dover, New Jersey. This assignment allowed him to bring some of his combat sketches to New York City galleries. Again, he was met with rejection. Stallings, however, saw Thomason's press releases about his shows and asked to see his portfolio. Impressed, Stallings took the portfolio to *Scribner's Magazine*. Equally impressed, the editors of the magazine paid a good sum for the illustrations, but wanted some text to go with them. Stallings asked Thomason to supply a narrative for the work. Thomason then submitted the short articles other magazines had rejected. The editors at Scribner's were "dumbfounded; their unknown artist could write even better than he could draw." Thomason was assigned to Maxwell Perkins, the brilliant editor who handled Hemingway and other major writers of his time. The pieces ran as articles and caused a stir, especially among those who had served in combat in World War I. Perkins began to think about a book based upon the short stories and drawings. It eventually became *Fix Bayonets!* and was released to great critical acclaim. It went through three printings of fifteen thousand each in only ninety days. From this point on, Thomason never had the financial worries of his brother officers. He might well have resigned his commission and become a successful writer and artist, but, until the end of his life, he thought of himself as a U.S. Marine Corps officer.[18]

Thomason eventually served at sea, in China, attended the Naval War College, served as the Marine Corps Aide to the Assistant Secretary of the Navy, and eventually commanded a rifle regiment at Camp Pendleton, near San Diego, California. By this time, he had attained the rank of lieutenant colonel. In June of 1940, he was relieved of command of the regiment and assigned to the Latin American desk of the Office of Naval Intelligence in Washington, D.C. Such a duty assignment for an officer of Thomason's rank meant a crushing blow: he was on the desk of a sideline to a sideline. Even though he was considered the most famous marine in the Corps and had a service record that was outstanding, he had a serious drinking problem. If a service member drank to excess but could show up for work and not bring dishonor to the organization, excessive drinking was overlooked, or even in some cases, the person was given medical help. In such cases the medical record had a euphemism. Thomason's record shows a number of hospitalizations to "recover from exhaustion." Those in higher command knew this other side of Thomason's record.[19]

Admiral Chester Nimitz, an old friend, offered Thomason the position of war plans officer and inspector of Marine bases on his staff at Pearl Harbor. In his normal way, Thomason managed to visit combat units while they were engaged in battle. Shortly thereafter he was hospitalized in Australia with double pneumonia and sent back to Pearl Harbor. He died in the naval hospital in San Diego on March 12, 1944, at the age of fifty-one.[20]

Writer David Morris points out that Thomason "apparently never received a bad review." He was, Morris said, a "hugely competent writer, if not from the top literary drawer, at the very top of the second."[21]

After World War II, Hemingway enjoyed taking *Pilar* to an area just west of Bahía Honda. As mentioned earlier, guests from Havana would stop at Mariel, purchase ice and then travel to the Port of Mulata, where the Hemingways awaited their friends. Their destination was Cayo Paraíso, where, according to the Cuban writer Noberto Fuentes, Hemingway had visited as early as 1935 and during World War II had planted pine trees on the island as they would provide a point of reference while searching for submarines among the treeless islands. Once at this location, Hemingway and his guests would enjoy the white sandy beach and the clear, pristine sea.[22]

After soaking in the beauty of this area, the traveler can return to Havana either by the same route that, basically, stays close to the sea or continue on the route to just south and east of Mariel and connect with the much faster Autopista de Pinar del Río. This ended my search for places dealing either directly or indirectly with Ernest Hemingway to the east and west of Havana. The "expedition" helped in further understanding why the writer loved Cuba and its people. Anyone traveling along the cayos of the north coast of Cuba can see the beauty and, especially after reading *Islands in the Stream*, can see how the area affected his writing. Moreover, the tracker who visits the city of Trinidad, the Valle de los Ingenios and is lucky enough to see a traditional farm in the Sierra del Escambray, or travel the "blue highway" between Mariel and Bahía Honda, can quickly recognize the beauty of the country and understand why Hemingway loved the land. In this completed journey, I recognized that while relations between Cuba and the United States have been strained, to say the least, for over a half century, the people, especially in the rural areas, are the friendliest one could hope to meet. In Hemingway's day to the present these people will, even though they have very little, offer whatever they have to a visitor just as Hemingway found when speaking with the fishermen along the north coast. Today's Hemingway tracker can see it even in little things such as Cubans offering up their place in line to a person from another country. All of this makes the long trip outside of Havana well worth the time.

As mentioned, there are three sites in the Havana area for the person who has time for only a week in Cuba should visit. It is time for the last: a short drive to the village of Cojímar.

◈ 7 ◈

Cojímar

One of the best ways for anyone to understand why Cubans still speak glowingly of Ernest Hemingway is to spend time in the north coast village of Cojímar, an easy drive from Old Havana. Depending on the weather and his schedule, Hemingway had four places he moored or anchored *Pilar*. Three of the locations have already been visited: Casablanca; Regla, with its yellow church; and the third, near the wharf at Plaza de San Francisco. The fourth, the pier at the village of Cojímar, lies approximately seventeen miles (27 kms) east from Old Havana and at least nine miles (14 kms) from Hemingway's home at Finca Vigía. The location allowed him to write in the morning and, if he desired, fish in the afternoon.

Cojímar remains, basically, the small fishing village Hemingway knew so well; there is little doubt he used the town as part of the setting for *The Old Man and the Sea*. The entrance to the harbor has a Spanish fort—the Castillo—built around 1643. A 1922 travel guide mentioned that some Cubans called the structure "Little Moro" after the larger fort guarding Havana's harbor. In Hemingway's day, the modest homes of fishermen dotted the hills surrounding part of the harbor. The Cuban fishermen of the village started their day in the dim light of the rising sun as described so well by Santiago, the protagonist of *The Old Man and the Sea*, as he makes his way to his fishing craft. The men pursuing marlin usually went to sea alone in small wooden boats, fishing with hand lines; at other times, they used throw nets at the entrance to the harbor.[1]

The interaction of the fishermen and other residents of Cojímar with Hemingway can provide an insight as to how Cubans felt about the American writer. Take, for example, one of the famous Cubans of the village, Raúl Corral Fornos. Born on January 29, 1925, in Ciego de Ávila, he began as a lab assistant and photographic reporter in 1944. Raúl made his home in Cojímar beginning in the 1940s. He eventually gained an international reputation as one of Cuba's top photographers and along the way adopted the "artistic name" of Raúl Corrales.

Like others who lived in Cojímar, Corrales was poor. The cost of film and chemicals for lab work remained high, compelling him to take extra time to carefully compose a photograph before he snapped the shutter. Raúl's daily routine included visiting Cojímar's waterfront area to record the lives of the fishermen and their families. One of his photographs captures eight fishermen with a marlin on a board, struggling up a hill from the harbor of Cojímar; it exemplifies the scenes of the village in *The Old Man and the Sea*. Corrales's photograph also confirms the accuracy of Hemingway's descriptions of these men. The photographer captioned the image of one fisherman, Anselmo Hernández, as the "*pescador de Cojímar que inspiró el personaje de Santiago en El viejo y el mar* "("The Cojímar fisherman who inspired the Santiago of *The Old Man and the Sea*"). While there are many older fishermen of this village who have, at one time or another, been called the inspiration for *El viejo y el mar*, a careful examination of Corrales's series of images of Anselmo Hernández reveals the fisherman's leathery face and gnarled hands from a lifetime of working in salt water. Raúl recognized Hemingway as a fellow artist. It is little wonder that the first photograph in one of Corrales' books about his village shows Ernest Hemingway garbed in his normal attire for a day of fishing—shorts, a loose shirt and vest, long-billed hat, and sockless moccasins—on the pier gesturing as he explains something about *Pilar* to a rapt audience of people from Cojímar.

Before Corrales had achieved fame, he wrote that one day he "was at the pier with my camera, as usual, and [Hemingway] said to me: 'Come, climb [aboard],' and I did." Corrales spent most of the day at sea in *Pilar* with only one roll of film; one can only imagine how discerningly he would have been with his shots. The photographs, as befitting a great artist, are some of the best professional images of Hemingway at sea. Many of Corrales's photographs of the people of Cojímar and, of course, Hemingway, have been compiled in a volume titled *Hemingway y Cuba: Fotos de Raúl Corrales* (*Hemingway and Cuba: Photographs of Raúl Corrales*).[2]

Even though Hemingway always insisted that Santiago was not drawn from any particular person, the debate among scholars continues, not only about the inspiration for Santiago, but other characters in the book. For example, Hemingway employed a boy named Manolito, the son of a Cojímar café owner, as a deck hand on *Pilar*. Prof. Carlos Baker, who wrote the classic biography of Hemingway, says that Manolito "probably served as a rough model for the boy." Speculation continues about the model for the Old Man: is it Carlos Gutiérrez, another fisherman employed earlier by Hemingway? or Anselmo Hernández? or especially Gregorio Fuentes?[3]

"Early on, Ernest had mastered the theory and practice of navigation and seamanship," Walter Houk observed, "yet *Pilar* could not have run nearly as smoothly without Gregorio Fuentes." In Hemingway's 1956 speech, when awarded Cuba's San Cristóbal Medal, he recognized "my old comrade in arms, Gregorio Fuentes." Gregorio is yet another reason Cojímar is important to the story of Hemingway in Cuba.[4]

Gregorio Fuentes, born in the Canary Islands on July 11, 1897, went to sea at a young age, working alongside his father. When Gregorio was ten years old, his father decided they would immigrate to Cuba. Tragically, his father died on the voyage and Gregorio arrived in his new country an orphan, but was taken in by former Canary Islanders then living in Cojímar.

Hemingway first met Fuentes when fishing out of Key West in 1931. The fishing party ran out of Bermuda onions, a favorite of Hemingway, while at the Dry Tortugas. Hemingway went to a nearby Cuban fishing boat to see if they had any onions to spare. Gregorio, captain of the craft, not only gave Hemingway what he needed but threw in some rum and refused payment for any of it. During the exchange, Hemingway noticed the cleanliness of the fishing vessel.[5] When Hemingway looked for a new mate to replace Carlos Gutiérrez in 1938, he recalled the shipshape fishing vessel's captain and hired him to be the mate of *Pilar*. Later, Hemingway remarked that Gregorio was "the pillar of the *Pilar*." In a 1949 article in *Holiday* magazine, Hemingway gave Gregorio's age as fifty. His nickname for him was "Gregorine."[6]

When Houk first met Fuentes, in 1951, Gregorio was fifty-three. Houk described the mate as having dark "grizzled" hair, a face "seamed and leathered by a half century of sun and salt breeze" and "a mariner's clear and untroubled eyes." Despite his advancing years, he moved easily around *Pilar*. Like old school sailors, he preferred to go barefoot at sea, but, at times, he wore rope-soled *alpargatas* for a better grip on wet decks. Gregorio knew little English. Although "affable if not talkative," he preferred to do his work on *Pilar* without socializing with the guests, even the ones who spoke Spanish. At sea, Fuentes usually wore "a cotton shirt," very faded blue trousers and either a "visored cap or sometimes a brimmed hat." Like many Cuban fishermen he "usually had a cigar in his mouth."[7] Hemingway felt Gregorio would rather keep a clean ship than fish, but he would rather fish than eat. From the date Gregorio signed on *Pilar*, there are very few pictures of Hemingway in his craft without Fuentes nearby. He not only helped Hemingway's education on marlin and la mar, but was also *Pilar*'s bartender and, by all accounts, a very good cook.[8]

In the same article in *Holiday*, Hemingway mentioned how Gregorio saved *Pilar* during a particularly savage hurricane in 1944. As the storm lashed Havana with winds of 180 miles per hour, Fuentes moved *Pilar* to a swampy area in the harbor and dropped anchor and then set about tying ropes to every pole, rock, and tree he could find. "When I was through," Fuentes recalled to Cuban writer Norberto Fuentes (no relationship), "it looked like a yacht caught in a spider web." *Pilar*'s secure location gave shelter to six other damaged fishing boats and Fuentes invited the skippers of these boats to ride out the storm with him in *Pilar*.[9]

While there is no doubt a special friendship existed between Gregorio and Hemingway, it does not mean they never had disagreements, as anyone who has spent time in a boat for a prolonged time knows it can be difficult to always remain cheerful. Norberto Fuentes recorded that once while Gregorio was engaged in a strong argument with the captain of a nearby boat, Hemingway intervened in such a way that Gregorio thought showed "a lack of respect" for him. Fuentes asked for the wages due him, as he was resigning from *Pilar*. Hemingway came back three or four times trying to make up. Once Hemingway said if Gregorio did not return he would "burn down the farm and the yacht"; the argument finally settled, Gregorio would later say, "Once in a while old Hemingway was strange."[10] With the wages Fuentes earned from Hemingway—by 1950, he earned $155 a month, "three times what any Hemingway household employee got paid"—he bought a pastel-colored home at 209 Calle Pasuela in Cojímar, and called the fishing village his home.[11]

As he grew older, Fuentes sometimes brought a boy along from Cojímar to work as a deck hand. One was Manolito, and the other Felipe, who "Papa found strange." Many times Felipe piloted Mary Hemingway's small boat, the *Tin Kid*.[12]

After Hemingway's death, Mary Hemingway became the sole beneficiary of the estate. On August 24, 1961, a day before a copy of Ernest Hemingway's will was published in the *New York Times*, Mary, following instructions in a letter from Hemingway that accompanied his will, gave *Pilar* to Fuentes. This began what writer Paul Hendrickson labels "The Curious Afterlife of *Pilar*."

In her memoirs, Mary related one story concerning the fishing craft. This account stated that, upon her return to Cuba to retrieve material from the finca, Gregorio visited with her and they discussed the fate of *Pilar*. Her book clearly says she wanted the boat sunk. Mary did not say why this did not happen: "The Cubans used *Pilar* as a workboat for a while, and then installed her (poor thing) as an exhibit on the [finca's] lawn, so I was told."[13] The Cuban writer Fuentes, however, notes Gregorio worked *Pilar* after Hemingway's death, but eventually could not afford the upkeep and gave it to the Cuban government, who transported it to the former tennis court of the finca. René Villarreal, Hemingway's long-serving majordomo and, for a period, director of the Museo de Ernesto Hemingway, related that Gregorio showed up at the finca. He had been unable to keep *Pilar* due to the cost of repairs and wanted to turn it over to the government. He wanted a smaller boat to "join the cooperative of fishermen from Cojímar."[14]

It really does not matter who owned *Pilar* after Hemingway's death. As the years passed, Gregorio Fuentes became the only living link to Hemingway, *Pilar*, and Cojímar. Many still believe him to have been the model for Santiago and he does seem to fit Hemingway's description of the old Cuban.

Gregorio Fuentes lived a long life. In his old age, he supported his family by charging tourists, Hemingway aficionados and scholars for interviews and pictures, becoming "a national treasure." Fuentes remained loyal to Hemingway to the end of his life. If someone said something against the writer, Gregorio, with eyes flashing, retorted, "Did [that person] know [Hemingway]?"[15] On January 13, 2002, Gregorio Fuentes died at the age of 104. "He died in the house he had always lived in," said his grandson Rafael Fuentes. Gregorio Fuentes is buried in the nearby village of Guanabacoa.[16]

The interior of the restaurant La Terraza (The Terrace), in Cojímar. Cojímar is one of the locations Hemingway kept his fishing craft *Pilar* and is the model for the novella *The Old Man and the Sea*. The restaurant is mentioned in his novella and Hemingway reportedly sat at the table in the corner shown in the right background of the photograph (note the draped chairs). The local Cuban fishermen used the bar and, from them, Hemingway gained knowledge about marlin. When La Terraza fell into disrepair, Fidel Castro ordered it to be restored to how it was when Hemingway patronized the establishment—and with the same type of menu. (Photograph by Víctor Pina Tabío.)

While a number of tour buses and guides usually first bring tourists to one location in Cojímar—La Terraza (The Terrace)—the person interested in the story of Hemingway in Cuba and how the village of Cojímar fits into the narrative should instead first take the time to see the village. Start by driving to a small active church away from the harbor and then drive around the village, working slowly toward the sea. On this drive one may, at times, come upon young people in gray uniforms, searching for something. These are young men and women from the Ministry of Health performing what is known as *"Campaña Anti-vectorial"* (Anti-vectorial Campaign). Vector is a term in epidemiology to denote the agent responsible for the spread of diseases. The young people carry identification to show before they enter houses to search for any reservoirs of water that breed the mosquito *Aedes aegtoti*. This mosquito transmits dengue fever, along with *chikungunya* and yellow fever viruses. One of the problems the young Cubans face in their undertaking to eradicate the insect is that some Afro-Cuban religious practices fill jars of various sizes with water and flowers. These jars offer perfect breeding conditions for mosquitos. The inspectors check the water and insist it must be changed regularly. At times the army helps in the work and, when that happens, the soldiers wear a beige uniform instead of the normal olive green.[17]

Cruising the back streets of Cojímar, Víctor and I observed many of the buildings and homes that had seen better days, but then the next street might reveal a cluster of homes as carefully maintained as in any middle-class neighborhood in any country. While we drove through the different neighborhoods, I had Víctor stop the car at a street leading downhill to the sea. I walked a short distance down the road and stopped for a bit, looking at the water in the distance. It does not take long for the mind's eye to see Santiago making his way through the early morning light, carrying his mast, sail, and bait to his boat as he prepares to venture out onto la mar, even though it has been eighty-four days since he last caught a marlin.

For the next stop in my visit to Cojímar, I had Víctor drive to the street bordering the harbor until reaching one of the important Hemingway Cuban landmarks, a golden-cream colored two-story building. Santiago and Hemingway would have sailed past this building. The second story has balconies that overhang the sidewalk with white columns from the sidewalk to the balconies, forming the colonnades, familiar to Cuban architecture. A blue-and-white sign with a fighting marlin upon it proclaims: La Terraza. In Hemingway's years in Cuba, it was a fisherman's bar and restaurant with a ceiba tree that grew at the back of the restaurant. Under the large spreading tree, Cuban fishermen gathered to discuss the day's events. La Terraza is mentioned a number of times in *The Old Man and the Sea*.

Walking beneath a blue-and-white-striped awning, one enters La Terraza, and to the right is a bar. While Hemingway did dine here, he also used the bar as another location where he could learn more about la mar and marlin from the tough Cuban fishermen who put out to sea in pursuit of the fish.

Passing through the bar area, there is a hallway and on the right-hand wall hangs a painting of Hemingway; continuing onward, one enters the restaurant. The tall ceiling has large slowly rotating wooden paddle fans. Windows grace the side of the restaurant overlooking the harbor and out toward the sea. The two other sides of the room away from the windows have walls covered with poster-sized photographs by Raúl Corrales, most of which are images of Hemingway at sea. The floors are in a pleasing pattern of contrasting colored squares. Waiters, wearing their white guayabera shirts, hover nearby.

According to legend, the table in the left-hand corner is where Hemingway sat when he dined in the restaurant; it has windows on two sides of the corner. At this table, Hemingway could see part of the entrance to the actual harbor, the approach, out to sea and part of the immediate shoreline: a perfect location.

If you arrive late, there is apt to be a crowd of people sitting in long tables at the back of the restaurant. Tour buses drop many out-of-towners in front of or nearby La Terraza, with the inevitable Cuban band playing for the visitors. The table in the righthand corner is quickly occupied. However, in 2010 and 2011, Víctor and I arrived early and the waiters, who thought I looked like Hemingway, sat us at the coveted table. Information relayed to me in 2012, however, indicates the table has since been formally set aside, with a rope preventing anyone from sitting there: a plaque on the table stating this was where Hemingway dined.

Once finished with an excellent meal, I stepped outside to view the surroundings. As mentioned, in Hemingway's day the Cuban fishermen gathered beneath a spreading ceiba tree to discuss fishing, and Hemingway, as he did in the cayos throughout the north coast, never missed an opportunity to learn about marlin from these men. Unfortunately, the ceiba tree is now gone. No one recalls when it was removed. Hemingway also did spend some time on the sea near La Terraza. (Two photographs in the Hemingway Collection at the John F. Kennedy Library in Boston show him pulling in a net with some fishermen of Cojímar, possibly near the restaurant.)

After viewing the immediate surroundings of La Terraza, I walked a few feet away from the restaurant for a better view of the castillo that overlooks a cement pier, formerly made of wood. This is where Hemingway kept *Pilar*. One of Corrales's photographs shows *Pilar* pulling away from the dock in the early-morning hours, a part of the many small Cuban fishing craft. In February 2011, I observed a few Cubans trying their luck at fishing from the pier and a few tourists stood on the structure—when a tour bus is in Cojímar, however, the number of tourists on the dock naturally increases. In 2011, the castillo had a number of antennae protruding from the top and at least one army vehicle

From near La Terraza and across the bay a visitor can view the Spanish fort built around 1643 and called the Castille. To the left a white rotunda contains ... [see facing page]. (Photograph by Víctor Pina Tabío.)

7. Cojímar

parked alongside the structure. (Reports in 2012 that the antennae and military vehicle were no longer visible.)

Located a few feet from the castillo is a small rotunda-shaped structure with some of its original blue paint still in place. The building contains a bust of Hemingway on a stone plinth. In the stone is carved "Ernest Hemingway 1898–1961." (His birth date is actually 1899.) On the opposite side, in Spanish, is a plaque explaining how and why this structure and the Hemingway bust came to be in this small fishing village.

Upon learning of the death of Ernest Hemingway in 1961, a group of the Cojímar fishermen met to discuss how they could honor "the

... a bust of Ernest Hemingway on a plinth. The poor fishermen of Cojímar, upon hearing of Hemingway's passing, wanted to do something to show their respects to the American they considered a fellow fisherman. When they found they could not obtain the metal needed for the sculpture, they willingly melted some of their fishing gear to produce the bust. This act is illustrative of how Cubans in Hemingway's time felt about the writer. (Photograph by the author.)

The bar area of Hemingway's favorite bar/restaurant in Havana, the Floridita. The bust on the wall has been there many years. The statue of Hemingway at his favorite location is relatively new. (Photograph by Víctor Pina Tabío.)

American," whom they viewed not as a famous writer, but as a fellow fisherman. The meeting decided upon some type of sculpture to be erected near where Hemingway's *Pilar* moored at Cojímar. There was a structure there already, close to the castillo. No one seemed to know why the rotunda-like edifice had been placed there, but this seemed the logical location for what they wanted to accomplish. The delegation from Cojímar met in Havana with the sculptor who earlier had created a bust of Hemingway for the Floridita. The artist said he would be willing to do the bust, but the United States embargo had made the required bronze for the sculpture too difficult to obtain. These tough, hard-working, poor fishermen who risked their lives in the attempt to support their families hit upon an amazing solution: they would contribute bronze fishing equipment to be melted down for the bust. The sculptor was so moved by this offer he did the work for no charge.[18]

The bust was placed upon the stone column facing the pier area and the sea. Fittingly, Gregorio Fuentes unveiled the sculpture at the dedication of the Hemingway Park in Cojímar, in 1962. Raúl Corrales has at least two photographs of the event: one with Fuentes removing the veil covering the bust and the other of the large festive crowd next to the rotunda and a small girl holding flowers ready to lay them near the bust.[19]

Hemingway's love of the village is illustrated in an interview he gave on Cuban television upon receiving word of his selection for the Nobel Prize in Literature in 1954; at his request the interview was conducted in Spanish—further endearing him to the Cuban people. During the telecast, Hemingway mentioned he was the "first *Cubano sato* to win the Nobel Prize"—in Cuba, *sato* usually means common. A smile spreads over the Cuban interviewer's face at Hemingway's comment. Cubans have repeated the Nobel Prize–winning writer's simple statement many times to me in their efforts to explain why they love Hemingway.[20]

In 1956, Hemingway received the Cuban medal of San Cristóbal at the Sports Palace in Havana. In his short speech, Hemingway said he accepted the award in the name of all the marlin fishermen of the north coast of Cuba, from Puerto Escondido to Bahía Honda. He also named many of the fishermen of Cojímar: Anselmo, Figurín, El Sordo Marcus Puig, and "all others alive and dead" from Cojímar. He also stressed that "Cojímar is my second country."[21]

Gladys Gonzáles, former director of the Museo de Ernesto Hemingway, and an expert on Hemingway's time in Cuba, remarked that the writer liked the country because of the weather and the closeness to the Gulf Stream for marlin fishing. Also, his home was located in an ideal place for a writer. Hemingway's Cuban neighbors did not bother him, and the early-morning hours proved an excellent time to work. Ms. Gonzáles rightfully observed, however, that the main reason he loved Cuba was because of the people, especially the people of Cojímar. Indeed, during the Cuban television interview, Hemingway spoke of the "many kind-hearted people along the north shore of Cuba." At the end of the interview, when asked what message Hemingway would give young Cuban writers, he replied, "If the younger generation of Cuban writers wants a message, look at the fishermen of Cojímar, you can't fail."[22]

Someone once remarked that Ernest Hemingway's writing about the city and countries he loved most, Paris, Spain, and Cuba, "more or less devoured [them] ... not exploited them, but made love to them as if they were women. He caressed each country and we got to know them through his eyes, his body, his sentences and his great gift of language."[23] Even I, a Hemingway novice aficionado, who took the time to visit both the tourist locations and the out-of-the-way locations in the country that had something to do with the writer, recognize the amount of knowledge he absorbed about Cuba and its people, especially the fishermen.

It is obvious that the Cuba of Hemingway's day was far different than the country of the 21st century, but at least three important things today remain the same. The first is la mar. Hemingway began his initial research of the sea while still living in Key West, but this deepened during his long years in Cuba and, in general, took place along the north coast of the country. Hemingway scholar Mark P. Ott points out Hemingway's writing style has been compared to the art of Paul Cézanne—that is, abstract—but by the time he wrote *The Old Man and the Sea*, and after years of fishing in the Gulf Stream off Cuba's north coast, it would be more fitting to liken his style to that of Winslow Homer, the American painter—realistic.

The second item concerns the Cuban people's great ability to persevere with very little. To verify this, visit Ediciones Vigía, in the city of Matanzas, to see what local artists have been able to produce given their limited means. Although lacking many things that people who live in the United States take for granted, most Cubans, especially those who live in the rural areas, will go out of their way to cheerfully greet and help a stranger. As mentioned, some fifty-seven years after Hemingway's death, Gladys Gonzáles, former director of the Hemingway museum, rightly pointed out the main reason Hemingway loved Cuba was because of the Cuban people.[24]

Third, and finally, there is the rich history of the country. Havana offers much history and beauty with the views from the Malecón and, of course, the colonial architecture, especially in La Habana Vieja. Travel outside of the capital city and the visitor will find the combination of great beauty and history, with Trinidad and the Valle de los Ingenios as examples. Trinidad shows colonial buildings with a history dating back to at least 1514, while the valley illustrates the importance of the sugar industry and the splendor of the vale, all of which have been confirmed by UNESCO designating the two locations as World Heritage Sites. Then there is the farm with its traditional bohíos set against the Sierra de Sancti Spiritus, a part of the majestic Sierra del Escambry. While each person will have his or her own location that says something about Cuba, for me, the farm and its location best illustrates the beauty and history of the country.

An important part of the genius of Ernest Hemingway, as mentioned, was his ability to use what he observed and produce works such as *To Have and Have Not*, *Islands in the Stream*, but especially *The Old Man and the Sea*. After reading that Pulitzer Prize–winning novella, and spending time in Cojímar, one can begin to understand Hemingway's genius for turning observation and knowledge of la mar into literature. It is also important to see his love of Cuba and Cubans and how one small village returned his affection.

Hemingway's bust on a plinth overlooking Colima's harbor is arbuably the best memorial to Ernest Hemingway and should be on every list of Hemingway places to visit. It is also only fitting that the best memorial is in the country he loved the longest of all the locations he lived as an adult. It is no wonder Hemingway said "Cojímar is my second country."[25]

Fidel Castro in 1970 toured the area of Cojímar. Castro, an admirer of Ernest Hemingway, asked what had become of La Terraza since Hemingway's death? His staff informed him that it was now a roadhouse "where great quantities of beer were sloshed down in paper cups." Castro then ordered the establishment restored to the condition it was in when Hemingway patronized it, including the same type of menu as in Ernest Hemingway's day. One must go to La Terraza in Cojímar where one can visit and think about Ernest Hemingway in Cuba.

Appendix A
A Short History of Ernest Hemingway

Ernest Miller Hemingway entered the world on July 21, 1899, in Oak Park, Illinois, a middle-class suburb of Chicago, the second child of six. His physician father, Clarence Edmonds ("Ed") Hemingway, eventually kept his office in the substantial home. His mother, Grace Hall Hemingway, had musical talent. Though he eventually rebelled against the conservative Oak Park, the young Hemingway led a comfortable life denied to many at the beginning of the 20th century. In elementary school in 1908, he wrote in a notebook: "I intend to travel and write." Nineteen days before his sixty-second birthday, Ernest Hemingway took his own life at his home overlooking the beautiful Wood River in Ketchum, Idaho. In this remarkably short span of time Hemingway received the Pulitzer Prize in 1953 and, a year later, the Nobel Prize for Literature. He was born at the end of the 20th century and by the first decade of the 21st century his major novels have not gone out of print. He is still read throughout the world.[1]

Ask anyone who has had any exposure to Ernest Hemingway's writings to describe the man and they will invariably give a description close to the portrait taken by the famous photographer Yousuf Karsh in 1957. Hemingway is posed in a bulky sweater, unsmiling, with a prominent full beard. The picture suggests a mature man who has seen and experienced much in his life, who would command attention in any gathering of people. Indeed, this description fits well into an overview of Hemingway's short life span.

Throughout his adult life, Hemingway never ceased to proclaim his dislike for his mother, Grace Hall Hemingway. The American writer John Dos Passos said Ernest was the only man he had met who really hated his mother. Hemingway felt Grace had to dominate everything and that she drove her husband to suicide.[2]

Grace Hall was born on June 15, 1872, in Chicago, to Ernest Hall and Caroline Hancock, English immigrants. Her father became financially comfortable. At the age of fourteen, Grace's family moved into a large six-bedroom house at 439 North Oak Park Boulevard, in the village of Oak Park, Illinois. Oak Park had not yet felt the encroachment of the growing Chicago. Grace grew into a "tall and buxom [woman] with English coloring—clear blue eyes, rosy cheeks, and abundant brown hair."[3]

Not an academic scholar, Grace barely passed Latin and science, but liked history and literature. Music, however, dominated the Hall household. Grace's mother, Caroline, recognized her daughter's talent and encouraged her to practice the piano and violin, and to take singing lessons. Caroline, contrary to the general opinion of the role of women in the late 19th century, did not expect Grace to learn to cook and told her to "tend to your practicing." Caroline felt, if possible, women should keep away from domestic chores. Upon Grace's graduation from high school in 1891, Caroline urged her daughter to take additional voice lessons and foreign language studies in preparation for a career in opera. To earn additional money, Grace gave recitals and lessons as a voice teacher.[4]

Across the street from the Hall residence lived the Anson Hemingway family. Anson, a Civil War officer, was deeply religious. He spent ten years forming the Chicago YMCA before turning to real estate in Oak Park and becoming respected in local political issues. Anson married Adelaide Edmonds, a trained botanist, who passed her knowledge of the subject on to her children and grandchildren. Anson and Adelaide raised six children, two girls and four boys. All six attended Oberlin College in Ohio. Oberlin College is noted for being the first coeducational college to grant baccalaureate degrees to women. Born into this interesting family in 1871, Clarence Edmonds "Ed" Hemingway loved collecting stamps, coins, arrowheads, and practiced taxidermy. Above collecting, Ed's primary interests centered on hunting, fishing, and cooking, especially all types of game and fish. Grace and Ed had what appeared to be a casual relationship during their high school years.[5]

Ed did premedical work at Oberlin College. After graduation, he and some companions camped in the Great Smokey Mountains of North Carolina. One day Ed amazed his friends by preparing a repast made up of a fresh blackberry pie, sweetened with wild honey from a nearby tree, while a squirrel stew simmered nearby. "He had rolled out the pie crust on a peeled log with an empty beer bottle."[6]

Ed Hemingway obtained his medical degree from Rush Medical College, in Chicago. By this time, Ed and Grace had entered into a relationship. Dr. Hemingway, at the age of twenty-six, stood six feet tall, with a barrel chest and powerful arms. An older Oak Park physician took Ed Hemingway on as an assistant in 1894. In the same year, Grace learned her mother had cancer. The young Dr. Hemingway made many house calls to the Hall household and helped with Grace's depression over what proved to be a long vigil beside her mother's sickbed.

In the summer of 1895, Dr. Hemingway traveled to a medical center in Edinburgh, Scotland. While there, he continued to correspond with Grace. Upon his return to Oak Park near the end of August, he wanted to renew the relationship, but in September Grace's mother died. A few weeks later Grace left for New York City to study voice under Madame Louisa Cappianni. Cappianni had prepared Amelita Galli-Curri, perhaps one of "the greatest coloratura sopranos of all time." Impressed with Grace's contralto voice, her coach arranged an audition with the Metropolitan Opera and a chance for a contract seemed in the offing for Grace.[7]

During this period, Grace and Ed continued their correspondence. Later, she told her children that Ed pleaded with her to marry him. Even with her family's help, Grace owed Madame Cappianni a considerable sum for her lessons, so she scheduled a concert in Madison Square Garden. Though she received favorable notices, the strong lights hurt her weak eyes. After the performance, her father invited her to travel to Europe with him for the summer. Sometime during the time of the recital and the journey to Europe, Grace decided to marry Ed. They took their vows on October 1, 1896, in Oak Park. Grace convinced Ed to move into her father's house. Four of their six children were born in this house. Later, they would move into their own house at 600 North Kenilworth, still in Oak Park.[8]

While Ernest Hemingway only reluctantly admitted that his mother's insistence on learning a musical instrument—the cello— helped in his writing, Grace's desire to have a home that stressed music and an artistic atmosphere for her children influenced his life. The large record collection still at Hemingway's house at the Finca Vigía, in Cuba, plus the extensive art collection that had hung on its walls during the years he lived there, is witness to Grace's influence. Grace continued giving voice lessons after she married, at times receiving "as much as a thousand dollars a month," much more than her doctor husband earned when he began his practice.[9]

In 1898, Ed and Grace purchased two-hundred feet of waterfront property at Walloon Lake (then named Bear Lake) in the northwestern part of Michigan's Lower Peninsula, near Petoskey. In September 1899, the Hemingway's brought the six-week-old Ernest with them as they finalized their purchase and arranged for the construction of their cottage, which they named Windemere. The next year the family spent their first summer there. Every summer until he left home at the age of eighteen, Ernest journeyed from Oak Park, Illinois, by train and then transferred to a steamer crossing Lake Michigan. Arriving in Michigan, he then continued the voyage to Windemere by "two little trains" to Walloon Lake and, lastly, a "little steamer to the cottage." Ernest explored the nearby forests, streams, and communities. He continued his time in Michigan after returning home from World War I and married his first wife near Windemere. While Ernest's fiction did not deal with Oak Park, his experiences in Northwestern Lower Michigan or the Upper Peninsula of Michigan, however, played an important part and continued with him for the rest of his life.[10]

At the time the Hemingways began making their yearly journey to the forests and waters of Michigan, the urban area of Chicago had already begun its encroachment upon the former prairie surrounding Oak Park. It is little wonder that Ed Hemingway would enjoy the Michigan interlude and pass on his knowledge of hunting, fishing, and his love of nature. This is where his Ernest "learned to regard nature as a source of refreshment and healing."[11]

In his later years, when asked about writing, Hemingway stressed a fiction writer should first describe the country. It is not hyperbole to state the Michigan forests, streams, and lakes provided the foundation for Ernest's genius at describing a country. While Hemingway's early work described the north as a frontier, by the time he started noticing his surroundings in the Walloon Lake region, logging had removed all but a few pockets of the great White Pines. The first Europeans to see what is now Michigan thought it would take forever to cut the timber they viewed. Petoskey-born Pulitzer Prize-winning historian Bruce Catton, however, described how reality proved otherwise. By 1897, two years before Hemingway's birth, Michigan "in less than half a century," had produced "more than a hundred and sixty billion feet of pine boards ... enough lumber to build a solid pine floor over the entire state of Michigan, with enough left over to floor all of Rhode Island as well; or ... to build fifty plank roads, each fifty feet wide, from New York to San Francisco." This writer can recall in the middle 1950s the sight of blackened and weathered stumps of some of the huge trees that once covered the Kalkaska region, not far from Walloon Lake. This does not mean that the land is barren of trees. The second growth of timber in the Michigan forests of today can still inspire anyone who takes the time to walk in them.[12]

Ernest grew into a young man during a period of strong national interest in nature study. Grace kept five scrapbooks of Ernest's youth. She proudly recorded that her nineteen-month-old son, when shown pictures of birds, knew the names of many of them. At four years of age, Ernest was, according to Grace, developing into a naturalist and enjoyed everything dealing with the surrounding natural environment.[13]

Ed Hemingway's medical degree and a love for the natural world gave him a scientific outlook of nature. While at Oberlin, Ed joined the Agassiz Association. Named in honor of the Swiss-American scientist Louis Agassiz, the association emphasized amateur nature study through work in the outdoors. It stressed teaching children a minute examination of nature, both through description and dissection. Feeling strongly about the association, Ed Hemingway founded an association chapter in Oak Park before marrying. Grace's scrapbooks record Ernest's progress in the association under the tutelage of his father. Adding to this hands-on approach to the study of the natural world, the schools of Oak Park also stressed the method in their science courses. Ernest Hemingway "remained throughout his life first and foremost an Agassiz-trained naturalist, keenly observant of detail, seeing the relationship between form and function, always in pursuit of inspiration from nature." This becomes very clear in the coming years while fishing for marlin off the coast of Cuba.[14]

Upon Ernest Hemingway's graduation from high school in June 1917, he worked briefly as a reporter for the *Kansas City Star*. Hemingway later stated he chose not to attend college because he wished "to leave the confines of the library and the school" and "meet Nature face to face." His poor eyesight kept him from military service in World War I, but in 1918 Hemingway volunteered to serve as an ambulance driver in the American Red Cross in Europe. He eventually arrived in Milan, Italy, and soon thereafter received orders to proceed to Schio, in northern Italy, northwest of Venice and surrounded by the Little Dolomite Mountains and Mount Pasubio. His section consisted of seventeen Fiat and six Ford ambulances. Ernest took turns driving the sharp curves of the mountain roads of Mount Pasubio, taking wounded Italian soldiers to medical reception centers.[15]

The narrative of this book and Appendix A deals with Hemingway's life through his years until leaving Cuba at the time of Fidel Castro taking control of the Cuban government in 1959.

"Fifty-one years old, sicker than most knew, and eleven years without a successful novel, Ernest Hemingway seemed to have reached the end of his career." Some literary scholars and writers feel Hemingway's genius ended even before he turned fifty-one. "The great novels were all before 1940," writes novelist Howell Raines, "and even his last generally admired book, 'The Old Man and the Sea,' in 1952, was conceived in 1936." Over a half-century after his death, literary critics, biographers, and pundits seemed to emphasize only the negative aspects of Hemingway's personality. Not for him were "the long productive career and cuddly tolerance enjoyed by fellow giants like Picasso and Yeats." Moreover, the "alcoholism, depression, adulteries, public spectacles, literary failures, senescent romances and Hollywood sell-outs of Fitzgerald and Faulkner have been portrayed with indulgent sympathy given to quirky geniuses." Further, some used psychoanalytic studies that "made it popular to put Hemingway the man on the couch so as to diminish Hemingway the writer."[16]

Glimpse Ernest Hemingway's life after 1940 and it is amazing that he accomplished anything during the twenty-one years remaining to him. World War II interrupted Ernest's life, as it did to almost everyone in those years. During 1942 and 1943, as shown in Chapters 5 and 6, he sailed *Pilar* in anti-submarine patrols. Hemingway departed for Europe in 1944 and returned in 1945. Upon his return to Cuba, he continued to work on a manuscript he had begun before the war entitled "Bimini," which eventually became *Islands in the Stream* and was published after his death.

A Short History of Ernest Hemingway

Shortly after receiving the Pulitzer Prize for *The Old Man and the Sea*, on May 4, 1953, Ernest and Mary departed for a tour of Europe, including a trip to Pamplona, Spain. This was Ernest's first visit to the city since 1931 and the site of his novel *The Sun Also Rises* that marks his beginning of fame. The European trip ended in August and the Hemingways left for an African safari that stretched until near the end of January 1954.

After the end of the safari, Ernest and Mary began taking low-level flights with bush pilot Roy Marsh in his Cessna aircraft. At first nervous about flying low, Ernest began to enjoy it so much that he promised Mary a low-level flight over Africa. On Thursday, January 21, the three took off from Nairobi on the way to Murchison Falls. It took two days to reach their destination. Flying near the falls, a flight of black-and-white ibis rose in front of the Cessna and Marsh dove beneath them to avoid a collision. The aircraft struck an abandoned telegraph line, causing it to crash. Mary suffered from shock and two cracked ribs. Although suffering severe back, arm, and shoulder pain, Ernest helped Marsh move Mary and establish a camp in a clearing. Marsh used his weak radio to broadcast distress signals, which went unanswered. A commercial airliner, however, spotted the wreckage and announced no survivors. Newspaper editors began setting up headlines on the death of Papa Hemingway. Meanwhile, at the survivors' camp, Ernest awoke Mary in the night telling her "not to snore because the noise" was making a nearby elephant herd "curious."[17]

Spotted by a charter boat the next day, the survivors arrived in Butiaba, Uganda. There they met Reggie Cartright, who had been searching for the downed trio in a twin-engine de Havilland aircraft. Cartright claimed his craft was capable of taking everyone off from the rough dirt strip. The de Havilland, with Cartright at the controls, and Marsh, Mary, and Ernest in the passenger seats, bounced as it tried to get airborne. Just as the aircraft lifted into the air it nosed down and crashed. The left engine burst into flames, igniting fuel from a ruptured fuel tank. Finding the left door of the aircraft jammed, Marsh pushed Mary forward and they squeezed out a broken window. Ernest's height and weight stopped him from crawling out the small window. As the de Havilland filled with smoke and fire, Hemingway struggled with the door, but the earlier crash injuries weakened him and he could not budge it. He desperately began butting the door with his head as the flames increased. Ernest managed to get the door open enough to escape. Years later, British television and movie star Michael Palin interviewed a resident of Butiaba on what he recalled of the crash. "Mr. Hemingway was the last to come out of the plane," said the witness. "He came running towards us. His hair was on fire and he was crying."[18]

Ernest suffered a number of injuries: yet another concussion, liquid was leaking from a scalp wound behind his left ear, one of his kidneys was badly hurt, his liver damaged, his shoulder dislocated, his lower intestine collapsed, and he suffered temporary loss of hearing in his left ear and vision in his left eye. Later, X-rays found two crushed lumbar vertebrae. At "fifty-four, he was in worse physical shape than when he was blown up at eighteen." Writer Paul Hendrickson feels it "seems inarguable now ... that Hemingway never recovered mentally or physically from those back-to-back plane crashes in early 1954 in Africa." But no one realized this at the time.[19]

Despite everything Hemingway endured during this period and, despite what critics have said, Ernest still continued to write, especially after 1957. He wrote two new short stories, had in draft form a three-part manuscript; an African novel of 200,000 words in manuscript form; a large amount of what would be published posthumously as *The Garden of Eden*; and had started work on what would later become *A Moveable Feast*. This proves that despite injuries and disparaging remarks from critics, he could still produce credible work.[20]

The period between 1955 and 1961 in Ernest Hemingway's life is a downward spiral of paranoia and depression, interspersed with "euphoric writing." One of the major reasons for his decline began in 1957 when Fidel Castro's guerrilla operations against the government of Fulgencio Batista began to heat up in Cuba. Hemingway felt his fame and citizenship would not protect him should the revolution spread. One of the things he did was took *Pilar* out to sea and dumped rifles, sawed-off shotguns, and other ammunition over the side so the police or army would not confiscate them. Ernest also began to make preparations to ride out the unsettled period in some location in the United States. He chose Ketchum, Idaho, as it was close to Sun Valley and the surrounding region made for good bird hunting. He had visited the area off and on since 1939.[21]

In 1958, Ernest and Mary arrived in Ketchum. The news of Batista fleeing the country and Castro's victory in January 1959 prompted news organizations to contact Hemingway and ask his opinion of the revolution. He said, "I believe in the historical necessity for the Cuban revolution and I believe in its long range aims. I do not wish to discuss personalities or day to day problems." Later, in a telephone interview with the *New York Times*, Ernest said he was "delighted" with the news. Mary, however, felt this might convey the wrong impression and she convinced him to change it, which he did by substituting the word "hopeful" for "delighted."[22]

It does seem that Hemingway supported the revolution, or at least the early stages of it. He felt the largest problem facing Castro was not Batista's former government, but the strong United States interests, such as United Fruit, which would be difficult to replace. When Castro announced he would make a trip to the United States to tell his large neighbor to the north the truth of his revolution, Hemingway wanted to brief him on American politicians and the American people. Castro appointed Vazquez Candela, assistant editor of the newspaper *Revolution*, to interview the writer. Fidel listened to what was relayed to him. When Castro was asked a difficult question on the United States television program *This Is Your Life* he began his response: "Let me tell you what Hemingway thinks about this...."[23]

Mary urged Ernest to move as many of their important possessions from the finca as possible, but "he refused to consider the idea." Hemingway knew what could take place in the unsettled time after a revolution, but there seems little doubt he felt he belonged in his beloved Finca Vigía and Cubans would accept him once the heat of the final events of the revolution passed and Fidel Castro's government settled in to govern. In 1960, Ernest flew into Havana and was greeted by a large welcoming crowd. Reporters asked him what he thought of the growing tensions between the United States and Castro's government. Ernest replied he did approve of the new government and that after twenty years of living in Cuba, he considered himself a true Cuban. After saying that, he then "kissed the hem of a Cuban flag." He did this so abruptly that the assembled photographers did not have time to capture the moment. They clamored for him to do it again. His reply: "I said I was a Cuban, not an actor."[24]

In 2004, Valerie Hemingway, Ernest's daughter-in-law, wrote *Running with the Bulls: My Years with the Hemingways*. In the book, she tells of the last United States Ambassador to Cuba, Philip Bonsall, having dinner at the finca. Bonsall brought an "informal message": the diplomatic relationship between the two countries was at the breaking point. Officials in Washington felt that as the highest profile American living in Cuba he should not only leave the country, but also renounce Castro's government. Hemingway refused. He pointed out the finca was his home, the Cuban people were his friends, and he was a writer and not politico. Furthermore, he had always shown his loyalty to the United States and his reputation was as an American writer. While Bonsall seemed to understand Ernest's comments, the ambassador pointed out some officials in Washington did not see it as Hemingway did and the "word *traitor* [Valerie's emphasis] had come up."

On Bonsall's next visit to the finca, he said he had been recalled. The departing ambassador stated what he had said previously. Furthermore, with the now-severed diplomatic relationships, Ernest must very clearly make his choice "between his country and his home."

Three years after Valerie wrote her book, she again returned to Cuba and wrote of her experiences in *Smithsonian* magazine. She reiterated Bonsall's comments, except in this publication she has Ernest resisting the suggestion "fiercely."

Valerie Hemingway writes that only the Hemingways and she were present when Ambassador Bonsall passed on his information. In his classic biography of Hemingway, Prof. Carlos Baker does not mention the conversation, nor does Mary Hemingway in her memoirs. Michael Reynolds, in his five-volume work on Hemingway, does not mention this, nor does he have Bonsall in his index.

Valerie Hemingway's disclosure may explain why Hemingway left almost everything he owned at the finca. He may have felt things would eventually ease and he could return. Unfortunately, the abortive CIA-sponsored invasion of Cuba at the Bay of Pigs in April 1961 dashed Hemingway's hopes for a reconciliation and probably his chance to return to his home. This did not help his mental condition in the last years of his life.[25]

By 1960, "Ernest Hemingway was ... a writer unable to outrun his demons." He fretted constantly and unnecessarily about money. Reynolds points out that in January 1959 Ernest's six-month earnings from Scribner's was "slightly more than the $20,000 annual median family income of the top 5 percent of the nation." Furthermore, he usually had more money in his special tax account "than 99 percent of the nation made in a year."[26]

His paranoia increased. Most of it focused on the FBI. Hemingway saw agents everywhere and thought the bureau kept a constant surveillance on him, while tapping his telephone, his car, plus opening his mail. One night, for example, while driving through Ketchum, Hemingway saw lights on in the local bank. This upset him greatly. He told Mary the FBI was checking his bank accounts as "they wanted to get something on us." Until near the end of the 20th century, researchers of Hemingway's life pushed aside any notion of the FBI's interest in the writer, feeling the comments came from a delusional man.

From 1959 onward, the combination of paranoia, depression, his increasing mood swings, and his continued consumption of alcohol combined with the taking of a "pharmacological stew" led to Ernest's further deterioration. Friends noticed he seemed to age prematurely; he lost weight and seemed fragile. By November 1960, Dr. George Saviers, who was Hemingway's doctor in Ketchum, talked his patient into flying to the Mayo Clinic in Rochester, Minnesota.

Hemingway entered the Mayo clinic under the name George Saviers. Shortly after settling into the clinic, electroshock therapy began, at least ten sessions. The press soon learned the true identity of the patient and, eventually, the Mayo Clinic released a statement that Hemingway was undergoing treatment for hypertension, the results of which were regarded as "satisfactory." He was released on January 22, 1961.[27]

By March, Hemingway was exhibiting more symptoms. He was first brought to the small ten-bed hospital in Ketchum. As was customary, only one nurse had duty that night: Monica Mollner, who had just graduated from Creighton Memorial St. Joseph Hospital School of Nursing in Omaha, Nebraska. Years later, Monica recalled Hemingway was "diagnosed with severe depression. We had to keep him overnight and then he would be flown out the next day.... We had him on a suicide watch. At the same time, we had a woman in labor and about ready to give birth."[28]

Realizing that Monica could not watch the woman and Hemingway at the same time, the hospital "hired a girl from high school to come in and watch him from the hall." Monica took short breaks from the woman and looked down the hall "to see this girl sitting there."

At one of these glimpses, Nurse Mollner did not see the girl. Monica quickly "went down to the room and did not see Papa. He was in the only private room in the hospital. I thought the girl had gone down to the kitchen to get him some food, so I ran down there. I told her she was never to leave him unattended."

Monica then "ran back to the room. I was thinking, 'My first job and I lose Papa Hemingway. I will be fired in the morning.'

"There was a door just outside of the room that led to the golf course. I knew Papa liked the Sawtooth Mountains, so I went out the door and found him a short distance away. I spoke with him briefly, talking about the ambience [of the area], and then sliding my arm inside of his, gently guided him back inside."

He was again flown to the Mayo Clinic. At one stop along the way, he tried to walk into the turning propeller of an airplane. He was released from the clinic again on June 30.[29]

The comments of one biographer, A. E. Hotchner, who was also a friend of Hemingway's for fourteen years, are a good example of what took place in many people's minds concerning these final years. Hotchner had listened to Ernest's comments about the FBI bugging his room while in the hospital at Rochester, Minnesota. Hemingway even believed the FBI tapped the public telephone outside his room. Like others, Hotchner dismissed the comments. On July 2, 2011, however, in an opinion piece in the *New York Times*, Hotchner commented upon the results of the Freedom of Information Act that requested the FBI to disclose any file on Hemingway. The piece brought out that since 1940 "agents filed reports on [Hemingway] and tapped his phones. The surveillance continued all through his confinement at St. Mary's Hospital. It is likely that the phone outside his room was tapped after all." The FBI's file, interestingly enough, even contained information on Mary's supposed comment on "stupid British colonials" and actress Ava Gardner's visit to the finca.

In 1961, another report entered the FBI file. The Minneapolis office of the bureau sent a report that the doctor treating Hemingway said his patient was worried about the FBI investigating him as he was registered at the hospital under an assumed name. The doctor wanted authorization to tell Hemingway that the FBI was not concerned with him being in the Mayo Clinic under an assumed name. In writer Paul Hendrickson's words, "in some weird, other clairvoyant sense, not so paranoid an idea at all."[30]

July is a memorial month for Hemingway. He was born in July; on the first of July of each summer of his youth he journeyed from Oak

Park for two wonderful months in Michigan; and in July he visited Pamplona, the location that provided him the material for his first major novel, *The Sun Also Rises*. On the morning of Sunday, July 2, 1961, Ernest Hemingway awoke early, put on his bathrobe and slippers and made his way downstairs from his bedroom. On this July morning, he went to the kitchen and found a ring of keys. Ernest then went to the basement and unlocked a storeroom. He picked out his favorite Boss shotgun and two 12-gauge shells and made his way upstairs. Ernest stood in the foyer, opened the breech of the Boss, loaded the shells and closed the breech. Ernest Hemingway put the ends of the double-barreled shotgun in his mouth and, at 7:30 a.m., pulled the trigger.[31]

Appendix B
The Hemingway Women

Agnes Hannah von Kurowsky

In World War I, while serving in the Red Cross near the Peave River, Italy, Ernest Hemingway was wounded. Ernest's transport from the battlefield took him, via ambulance and hospital train, to the *Ospedale Croce Rosa* (American Red Cross Hospital) at 10 Via Manzoni, Milan. There he met Agnes Hannah von Kurowsky, an American Red Cross nurse, who became his first love as an adult.

Paul Moritz Julius von Kurowsky, a naturalized American of Polish, Russian, and German ancestry, came from Königsberg around 1890. According to Agnes, her father had gambled and lost all his family's money and property. Until he lost everything, von Kurowsky had served in what she called "a rich regiment" of the German Army and, rather than be forced by his penury into a "poor regiment," he immigrated to the United States. While teaching German at the Berlitz School in Washington, D.C., he fell in love with one of his students, pretty American debutante Agnes Theodosia Holabird. They married against the wishes of the bride's father, Brig. Gen. Samuel Holabird, who was suspicious of anything German.[1]

Agnes's grandfather graduated from West Point in 1849 and immediately began what would eventually be almost a decade of service on the Texas frontier. He led scouting parties and then, in 1852, began working in quartermaster (supply) assignments. He then received orders to other assignments, but by 1861 he again returned to quartermaster duties. He remained in the supply field throughout the Civil

War, where he received numerous brevets for his work concerning supply and for being the aide-de-camp to Maj. Gen. N. P. Banks. He was also recognized for his participation in the battle of Antietam. After the war, he continued in supplies and eventually became the Quartermaster General of the U.S. Army.

Gen. Holabird retired on June 16, 1890. He settled in Evanston, Illinois, where his son William, a noted architect in Chicago, lived. Later, Gen. Holabird moved back to Washington, D.C., where he amassed a library of seven thousand volumes.[2]

Agnes Hannah von Kurowsky was born in the Germantown Section of Philadelphia on January 5, 1892, the younger of two daughters. Paul von Kurowsky obtained a position in the civil service and then was assigned to the U.S. Army. His duties took him to an isolated post at St. Michaels, Alaska, in 1898 and, several years later, to Vancouver, Washington. While living in Vancouver, the children were struck with illness. Agnes barely escaped from diphtheria, while her sister died from the complications of scarlet fever. After Gen. Holabird retired, Paul requested and received a transfer to Washington, D.C., so his wife could be near her aging father. Agnes's grandfather arranged for a private French language tutor and gave her open access to his large library.

Gen. Holabird died in 1907 and, tragically, so did Agnes's father, Paul, who succumbed to typhoid fever. With no other place to go, Agnes's widowed mother moved with her daughter into an apartment. They lived on a small trust fund. Agnes graduated from the Washington, D.C., Fairmont Seminary for Girls. She became a librarian, perhaps influenced by her grandfather's love of books.[3]

Agnes worked as a cataloguer in the District of Columbia's Public Library. After four years of cataloguing books, the "sociable young woman with curling chestnut hair and alert blue-grey eyes," who spoke in "softly cultivated tones with a southern inflection," decided library work was "not active enough" and decided to go into nursing. She graduated from the Bellevue Nursing School, New York City, in July 1917.[4]

On January 2, 1918, Agnes applied to the director of the American Red Cross Nursing Service for a position as an overseas Red Cross nurse. She described herself as "5'8", 133 pounds, and fluent in French and German." When she departed the United States, a doctor in New York considered himself engaged to Agnes. Apparently, the young nurse led him to believe this, although later, upon leaving the United States, she admitted she felt "free to enjoy the company of other young men."[5]

Agnes eventually arrived in Milan at the American Red Cross Hospital on July 11, 1918. Less than a week later, the hospital train brought the wounded Ernest Hemingway to Milan and to the hospital. Hemingway soon made a hit with all the nurses, but his attention focused on Agnes. From his room on the fourth floor of the hospital Ernest began writing at least three, sometimes four, letters a day to Agnes on the third floor. By the third week of Hemingway's stay in the hospital, nurses and patients talked about how Nurse Von Kurowsky noticed Ernest.

"No one has suggested that it was a fully realized love affair." It appears that Agnes returned his affection, but not with the intensity of the younger Hemingway.[6]

Orders detailing Agnes to a hospital in Florence briefly interrupted their time together. The two continued a strong correspondence. Writer Bernice Kert has pointed out that Hemingway failed to see the hints that Agnes put in her letters. She worried about the differences in their ages: she was seven years older than Ernest; Agnes still had not broken with the doctor in the United States; and she loved nursing and had no intention of giving it up. Years later, when asked to describe herself back in 1918, Agnes replied, "I was looking for adventure ... and I was very fickle." Ernest, however, continued his assumption that they would marry. But, as Kert has pointed out, by November 1918, the "mood of the lovers ... was not synchronous."[7]

About this time, Hemingway received an offer from Capt. James Gamble, a "wealthy young man whose family ran the soap manufacturing firm of Procter and Gamble." Gamble, Hemingway's officer on the Piave River area, offered to pay all expenses if Ernest would accompany him on a yearlong traveling trip throughout Europe. Agnes felt that living off someone else would ruin Ernest. She insisted he return to the United States and start a career.[8]

Agnes received orders to the Army base at Treviso, outside the city of Padua, near Venice. This allowed her to put on hold her decision about the young Hemingway. In December 1918, Ernest decided to take Agnes's advice and began his journey to the United States. Meanwhile, Agnes moved to another hospital at Torre de Moste, in the province of Venice.

At Torre de Moste, Agnes met *Teniente* (Lieutenant) Domenico Caracciolo, a Neapolitan. Unaware that Caracciolo was the heir to a dukedom, she started an affair with him. Even after learning of the differences in their backgrounds, the two became engaged. In March 1919, Agnes sent a letter to Ernest that she expected to be married in the spring. The marriage was not to be. When Caracciolo returned home on leave, his mother convinced him he should not marry the American nurse. Agnes did not hear from Domenico Caracciolo again. The only communication she received: a formal letter from his mother saying what took place was only a wartime love affair that would be best forgotten. Shortly thereafter, Agnes returned to New York.[9]

Ernest did not see Agnes again. Literary scholars have, however, pointed out that Hemingway used Agnes as the model for the character Catherine Barkley and killed her in his novel *A Farewell to Arms*. As with most interpretations of Hemingway's works, scholars are divided on this subject, but do point out that he used her in two stories, "A Very Short Story" and "The Snows of Kilimanjaro."

Much has been made of the Italian years and their influence on Ernest's life and writing. Some literary scholars point out that, for whatever reasons, he exaggerated his wounds and his affair with Agnes. Prof. James Nagel observed, "The true story is in many respects more moving and more dramatic." He had volunteered for hazardous duty, was wounded and, while suffering from his wounds, performed an act of bravery. Once Hemingway arrived at the hospital in Milan, he met his first love, proposed marriage and was rejected. Novels and movies have been produced on much less.[10]

Agnes continued in nursing. She took a position with the Red Cross in Haiti and, while there, met and married Howard Preston Garner on November 24, 1928; she divorced him after her assignment in Haiti. In 1934, she married William Stanfield, a hotel manager and widower with three children. During World War II, Agnes worked at the Red Cross Blood Bank of Fifth Avenue in New York City.

Agnes and William eventually moved to Key West, Florida, not far from the Hemingway home in that city. She reconnected with Henry Serrano Villard, whom she knew when he was a patient in the Milan Hospital with Hemingway. Agnes wanted to be buried in the United States Soldiers' and Airmen's Home National Cemetery in Washington, D.C., alongside her grandfather, mother, and father. This was denied. Villard, a former ambassador, successfully interceded on her behalf.

Agnes Von Kurowsky Stanfield died on November 25, 1984, at the age of ninety-two, and is buried where she wished to be.[11]

Elizabeth Hadley Richardson

Elizabeth Hadley Richardson was born November 9, 1891, in St. Louis, Missouri, the youngest of four children. She grew up in the "bosom of upper-class St. Louis." Her maternal grandparents came from old-line American families; both grandparents were descendants of Pilgrims that had settled the Massachusetts Bay Colony. Her grandfather, Edward Wyman, was a noted educator. He married Elizabeth Florence Hadley, after whom she was named. Their only daughter, Florence, attended Mary Institute, a prestigious girls school founded in 1859 by William Greenleaf Eliot, the poet T.S. Eliot's grandfather. William Eliot felt girls should receive the same rigorous education as boys. The graduates were not expected to use this education, however. "We were trained to be wives and mothers," one graduate recalled. To graduate from Mary Institute, a girl had to pass tests in Greek and Latin, plus "bake an edible loaf of bread." Florence proved a serious student. She began studying music at the tender age of eight, exhibiting genuine talent. She became well known within the upper levels of St. Louis society for her musical abilities, and her teachers encouraged her to study abroad. Instead, she married James Richardson, Jr., in 1878.[12]

James Richardson, Sr., also came from an old-line Massachusetts family. He began as a teacher and eventually moved to St. Louis, where he founded the Richardson Drug Company, which became the largest pharmaceutical company west of the Mississippi. By 1885, its stock was valued at half a million dollars (more than $12,900,000 in 2016 dollars).

James married Laura Clifford, and the couple had two sons and two daughters. The oldest boy, James, Jr., did not live up to his father's expectations. The less ambitious young man eventually received an appointment as secretary and treasurer in the Richardson Company as a sinecure created by his disappointed father. His chief interests seemed to be gambling, drinking, and carousing.[13]

Even from the beginning of their marriage, the couple seemed unhappy. According to Hadley's biographer, Gioia Diliberto, Florence was "austere and sexually repressed." She was a leader of St. Louis's suffragists. Florence also is noted for becoming one of the founding members of the St. Louis Symphony, and a popular lecturer. Some of the descendants of James and Florence point out that she "was a difficult, controlling woman."[14]

James rebelled against Florence's values. He tried to work up enthusiasm for the drug business, but that proved unsuccessful. In 1899, a fire destroyed the company's warehouse, closing the St. Louis office. James eventually took on a consulting job for another drug firm, but spent most of his time playing the stock market and drinking. Florence continued her hatred of men and loathing of sex.[15] Despite this, the couple had five children, two of whom died in infancy. Hadley, the youngest of the family, spent her first years in luxury, due to the estates of both the Wyman and Richardson families. Music played an important part of her upbringing as their house included a music room with two Steinway pianos.[16]

The dynamics of the family had all the ingredients of a daytime television soap opera. As a young girl, Hadley and her next oldest sister, Fonnie, seemed inseparable. As they grew older, however, friction developed between the two siblings. By this time Hadley was a "vividly pretty" redhead, possessing an independent personality with musical talent. Fonnie, however, did not have Hadley's looks or talent, and possessed an "obedient, subservient" personality. Florence doted on Fonnie largely because of her personality. Years later Hadley felt that Florence and Fonnie worked together to make her life miserable. Eventually, Hadley admitted that "she didn't like" either her mother or Fonnie. However, like their mother, both Hadley and Fonnie attended Mary Institute.[17]

As the years passed, Florence focused on James Richardson's drinking. She continued her struggle to dominate the household. Meanwhile, a branch of the Richardson Drug Company in Omaha, Nebraska, despite the fire in the warehouse at St. Louis, continued to do well, netting both James and his brother, Clifford, immense yearly incomes of $30,000 (about $815,000.00 in 2016 dollars.) In 1904, a worker in manufacturing brought home an average annual income of $538. Clifford invested some of his income to establish the Chemical National Bank of St. Louis, which grew into one the city's largest banks. James continued to play the stock market, constantly losing.[18]

In 1904, James borrowed close to $30,000, using his stock as collateral. He lost it all. He complained of constant illness and insomnia, and on February 7, 1905, James, while at home, took a pistol and committed suicide.[19]

Florence managed to pay off James's debts, sold their large home, and bought a smaller house in a "less fashionable" middle-class neighborhood and paid off the mortgage. She entered into intellectual interests, but her focus centered on woman's suffrage. Fonnie joined her mother in this. Hadley, not interested in feminism, found herself looked upon as an outsider by both Florence and Fonnie. Florence began treating Hadley as if she were weak and an invalid. Her mother kept Hadley at home from school so often that she had to repeat her senior year and did not graduate until she was eighteen.

At Mary Institute, Hadley proved a good student and had a natural talent for the piano. One teacher suggested that she study music abroad, in Germany. Eventually, Hadley entered Bryn Mawr, near Philadelphia, Pennsylvania. She did not adjust well to college life and withdrew, returning home to St. Louis.

Upon her return from college, her mother and sister continued their overprotection of Hadley, leaving her with very little social life or any physical activity. Her mother relented only once. One summer, Florence allowed Hadley to visit with her former college roommate, Kate Smith, in Vermont. There she enjoyed tennis and met the artist Maxwell Parrish. Hadley's mother again worried about her well-being and forced her to return home. Upon her return, Hadley began to immerse herself in trying to become a pianist, but abandoned that due to what she considered her lack of talent. After her mother contracted Bright's disease, a kidney ailment, Hadley nursed her until Florence's death in December 1920.[20]

Shortly after the passing of her mother, Hadley again visited with Kate Smith, now living in St. Louis. Smith's brother roomed with Hemingway, who worked as an associate editor for a monthly journal, *Cooperative Commonwealth*. Hadley and Ernest met through Kate's brother. Later, Hemingway wrote he "knew she was the girl I was going to marry." As he did with Agnes, Ernest brushed aside the difference in their ages, she being eight years older than he. Despite concerns from the friends of both Hadley and Ernest, the two were married at Horton Bay, Michigan, on September 3, 1921, and honeymooned nearby at the location of the Hemingway family's summer cottage. Hadley brought to the marriage a small inheritance that she believed would support both of them.[21]

The couple returned to Chicago and lived in a small apartment. Hadley received another inheritance from an uncle. The couple had met the writer Sherwood Anderson and he suggested the two live in Paris. Two months later, Hemingway was hired as a foreign correspondent for the *Toronto Star* newspaper. With a letter of introduction from Anderson to some of the writers living in Paris, Ernest and Hadley departed for the City of Light.[22]

In December of 1925, when Hemingway and Hadley made their second trip to ski at Schruns, Austria, Pauline Pfeiffer joined them. Ernest and Pauline began an affair, which Hadley discovered. Hadley and Hemingway made a trial separation and finally divorced on January 1927. Hemingway gave Hadley the royalties to *The Sun Also Rises*.

Hemingway's first wife, Elizabeth Hadley Richardson, remarried, to the poet and journalist Paul Mower on July 3, 1933. The couple eventually moved to Chicago. Once divorced and remarried, Hadley moved out of the spotlight of publicity. Paul Mower died in 1973, and Hadley died January 23, 1979, in Lakeland, Florida.[23]

Hadley did not have the sophistication, or wealth, of Hemingway's next wife, Pauline, or the writing abilities of his third and fourth wives, Martha Gellhorn and Mary Welsh. Hadley is, however, arguably the woman Ernest loved the most and felt the guiltiest about leaving. In his posthumous work, *A Moveable Feast*, Ernest says much about the young couple's life during the Paris years. It is in the last two pages of the book that he bares his feelings about Hadley when he returned to Paris: "I wished I had died before I ever loved anyone but her.... I loved her and I loved no one else and we had a lovely magic."[24]

Lady Duff Twysden

Before the writing of *The Sun Also Rises*, Hemingway seemed very interested in Lady Duff Twysden. Duff, born Dorothy Smurthwaite on May 22, 1892, was the daughter of a wine shop owner in Yorkshire. Her mother aspired to greater things and sought a social position. After her mother divorced, Duff took her mother's maiden name Stirling.[25]

Sent to Paris for her education, Duff spoke excellent French and had a flair for pen-and-ink drawing. She spent her summers in Scotland with her well-off grandparents. Her mother managed to get Dorothy presented at Buckingham Palace. At the time she was described as being tall with a "small exquisite head on a slender neck" and already showing a "natural style that became characteristic of her."[26]

Her first marriage, to Luttrell Byrom, covered the period of World War I. She performed volunteer assignments for the British Secret Service during the Great War, while carrying on with young naval officers.

Sir Roger Thomas Twysden, tenth baronet, and serving in the Royal Navy, became smitten with Duff. Despite loud objections from Twysden's family, they married after Duff's divorce from her first husband. The couple had a son thirteen months after their wedding. During their stormy marriage, she fell in love with a younger cousin, Pat Guthrie, an alcoholic. Twysden eventually sued for divorce on the grounds of adultery, naming Guthrie as co-respondent. She gave up her son to her grandmother and her former husband and moved with Guthrie to Paris.

It is in this period that Lady Duff became the talk of the café set in Montparnasse, Paris. The couple slowly worked their way downward from living at the Ritz to third-rate hotels. Constantly dodging creditors, she floated around café society with seemingly little concern about money. According to Bernice Kert, Hemingway seemed attracted to "her style, her unerring charm." Ernest introduced Duff to Hadley, who seemed to like her. Hadley also liked her because Duff felt that husbands were off limits. Hemingway, however, encouraged her friendship.[27]

At this time, Harold Loeb, of café society, became interested in Duff and moved in the same circles. He quickly fell in love with her and offered to take her away to Spain with him. They spent time together before she reminded Loeb she had to return to Paris and Guthrie. Loeb continued living in Spain by himself. During their time together, Loeb began to wonder if there was more than friendship between Ernest and Lady Duff.[28]

While continuing his tour of Spain, Loeb received a letter from Duff, saying she was coming to Pamplona with Ernest and others. Would he like to meet her there? Loeb had originally planned on meeting Ernest for fishing before going to Pamplona. He canceled this and decided instead to meet Duff and Guthrie at the train station and then drive them on to Pamplona. By this time, Hadley had begun to realize Ernest's interest in Lady Duff. Loeb, who valued Hemingway's friendship, worried about how the writer would take his infatuation with

Duff. Other problems plagued Loeb. It became obvious on the drive to Pamplona that Lady Duff was not going to leave Guthrie. But was she going to have an affair with Hemingway? A friend of Ernest's once said, "The question of Hem and Duff is a tricky one." Writers for years have tried to unravel this question.[29]

Readers of Ernest Hemingway's novel *The Sun Also Rises* can recognize the situation outlined in the previous paragraph. Lady Duff becomes Brett Ashley, Hemingway becomes Jake Barnes, Pat Guthrie becomes Mike Campbell, and Loeb becomes Robert Cohn. Sometime after the publication of the book, by the fall of 1925, Lady Duff Twysden drifted out of Ernest's life.

She fell in love with a young American painter, Clinton King. King came from a wealthy Texas family; he defied them by marrying Duff on August 21, 1928. This stopped his allowance from his family. The couple lived for a period of time on the shores of Lake Chapala, Mexico, and far differently than her days in Montparnasse.

In 1933, they moved to New York City. They lived a frugal life, but according to her friends, Duff had "a contentment about her, a sense of her own worth that had been sadly missing in her Paris days."[30]

On June 27, 1938, Duff Twysden King died of tuberculosis in Santa Fe, New Mexico, at the age of forty-five. Hemingway's *The Sun Also Rises* portrayed her wild years; what happened after she met and married Clinton King was far different. Kert has correctly written, "The legend of Duff Twysden was enshrined in the literature of the lost generation. The facts of her life were quite different."[31]

Pauline Pfeiffer

Pauline Marie Pfeiffer was born July 22, 1895, in Parkersburg, Iowa, to Mr. and Mrs. Paul M. Pfeiffer. Her father ran a pharmacy in Parkersburg. Five years later, the family moved to St. Louis, Missouri, where Paul's brothers, Henry and Gustavus, established Pfeiffer Pharmaceuticals. In 1902, Paul began purchasing land in Piggott, Arkansas, eventually acquiring more than 63,000 acres.[32]

In 1908, Pfeiffer Pharmaceuticals merged with William R. Warner. Five years later, the family moved to Piggott. In 1916, Henry and Gustavus Pfeiffer acquired the Richard Hudnut Company. Hudnut (1855–1928) is considered the first American to enter the cosmetics field in a major way. He introduced French-style perfumes and cosmetics to American women. Richard made a fortune with a reputation for high-end cosmetics. In short, Pauline came from a wealthy family.[33]

Pauline entered the Academy of the Visitation in St. Louis in 1901, graduating from the academy in 1913. She received a degree in journalism in 1918 from the University of Missouri. Eventually, Pauline landed in New York, where she worked for the *Daily Telegraph*, *Vanity Fair*, and *Vogue*.

Her abilities led to her receiving the position of assistant to the Paris editor of *Vogue*. In December of 1925, the second year Hemingway and Hadley went to ski at Schruns, Austria, Pauline Pfeiffer joined them. Ernest and Pauline began an affair, which Hadley discovered. Hadley and Hemingway made a trial separation and finally divorced on January 1927.

Ernest and Pauline had two sons, Patrick and Gregory. In December 1936, Hemingway met Martha Gellhorn in Key West, Florida.[34]

After Hemingway divorced Pauline Pfeifer, on November 4, 1940, she remained in Key West, opening a designer fabric, upholstery, and gift shop with Lorine Thompson. Pauline made many trips to California, where she kept an apartment in San Francisco. During a visit with her sister in Los Angeles, she died suddenly in St. Vincent's Hospital, on October 1, 1951. The surgeon's cause of death stated "hemorrhage into adrenal."[35]

The following women appear in the order they appear in Hemingway's life: Jane Mason, Martha Gellhorn, and Mary Welsh Hemingway. Information on these women is contained within the narrative.

Adriana Ivancich

In 1948, while touring and hunting in Italy, Hemingway met eighteen-year-old Adriana Ivancich. She had "rich black, long and lustrous hair, unusual green eyes, and Roman nose." Adriana had "unusual hollows under cheek bones and a curving mouth that smiled easily. Her figure was good." All this and "her coloring, bone structure, and classic Italian breeding" produced a very striking young woman who "had caused quite a stir in Venice" after her formal debut at the age of eighteen. Adriana had written poetry since the age of fourteen and could "draw very well."[36]

Not only did the young Venetian have beauty and intelligence, she also came from an illustrious family. The Ivanciches came from the island of Lussino, in Dalmatia, and were noted ship owners and captains. The family eventually moved their operations to Venice and became one of the five most important families in the city. By Adriana's birth, on January 1, 1930, the family's wealth had declined somewhat due to bad investments and the economic fallout from the Great War. Carlo, Adriana's father, however, helped keep the family's status in Venetian society. Her mother, Dora, also a great beauty, was noted for her kindness and wit. Adriana had three siblings, two brothers and a sister. She was next to the youngest, Giacomo, with Gianfranco the oldest and Francesca her older sister.

World War II radically changed the Ivancich family. Gianfranco fought in the Italian tank corps with German General Erwin Rommel's forces in North Africa. He was wounded in 1942 and sent home to recover. By September 1943, Italy went over to the Allied side. Gianfranco joined the United States Office of Strategic Forces (OSS) and eventually found himself in charge of all partisan activities in the Veneto. Dora worked as a volunteer nurse, and Adriana acted as a messenger for the partisans.

The strong resistance of the Germans in northern Italy eventually led to the destruction of the family estate near the village of San Michele on the lower Tagliamento River by United States bombing attacks. The greatest blow to the family came when Carlo was found murdered in an alley. Dora never recovered from his death. She did manage to hold onto the palazzo in Venice, hold her former position in Venetian society and, with a few remaining properties, educate the younger children.[37]

It is little wonder that Ernest was drawn to the young woman. Adriana introduced her brother Gianfranco to Hemingway and explained his military background. She also informed Hemingway that Gianfranco had an offer for a position in Cuba. Ernest told her that he liked her brother and would see him in Cuba.[38]

Hemingway met Adriana at least twice in Venice and once in Paris, where he professed his love for her, but also told her he "could not do anything about it." What he could do was invite both Adriana and her mother to visit him at the Finca Vigía. The mother and daughter stayed for two months.[39]

How much Ernest was smitten by the young Adriana is related by a small incident in René Villarreal's memoir. René said Hemingway had Mary shop for him at El Encanto, which was "one of Havana's finest clothing stores." There she bought him "new guayaberas, pants, shorts and shoes." Most of the people who have studied Hemingway have remarked on his careless approach to clothing. His sudden interest in new clothing is one small example of how much he cared to make a good impression on the young woman.[40]

The first of the Ivanciches to arrive, even while the Hemingways remained in Europe, was Gianfranco. Villarreal placed him in the newly decorated guest room. Gianfranco claimed he wanted to write, but René remarked although he left "a mess of crumpled papers," he had written nothing in his notebook. Villarreal, however, found Gianfranco an "easy person to get along with." Ernest's secretary, Nita Jensen, however, felt differently. In a letter to Hemingway while he was in Europe, she said she refused to stay in the house with Gianfranco, stating that "he's purely a sponger and taking every advantage he can of you." Because he stayed the longest at the finca, the guest room became known as the "Venetian Room."[41]

René Villarreal fell under the spell of the "beautiful, dark-haired, sultry siren." He became infatuated with her when they went riding through the countryside on horseback. This ride escalated his feelings and, over the next few months, after everyone in the house had retired for the night, René and Adriana met by the pool, remaining there until the early hours of the morning. Villarreal recalled that he did not know whether Hemingway ever learned of this relationship. When Adriana and her mother departed, René continued a correspondence for a few years, but the letters slowly halted.[42]

Adriana always insisted that she looked upon Ernest as a good friend and that nothing sexual happened between them. Many Hemingway biographers accept this as fact. When Adriana and her mother left Cuba, she never saw Hemingway again.[43]

Adriana Ivancich eventually published her autobiography *La Torre Bianca* (*The White Tower*) in 1980. In a letter to Bernice Kert, Adriana wrote that even penning the few lines of the letter were "a big effort." On March 23, 1983, Adriana Ivancich committed suicide by hanging herself from a tree at her farm in Capalbio, Italy.[44]

For many years, the women in Ernest Hemingway's adult life received very little attention from writers. Bernice Kert, whose work covers all of the women, writes, "Ernest Hemingway chose his wives well. They were adventurous, intelligent, resilient." Despite this "he could never sustain a long-lived, wholly satisfying relationship with any one of them." Writer Paula McLain, writing in the *Huffington Post*, comments, "Each of his wives was magnificent in her own way.... He loved them each deeply and inexpertly.... Perhaps his true love could only ever be his work, which mattered more than living." When depression and an inability to write closed in upon him and he thought of suicide, there "was no woman, and no amount of love, that could save him from himself."[45]

Chapter Notes

Chapter 1

1. McIver, *Hemingway's Key West*, 11; McLendon, *Papa*, 19–22; Palin, *Hemingway Adventure*, 18.
2. Reynolds, *Hemingway: Homecoming*, 169.
3. Quoted in Bruccoli and Trogdon, *The Only Thing That Counts*, 72.
4. McLendon, *Papa*, 8.
5. Reynolds, *Home Coming*, 172–173; Quoted in Bruccoli and Trogdon, *The Only Thing That Counts*, 72.
6. McLendon, *Papa*, 24–25, 27, 27–29.
7. Reynolds, *Homecoming*, 172.
8. McLendon, *Papa*, 30.
9. *Ibid.*, 42.
10. *Ibid.*, 30, 32–33.
11. "Measuring Worth"; "Hemingway Home"; McLendon, *Papa*, 68–76; McIver, *Key West*, 23–28.
12. McLendon, *Papa*, 80–81.
13. Fuentes, *Hemingway in Cuba*, 11.
14. Quoted in White, *By-Line*, 213.
15. Kert, *Hemingway Women*, 235.
16. Myers, *Hemingway*, 242–243.
17. Hemingway, Hilary, *Hemingway in Cuba*, 18. The authors do not cite their source.
18. *Ibid.*, 19–20.
19. "The Moro Castle," 1.

Chapter 2

1. "Old Havana and Its Fortification System," 2.
2. "Plaza de Armas," 1–2; Llanes, *Havana Then and Now*, 34–35; Hemingway, *Islands in the Stream*, 247–248.
3. Llanes, *Havana Then and Now*, 36–37; "Havana's Magic Ceiba Tree"; e-mail, Pina to Noble, February 23, 2011, in author's files.
4. "Old Havana and Its Fortification System," 2.
5. "Wifredo Lam," Guggenheim Museum, http://www.guggenheim.org/new-york/collections/collection-online/artists/bios/1544 accessioned December 15, 2015, pp. 1–2.
6. *Ibid.*; Llanes, *Havana Then and Now*, 40–41; "Cuban Culture," 1.
7. Llanes, *Havana Then and Now*, 42–43.
8. Hemingway, *To Have and Have Not*, 3.
9. Llanes, *Havana Then and Now*, 23–25.
10. Film at, www.youtube.com/watch?v=fEMYLKpYxx8; Cortanze, *Hemingway in Cuba*, 34; *Standard Guide to Cuba*, 19; Hemingway, *Islands in the Stream*, 247.
11. Fuentes, *Hemingway in Cuba*, 223.
12. *Ibid.*, 221–225, 228–229.
13. *Ibid.*, 230–233.
14. Feldman, "Leopoldina Rodríguez," 62–64, 67.
15. *Ibid.*, 67–68.
16. *Ibid.*, 65, 68, 70–72.
17. *Ibid.*, 72, 76–77.
18. Llanes, *Havana Then and Now*, 92–93.

19. *Ibid.*, 82–83.
20. *Ibid.*, 69.
21. *Ibid.*, 98–99, 136–137.
22. Gioseffi and Garcia, "Introduction: Pablo Armando Fernandez," 1.
23. Love, "Cuba, and an afternoon with poet Pablo Armando Fernádez," 1–2.
24. "José Rodríguez Fuster," 1.
25. "Sandra Dooley," http://Cuban art space.net/SandraDooley/sandradooley.php accessioned, December 6, 2015; "Jacqueline and Yamilys Brito," http://www.cubaartspace.net/old/exhibitions/sep_8_07.htm accessioned December 7, 2015, 1–3; e-mail, Víctor to Noble, December 5, 2015, in author's files.
26. Interview, Rojas by Noble, January 18, 2011; "A Humble Player on History's Stage: Marta Rojas," 1–2.
27. E-mail, Víctor to Noble, December 5, 2015, in author's files.
28. *Frommer's Cuba*, 83; "Old Havana and Its Fortification System," 2.
29. "Humboldt's Cuban Footprint," 5; Gillis, "Humboldt in the New World," 1–6.
30. E-mail, Pina to Noble, January 12, 2015, in author's files.
31. UNESCO Biosphere http://www.unesco.org/mabdb/br/brdir/directory/biores.asp?code=CUB+01&mode=all accessioned December 3, 2015; e-mail, Víctor to Noble, December 5, 2015, in author's files; "Cuban Flora Inspires Cuban Artist," http://www.dtcuba.com/shownews.aspx?/c=25405&Ing=2 accessioned, December 3, 2015; "Cuban Artist Jorge Pérez Duporte Featured in Pinar del Río Cuba]," http://havanajournal.com/culture/entry/cuban_artist_jorge_perez_duporte. Accessed December 3, 2015, 1–2.
32. Marquez, 8–9, in Introduction, Fuentes, *Hemingway in Cuba*, 8–9.

Chapter 3

1. McLendon, *Papa*, 15; Kert, *Hemingway Women*, 285; Moorehead, *Gellhorn*, 11–18.
2. Moorehead, *Gellhorn*, 11–18.
3. Kert, *Hemingway Women*, 295.
4. *Ibid.*, 285–286.
5. *Ibid.*, 286–287.
6. *Ibid.*, 287–291.
7. *Ibid.*, 289.
8. Moorhead, Gellhorn, 1–9, 420–424; "Flashback: Remembering Martha Gellhorn," 1–3.
9. Bruccoli, *The Only Thing That Counts*, 272–273; opting out of a tournament is in a letter from Hemingway to Thomas Shelvin, April 4, 1939, Baker, *Selected Letters*, 483–485.
10. Kert, *Hemingway Women*, 325; Fuentes, *Hemingway in Cuba*, 25.
11. Fuentes, *Hemingway in Cuba*, 24–28.
12. *Ibid.*, 31–31; Villarreal and Villarreal, *Hemingway's Cuban Son*, 13.
13. All material on Gellhorn's visit is in Gellhorn, "Cuba Revisited," 106–134.
14. Villarreal and Villarreal, *Hemingway's Cuban Son*, 13.
15. *Ibid.*, 102–103; 138–139.
16. *Ibid.*, 102–105.
17. *Ibid.*
18. *Ibid.*; Gellhorn, "Cuba Revisited," 136.
19. Fuentes, *Hemingway in Cuba*, 19.
20. *Ibid.*, 22–23; Gellhorn, "Cuba Revisited," 130.
21. Kert, *Hemingway Women*, 392–399.
22. *Ibid.*, 399.
23. *Ibid.*, 399–400.
24. *Ibid.*, 399–402.
25. *Ibid.*, 401–404, 424.
26. Fuentes, *Hemingway in Cuba*, 23–24.
27. Kert, *Hemingway Women*, 504–505.
28. Houk, "Gulf Stream," Hemingway, Mary, "Girl at Sea," 92.
29. Hemingway, Mary, "Girl at Sea," 92.
30. *Ibid.*, 92–93.
31. *Ibid.*, 52, 92–94; Houk, "Gulf Stream," 77. The picture accompanying the article by Mary Hemingway in *Cosmopolitan* shows *Pilar* towing *Tin Kid* out of Havana's harbor, with Moro Castle in the background. Ernest is on *Pilar*'s flying bridge; Gregorio is seen looking out a window below the flying bridge. In the small boat stands Mary.

At the stern of *Pilar*, with one leg on something, stands Walter Houk. According to Houk, Hemingway took great pains to set up this shot for the photographer, Houk, "Gulf Stream."
32. "Mary Hemingway Dies at 78," 1–2.
33. Quoted in Fuentes, *Hemingway in Cuba*, 20.
34. Burgess, *Hemingway and His World*, 13.
35. Hemingway, *A Moveable Feast*, 14–16.
36. Villarreal and Villarreal, *Hemingway's Cuban Son*, 14, 16, 18, 20–21; "The Collection: National Gallery of Art."
37. O'Rourke, "Evan Shipman," 155–158.
38. Hemingway, "The Farm," 28.
39. All material and quotes on Shipman's story is in O'Rourke, "Evan Shipman," 155–159.
40. Hemingway to Matisse, February 12, 1935, Series 2: Outgoing Correspondence, 1929–1942, Box 7, Folder 1035, Hemingway Collection, JK. See also, Hemingway, Colette, *in his time*, 20.
41. Hemingway, *Islands in the Stream*, 233.
42. Hemingway, Colette, *in his time*, 70–74; material on "Gattorno" and Hemingway is also found in *The Village Voice* (July 13, 1961), 1, 11; Series 2: Outgoing Correspondence, 1929–1942, Box 47, Folder 1934, Hemingway Collection, JFK.
43. Unless otherwise noted, material on "Gattorno" is found in, Poole, "A Cuban Painter for the World," in Poole and Cabral, "Gattorno," 273–276.
44. Hemingway, "Gattorno," 114; See also, Driscoll, Deconstructing Hemingway's America," for more information on Hemingway and "Gattorno."
45. e-mail Tatiana Fernandez, Prado Fine Art, to Dennis L. Noble, November 7, 2011, in author's files.
46. Reynolds, *Hemingway: The 1930s*, 191–192; "An Artist of Two Cities"; Martin, "Hemingway and Luis Quintanilla," 119.
47. Hemingway, "Quintanilla," 27; "An Artist of Two Cities."
48. "An Artist of Two Cities"; Baker, *Hemingway: A Life*, 392; Martin, "Hemingway and Luis Quintanilla," 128, 130.
49. "An Artist of Two Cities."
50. Hemingway, *in his time*, 24. "Mary refused to return Miró's *The Farm* to Hadley or Jack, who eventually relinquished his claim to the painting for a payment of $20,000." Meyers, *Hemingway*, 563.
51. Mary Hemingway, *How It Was*, 58–581.
52. *Ibid.*
53. *Ibid.*, 584–586.
54. Hemingway, Valerie, *Running with the Bulls*, 182–187.
55. *Ibid.*, 187–189.
56. The Ernest Hemingway Collection at the JFK in Boston lists in their collection the following works of art: André Masson, *The Throw of the Dice* and three other works by the same artist in what is entitled the "Forrest" series; Waldo Pierce, *Portrait of Ernest Hemingway*. Also listed is a watercolor by Antonio Gattorno, done in 1934, and donated by the artist and his wife. This is a watercolor of Hemingway wearing a beret. See, "Beret Project: Hemingway, Boina and Gattorno." In addition to the works mentioned in the narrative, Colette C. Hemingway notes that Hemingway purchased Gris's *The Bullfighter*, done in 1913, which was used as the frontispiece for *Death in the Afternoon*, "Ernest Hemingway and Art."
57. Hemingway, Colette., *in his time*, 85.
58. Hemingway, *Islands in the Stream*, 241.
59. *Ibid.*
60. May, *Manifest Destiny's Underworld*, 1–4.
61. Hemingway, *Islands in the Stream*, 246.
62. Quoted in *How It Was*, 348–349.

Chapter 4

1. Blas interview; Hemingway and Brennen, *Hemingway in Cuba*, 62; Robinson, "Memories of Playing," 1.
2. Blas interview; Hemingway, Valerie, "Hemingway's Cuba," 71.

3. Blas interview.
4. Hemingway, Valiere, "Hemingway's Cuba," 71; Hemingway, Hilary, and Brennen, *Hemingway in Cuba*, 62.
5. Hemingway, Hilary and Brennen, *Hemingway in Cuba*, 62. The authors do not cite where they obtained their quotes throughout their work.
6. Blas interview; Hemingway, Valerie "Hemingway's Cuba," 71; Robinson, "Memories of Playing," 3.
7. Hemingway, Hilary and Brennen, *Hemingway in Cuba*, 62.
8. Blas interview; Fuentes, *Hemingway in Cuba*, 36; Robinson, "Memories of Playing," 3.
9. Fuentes, *Hemingway in Cuba*, 34, 36.
10. *Ibid.*, 33–37; Blas disputes the comments about throwing firecrackers.
11. Blas interview; Valerie Hemingway, "Hemingway's Cuba," 71; Robinson, "Memories of Playing," 3.
12. Blas interview; Robinson, "Memories of Playing," 3.
13. Villarreal and Villarreal, *Hemingway's Cuban Son*, 32–34. Fuentes has a rather more dramatic scene for this tragedy, Fuentes, *Hemingway in Cuba*, 36–37.
14. Hemingway, Valerie, "Hemingway's Cuba," 71; Robinson, "Memories of Playing," 3.
15. Blas interview.
16. Fuentes, *Hemingway in Cuba*, 39.
17. Blas interview; Blas, *The Homerun Kid,* 29. Blas's memoir appeared just as the manuscript for this book was about to be sent off to the publisher.
18. Villarreal and Villarreal, *Hemingway's Cuban Son*, 23–24.
19. *Ibid.*, 28.
20. *Ibid.*, 37–38.
21. *Ibid.*, 55.
22. Mary Hemingway, *How It Was*, 213.
23. *Ibid.*
24. Fuentes, *Hemingway in Cuba*, 39; Villarreal and Villarreal, *Hemingway's Cuban Son*, 17–18.
25. Villarreal and Villarreal, *Hemingway's Cuban Son*, 95.
26. *Ibid.*, 101.
27. *Ibid.*, 123–128.
28. Fuentes, *Hemingway in Cuba*, 38.
29. *Ibid.*, 37.
30. Villarreal and Villarreal, *Hemingway's Cuban Son*, 136–139.
31. *Ibid.*, 143–144; Mary Hemingway, *How It Was*, 587.
32. Villarreal and Villarreal, *Hemingway's Cuban Son*, 147–149.
33. *Ibid.*, 11, 152–153.
34. *Ibid.*, 8, 153–154.

Chapter 5

1. "S. Kip Farrington, Jr."; Watson, "Hemingway in Bimini," 132.
2. Hendrickson, *Hemingway's Boat*, 12, 47–50, 51–54, 60–69, 70–71; "Measuring Worth."
3. Watson, "Hemingway in Bimini," 143.
4. Hendrickson, *Hemingway's Boat*, 60–69, 70–77; Reynolds, *Hemingway: The 1930s*, 169; "Measuring Worth."
5. Some of the sources for the boat's name: Baker, *Hemingway: A Life*, 259; Hendrickson, *Hemingway's Boat*, 9; Myers, *Hemingway: A Biography*, 280; Reynolds, *Hemingway: The 1930s*, 169; Watson, "Hemingway in Bimini," 133.
6. Hendrickson, *Hemingway's Boat*, 9; Houk, "Gulf Stream," 73.
7. "Other Materials," Hemingway Collection, JFK; for material on Houk: Hendrickson, *Hemingway's Boat*, 345–353; Houk, "Gulf Stream," 73.
8. Houk, "Gulf Stream," 70; Ott, *Sea of Change*, 34–35.
9. Hemingway, *The Old Man and the Sea*, 29.
10. Watson, "Hemingway in Bimini," 131.
11. *Ibid.*, 130–131, 133.
12. McIver, *Key West*, 41.
13. Samuelson, *With Hemingway*, ix.
14. Hemingway, "Monologue to the Maestro," 21; Samuelson, *With Hemingway*, 141.
15. Hendrickson, *Hemingway's Boat*, 104–136; Lacy, "Icarus," 214–221.
16. Samuelson, *With Hemingway*, 123–125.
17. *Ibid.*, 124–125.
18. Series 2: Outgoing Correspon-

dence, 1929–1942, Box 47, Hemingway Collection, JFK. See also Papers of Charles M. G. Cadwalader and Correspondence of Henry W. Fowler, Archives, Philadelphia Academy of Natural Sciences, Philadelphia, Pennsylvania; Samuelson, *With Hemingway*, 124–125.
 19. Martin, "Gulf Stream Scientist," 12.
 20. *Ibid*.
 21. Chakrabarty, "Papa's Fish," 111; Reiger, *Profiles*, 255.
 22. Churchill, *Memoirs*, 545; Hasslinger, "U-Boat War in the Caribbean," 3–4. The best novel of the battle against U-Boats in the Atlantic from the English viewpoint is Montserrat, *The Cruel Sea*.
 23. Kelshall, *War in the Caribbean*, 27–33; Hasslinger, "U-Boat War in the Caribbean," 7; Kelshall notes just the top twenty-five U-Boats in the "Caribbean Theatre by total tonnage sank" amounted to 268 ships sunk: Kelshall, *War in the Caribbean*, Appendix Two, 465–466.
 24. Morison, *Battle of the Atlantic*, 268–269.
 25. *Ibid*., 271–272; Mort, *Hemingway Patrols*, 111–112.
 26. Mort, *Hemingway Patrols*, 111–112.
 27. *Ibid*., 8–9, 112–113.
 28. *Ibid*., 115–119.
 29. *Ibid*.
 30. *Ibid*., 119–120.
 31. *Ibid*., 122.
 32. *Ibid*., 120.
 33. Noble, *The Beach Patrol and Corsair Fleet*, 3–4.
 34. *Ibid*., 4.
 35. Morrison, *Battle of the Atlantic*, 271–272.
 36. Mort, *Hemingway Patrols*, 160–161, 163.
 37. *Ibid*., 176n.
 38. *Ibid*., 79.
 39. *Ibid*., 80–81.
 40. *Ibid*., 228–230.
 41. *EdicionesVigía*.
 42. Cirules, *Hemingway in the Romano Archipelago*, 29. I am aware that there are those who doubt Cirules's work, pointing out that there has been no documentation uncovered as to Hemingway and Mason sailing in this region. Yet, in *Islands in the Stream*, Thomas Hudson pursues the survivors of a destroyed German submarine with many mentions of turtle hunters and good descriptions of the *Romano Archipelago*. Hemingway used his own experiences in his writings. True, he operated within the archipelago when hunting German submarines, but it seems the descriptions are from a more leisurely time in the region. Cirules, as mentioned, is from the region, and people would be very likely to talk to him. Until it can be proven that Hemingway was *not* in the region prior to World War II, I will use Cirules's information.
 43. *Ibid*., 44.
 44. *Ibid*.
 45. Mort, *Hemingway Patrols*, 209.
 46. *Ibid*., 210–216.
 47. Cirules, *Hemingway in the Romano Archipelago*, 29.
 48. *Casa Lancara*.
 49. Unless otherwise noted, all historical material on La Gloria, is in Adams, *Pioneering in Cuba*, passim.
 50. Deere, "Here Come the Yankees!" 729–765.
 51. *Standard Guide*, 145.
 52. "August C. Mayhew."
 53. "El Cobre, Santiago de Cuba," 1–3. See also Rooda, *Cuba, America, and the Sea*, 5.

Chapter 6

 1. DiGiantomasso, "Battle of Santiago," 1–19.
 2. "Battle of San Juan Hill," 1–11.
 3. "Trinidad and the Valley de los Ingenios," 1–3.
 4. Rodríguez, "Manaca Iznaga: A dream-like batey," 1–2.
 5. E-mail, Víctor Pina to Dennis L. Noble, February 5, 2012, in author's files.
 6. Fuentes, *Hemingway in Cuba*, 115–116; "Cuba's Sole Naval Academy," 1–2.
 7. On the Mariel Boatlift, see Chapters 2, 3, and 4, in Noble, *War on Human Smuggling*.
 8. "Log, *Pilar*, World War II, 1942," Hemingway Collection, John F. Kennedy

Library, Boston (JFK) and Mort, *Hemingway Patrols*, 184–191.
  9. FBI File June 13, 1943, Hemingway Collection, JFK.
  10. Quoted in Mort, *Hemingway Patrols*, 188n.
  11. Willock, *Lone Star Marine*, 26, 30–32; Morris, "A Texan Marine," 2.
  12. Willock, *Lone Star Marine*, 35–39.
  13. *Ibid.*, 42–44.
  14. Morris, "A Texan Marine," 2.
  15. *Ibid.*, 3.
  16. *Ibid.*, 4.
  17. *Ibid.*, 47.
  18. *Ibid.*
  19. *Ibid.*, 8–9.
  20. *Ibid.*, 9.
  21. *Ibid.*
  22. Fuentes, *Hemingway in Cuba*, 120.

Chapter 7

  1. Hemingway, *The Old Man and the Sea*, 29; *Standard Guide*, 102.
  2. Corrales, *Hemingway y Cuba*, 79, 118.
  3. Baker, *Hemingway: A Life*, 502.
  4. Fuentes, *Hemingway in Cuba*, 123; Houk, "On the Gulf Stream," 76.
  5. Hendrickson, *Hemingway's Boat*, 323; the author writes that the incidents related in this account took place in 1931, as does Baker, *Hemingway: A Life*, 222; Houk, however, places it in 1928, Houk, "On the Gulf Stream," 76.
  6. Fuentes, *Hemingway in Cuba*, 222; Houk, "On the Gulf Stream," 76; Quoted in White, *By-Line: Ernest Hemingway*, Hemingway, "The Great Blue River," 406–407.
  7. Houk, "On the Gulf Stream," 77.
  8. Hemingway, "The Great Blue River," 62; Houk, "On the Gulf Stream," 76.
  9. Fuentes, *Hemingway in Cuba*, 100.
  10. *Ibid.*, 108–109.
  11. Hendrickson, *Hemingway's Boat*, 323; Curtis, "The Real Old Man and the Sea," 12.
  12. Houk, "On the Gulf Stream," 77.
  13. Hemingway, *How It Was*, 586–587; Hendrickson, *Hemingway's Boat*, 503–507. By 2011, Pilar had been restored and looked like it was ready for Ernest Hemingway to come aboard and once again put out to the sea that he loved; much of the work was done by Prof. Elisa Serrano.
  14. Villarreal and Villarreal, *Hemingway's Cuban Son*, 147.
  15. Stoddart, "Our Old Friend; [Deathwatch] Gregorio Fuentes."
  16. "[Deathwatch] Gregorio Fuentes."
  17. E-Mails Víctor Pina to Dennis L. Noble, December 5–7, 2013, in author's files.
  18. Fuentes, *Hemingway in Cuba*, 124.
  19. Corrales, *Hemingway y Cuba*, 113–115.
  20. Interview with Gladys Gonzáles, former director of the Museo de Ernesto Hemingway, who gave the author a copy of the videotape, January 8, 2011, Havana, Cuba, hereinafter, Gonzáles interview.
  21. Fuentes, *Hemingway in Cuba*, 123.
  22. Gonzáles interview.
  23. Comments from an unidentified woman at a presentation of a new edition of *A Moveable Feast* at the John F. Kennedy Library, Boston, Massachusetts, videotaped by C-SPAN Book-TV. See, "A Moveable Feast," 289184–1-DVD, available from the archives of C-SPAN, the comment begins at about 1 hour and twenty-one minutes into the proceedings.
  24. Gonzáles interview.
  25. Fuentes, *Hemingway in Cuba*, 114.

Appendix A

  1. Quoted in Palin, *Hemingway Adventure*, 1.
  2. Kert, *Hemingway Women*, 21.
  3. *Ibid.*, 23.
  4. *Ibid.*, 22.
  5. Mellon, *Life Without Consequences*, 7–8; "About Oberlin: History"; Reynolds, *Young Hemingway*, 2–3.
  6. Baker, *Hemingway: A Life*, 2.
  7. "Galli-Curi"; Baker, *Hemingway: A Life*, 2.

8. Unfortunately, the correspondence between Grace and Ed has not survived. Kert, *Hemingway Women*, 25–26, 30–31.
9. Mellon, *A Life Without Consequences*, 6.
10. Jones, "A Moveable Michigan," 8.
11. Beegel, "Eye and Heart," 55.
12. Catton, *Waiting for the Morning Train*, 110–111. For additional material on Michigan forests, see, Dickman and Leefers, *The Forests of Michigan*; Meek, *Michigan's Timber Battleground*.
13. Scrapbook, Hemingway Collection, John F. Kennedy Library, Boston, Massachusetts, hereinafter, JFK.
14. Beegel, "Eye and Hart," 75; Scrapbook, Hemingway Collection, JFK.
15. Quoted in Beegel, "Eye and Hart," 87; Reynolds, *Hemingway's First War*, 3, 5; Baker, *Hemingway: A Life*, 40–43.
16. Hendrickson, *Hemingway's Boat*, 358; Rains, "Hemingway's Boat," 2.
17. Reynolds, *Hemingway: The Final Years*, 273.
18. Palin, *Hemingway Adventure*, 18.
19. Hendrickson, *Hemingway's Boat*, 459; Reynolds, *Hemingway: The Final Years*, 274.
20. Reynolds, *Hemingway: The Final Years*, 306.
21. Arnold, *The Idaho Hemingway*, 8–14; Mary Hemingway, *How It Was*, 517.
22. Mary Hemingway, *How It Was*, 527–528.
23. Reynolds, *Hemingway: The Final Years*, 343.
24. Reynolds, *Hemingway: The Final Years*, 343; Baker, *Hemingway: A Life*, 551.
25. Valerie Hemingway, *Running with the Bulls*, 106–107; Valerie Hemingway, "Hemingway's Cuba," 1; "U.S. Forced Hemingway to Leave Cuba."
26. Reynolds, *Hemingway: The Final Years*, 318, 344.
27. *Ibid.*, 348–352.
28. All quotes from interview with Monica (Mollner) Ostrom, by Dennis L. Noble, February 23, 2008, Sequim, Washington, in author's files; Reynolds, *Hemingway: The Final Years*, 355.
29. Reynolds, *Hemingway: The Final Years*, 355–358.
30. Hendrickson, *Hemingway's Boat*, 461; FBI File, Hemingway Collection, JFK; Mary Hemingway, *How It Was*, 481; Hotchner, "Hemingway Hounded by the Feds," A-19; Arnold, *The Idaho Hemingway*, 8–14.
31. Reynolds, *Hemingway: The Final Years*, 358–359.

Appendix B

1. Kert, *Hemingway Women*, 50.
2. "Brigadier General Samuel B. Holabird."
3. Kert, *Hemingway Women*, 50–51.
4. *Ibid.*, 51.
5. *Ibid.*, 51, 53.
6. *Ibid.*, 58.
7. *Ibid.*, 63.
8. *Ibid.*, 63–64.
9. *Ibid.*, 67–68.
10. Villard and Nagel, 262–263.
11. *Ibid.*, xi; Kert, *Hemingway Women*, 13, 496.
12. Dilberto, *Hadley*, 1–4.
13. *Ibid.*, 4.
14. Quoted in Dilberto, *Hadley*, 3.
15. Dilberto, *Hadley*, 4, 6.
16. *Ibid.*, *Hadley*, 8–11.
17. *Ibid.*, 11.
18. *Ibid.*, "measuring worth."
19. Dilberto, *Hadley*, 11.
20. *Ibid.*, 13; Kert, *Hemingway Women*, 84–85.
21. Kert, *Hemingway Women*, 88, 102.
22. *Ibid.*, 104–105.
23. *Ibid.*, 12.
24. Hemingway, *A Moveable Feast*, 210.
25. Kert, *Hemingway Women*, 156.
26. *Ibid.*
27. *Ibid.*, 158.
28. *Ibid.*, 159–160.
29. *Ibid.*, 160–161; quoted *ibid.*, 161.
30. *Ibid.*, 252.
31. *Ibid.*
32. *Ibid.*, 171.
33. "Richard Hudnut."
34. "Hemingway-Pfeiffer Timeline."
35. Kert, *Hemingway Women*, 373–374, 463–464; Hendrickson, *Hemingway's Boat*, 409–415.

36. Kert, *Hemingway Women*, 435–441.
37. *Ibid.*, 436–439.
38. *Ibid.*, 442–443.
39. *Ibid.*, 449–451.
40. Villarreal and Villarreal, *Hemingway's Cuban Son*, 81.
41. Reynolds, *Hemingway: The Final Years*, 217; Villarreal and Villarreal, *Hemingway's Cuban Son*, 82.
42. Villarreal and Villarreal, *Hemingway's Cuban Son*, 82–88.
43. Hendrickson, *Hemingway's Boat*, 337.
44. "Adriana Ivancich;" Kert, *Hemingway Women*, 13.
45. *Ibid.*, 12; McLain, "Hemingway Wives," 2.

Bibliography

Archival Material

John F. Kennedy Library, Boston, Massachusetts
    Ernest Hemingway Collection
Manuscript Division, Library of Congress, Washington, D.C.
    A.E. Hotchner Papers
    MacKinlay Kantor Papers
    Archibald MacLeish Papers
    Owen Wister Papers
Philadelphia Academy of Natural Sciences, Philadelphia, Pennsylvania
    Charles M.G. Cadwalader Papers
    Henry W. Fowler. Correspondence

Interviews

Ada Rosa Alfonso Rosales, Director, Finca Vigía, Museo de Ernesto Hemingway, San Francisco de Paula, Cuba. January 2011.
Ana Morales Arranda and Idalberto Sabina. Habana, Cuba. January 2011.
Prof. José Altshuler. Director, Sociedad Cubana de Historia de la Ciencia y la Tecnología. Habana, Cuba. January 2008, 2010, 2011.
José Armando. Director, Biblioteca Pública, Caibarién, Cuba. January 2011.
Pablo Armando. Habana, Cuba. January 2008.
Oscar Blas. San Francisco de Paula, Cuba. January 2010.
Isabel I. Ferreiro, Technical Deputy of the Finca Vigía, Museo de Ernesto Hemingway, San Francisco de Paula, Cuba. January 2008, 2010, 2011.
Esperanza M. García, Director, Hemingway Room Museum, Hotel Ambos Mundos, Habana Vieja, Cuba. January 2010, 2011.
Gladys Gonzáles. Former Director, Finca Vigía, Museo de Ernesto Hemingway. Habana, Cuba. January 2010.
Dr. Ing. Víctor Pina Tabío. Habana, Cuba. January 2008, 2010, 2011.
Marta Rojas. Habana, Cuba. January 2010.
Juan E. Sánchez. Caibarién Cultural Directorate. January 2011.
Prof. Elisa Serrano and Pablo Jane. Habana Vieja, Cuba. January 2008, 2010, 2011.

Guy M. Yudith and Camila García. Habana, Cuba. January 2011.
Ivon L. Zaldívar. Historian of Palma City, Cuba. January 2011.
Liliana Zerquera. Trinidad, Cuba. January 2011.

Books, Articles, Theses

Adams, James Meade. *Pioneering in Cuba: A Narrative of the Settlement of La Gloria, the First American Colony in Cuba, and the Early Experiences of the Pioneers*. Concord, NH: The Rumford Press, 1901.
Arnold, Tillie, with William L. Smallwood. *The Idaho Hemingway*. Buhl, ID: Beacon Books, 1999.
Baker, Carlos. *Ernest Hemingway: A Life Story*. New York: Charles Scribner's Sons, 1969.
___, ed. *Ernest Hemingway: Selected Letters, 1917-1961*. New York: Charles Scribner's Sons, 1981.
Brasch, James D. *That Other Hemingway: The Master Inventor*. Victoria, BC: Trafford Publishing, 2009.
Bruccoli, Matthew J., with the assistance of Robert W. Trogdon. *The Only Thing That Counts: The Ernest Hemingway-Maxwell Perkins Correspondence, 1925-1947*. Charleston: University of South Carolina Press, 1996.
Burgess, Anthony. *Ernest Hemingway and His World*. New York: Charles Scribner's Sons, 1985.
Chakrabarty, Prosanta. "Papa's Fish: A Note on *Neomerinthe Hemingwai*." *The Hemingway Review* 25, no. 1 (2005): 109-111.
Churchill, Winston S. *Memoirs of the Second World War*. Boston: Houghton Mifflin Company, 1959.
Cirules, Enríque. *Ernest Hemingway in the Romano Archipelago*. Translated from the Spanish by Douglas Edward LaPrade. Habana: Ediciones UNION, 1999.
Connett, Eugene V., III, ed. *American Big Game Fishing*. Lanham, MD: The Derrydale Press, 1999.
Corrales, Raúl. *Hemingway y Cuba. Fotos de Raúl Corrales*. Segunda Edición Mejorada. Habana [?]: Ediciones Aurelia, 2007.
Cortanze, Gerard de. *Hemingway in Cuba*. [?]: Editions du Chêne, 1997.
Deere, Carmen Diana. "Here Come the Yankees! The Rise and Decline of United States Colonies in Cuba, 1898-1930." *Hispanic American Historical Review* 78, no. 4 (November 1998): 729-65.
Diliberto, Gioia. *Hadley*. New York: Ticknor & Fields, 1992.
Driscoll, Sarah. "Deconstructing Hemingway's America: The Hemingway-Gattorno Relationships in the U.S.-Cuban Imagination." Master of Arts Thesis, Arizona State University, May 2011.
Federspiel, Michael R. *Picturing Hemingway's Michigan*. Detroit: Wayne State University Press, 2010.
Feldman, Andrew. "Leopoldina Rodríguez: Hemingway's Cuban Lover?" *Hemingway Review* 31, no. 1 (Fall 2011): 62-78.
Fernández Mesa, Oscar Blas, and Brian Gordon Sinclair. *The Homerun Kid: The True Story of Ernest Hemingway's Baseball Team*. Key West, FL: Whiz Bang, 2015.
Fitch, Noel Riley. *Sylvia Beach and the Lost Generation: A History of Literary Paris in the Twenties and Thirties*. New York: W.W. Norton, 1983.

Fuentes, Norberto. *Ernest Hemingway Rediscovered*. Photographs by Roberto Herrera Sotolongo. Translated from the French by Marianne Sinclair. New York: Charles Scribner's Sons, 1988.
_____. *Hemingway in Cuba*. Translated by Consuelo E. Corwin. Secaucus, NJ: Lyle Stuart, 1984.
Gannon, Michael. *Operation Drumbeat: The Dramatic True Story of Germany's First U-Boat Attacks Along the American Coast in World War II*. New York: Harper & Row, 1990.
Gellhorn, Martha. "Cuba Revisited." *Granta* (Winter 1986): 106-134.
Gingrich, Arnold. *The Well Tempered Angler*. New York: NAL Penguin, 1987.
Hemingway, Colette C. *In His Time: Ernest Hemingway's Collection of Paintings and the Artists He Knew*. N.p.: Kilimanjaro Books, 2009.
Hemingway, Ernest. *The Complete Short Stories of Ernest Hemingway: The Finca Vigía Edition*. New York: Scribner's, 1987.
_____. *Death in the Afternoon*. New York: Charles Scribner's Sons, 1932.
_____. *A Farewell to Arms*. Charles Scribner's Sons, 1929.
_____. "The Farm," *Cahiers d'Art*, IX (1934): 28.
_____. *The Fifth Column and the First Forty-nine Stories*. New York: Charles Scribner's Sons, 1938.
_____. "Gattorno: Program Note," *Esquire*, May 1936, 111, 141.
_____. "The Great Blue River." *Holiday*, July 1949, 60-63, 95-97.
_____. *Green Hills of Africa*. New York: Scribner's, 1935.
_____. *Hemingway on Hunting*. Guilford, CT: The Lyons Press, 2001.
_____. *Islands in the Stream*. New York: Charles Scribner's Sons, 2003.
_____. *Marlin!* Introduction by Gabriel García Márquez. San Francisco: Big Fish Books, 1992.
_____. "Monologue to the Maestro: A High Seas Letter." *Esquire*, October 1935, 21, 174A, 174B.
_____. *A Moveable Feast*. New York: Charles Scribner's Sons, 1964.
_____. *The Old Man and the Sea*. New York: Charles Scribner's Sons, 1952.
_____. "On the Blue Water: A Gulf Stream Letter." *Esquire*, April 1936, 31, 184-185.
_____. "Quintanilla." *Esquire*, February 1935, 26-27.
_____. *The Sun Also Rises*. New York: Charles Scribner's, 1926.
_____. *To Have and Have Not*. New York: P.F. Collier, 1937 [?].
Hemingway, Gregory H. *Papa: A Personal Memoir*. New York: Paragon House, 1988.
Hemingway, Hilary, and Carlene Brennen. *Hemingway in Cuba*. New York: Rugged Land, 2005.
Hemingway, Hilary, and Jeffry P. Lindsay. *Hunting with Hemingway: Based on the Stories of Leicester Hemingway*. New York: Riverhead Books, 2000.
Hemingway, John. *Strange Tribe: A Family Memoir*. Guilford, CT: The Lyons Press, 2007.
Hemingway, Mary Welsh. "Girl at Sea." *Cosmopolitan*, January 1952, 57, 92-95.
_____. *How It Was*. New York: Knopf, 1976.
Hemingway, Valerie. *Running with the Bulls: My Years with the Hemingways*. New York: Ballantine Books, 2004.
Hendrickson, Paul. *Hemingway's Boat: Everything He Loved in Life, and Lost, 1934-1961*. New York: Alfred A. Knopf, 2011.

Hotchner, A.E. "Hemingway, Hounded by the Feds." *New York Times*, July 1, 2011, A-19.
____. *Papa Hemingway*. New York: Random House, 1955.
Houk, Walter. "Lessons from Hemingway's Cuban Biographer." *The North Dakota Quarterly* 68 (Spring/Summer 2001): 132–155.
____. "On the Gulf Stream Aboard Hemingway's *Pilar*." *The North Dakota Quarterly* 65, no 3 (1998): 70–90.
____. "A Sailor Looks at Hemingway's Islands." *North Dakota Quarterly* 73 (Winter/Spring 2006): 7–74.
Kelshall, Gaylord T. M. *The U-Boat War in the Caribbean*. Annapolis, MD: Naval Institute Press, 1994.
Kert, Bernice. *The Hemingway Women*. New York: W.W. Norton, 1983.
Lacy, Robert. "Icarus." *North Dakota Quarterly* 70, no. 4 (Fall 2003): 214–221.
Lawrence, H. Lea. *A Hemingway Odyssey: Special Places in His Life*. Nashville, TN: Cumberland House, 1992.
Lyons, Nick, ed. *Hemingway on Fishing*. Guilford, CT: Lyons Press, 2000.
Martin, Lawrence H. "Ernest Hemingway, Gulf Stream Scientist: The 1934-35 Academy of Natural Sciences Correspondence." *The Hemingway Review* 20, no. 2 (Spring 2001): 5–15.
____. "Hemingway and Luis Quintanilla." *North Dakota Quarterly* (Fall 2003): 119–139.
May, Robert E. *Manifest Destiny's Underworld: Filibustering in Antebellum America*. Chapel Hill: University of North Carolina Press, 2002.
McIver, Stuart. *Hemingway's Key West*. Sarasota, FL: Pineapple Press, 1993.
McLendon, James. *Papa: Hemingway in Key West*. Marathon, FL: The Ketch & Yawl Press, 2006.
Mellow, James R. *Hemingway: A Life Without Consequences*. Boston: Houghton Mifflin, 1992.
Meyers, Jeffrey. *Hemingway: A Biography*. New York: Harper and Row, 1985.
Miller, Linda Patterson. "The Matrix of Hemingway's *Pilar* Log, 1934–35." *North Dakota Quarterly* 64, no. 3 (1997): 105–123.
Moorehead, Caroline. *Gellhorn: A Twentieth-Century Life*. New York: Henry Holt, 2003.
____, ed. *Selected Letters of Martha Gellhorn*. New York: Henry Holt, 2006.
Morison, Samuel Eliot. *History of United States Naval Operations in World War II*: Volume One: *The Battle of the Atlantic, September 1939–May 1943*. Boston: Little, Brown, 1984.
Mort, Terry. *The Hemingway Patrols: Ernest Hemingway and His Hunt for U-Boats*. New York: Scribner, 2009.
Myers, Jeffery. *Hemingway: A Biography*. New York: Harper & Row, 1985.
Noble, Dennis L. *The Beach Patrol and Corsair Fleet*. Washington, D.C.: U.S. Coast Guard, 1992.
____. *The U.S. Coast Guard's War on Human Smuggling*. Gainesville: University Press of Florida, 2011.
Nuffer, David. *The Best Friend I Ever Had: Revelations About Ernest Hemingway from Those Who Knew Him*. Bloomington, IN: XLibris, 2008.
Oliver, Charles M. *Ernest Hemingway A to Z: The Essential Reference to the Life and Work*. New York: Checkmark Books, 1999.
O'Rourke, Sean. "Evan Shipman and Hemingway's Farm," *Journal of Modern Literature* 21 (Summer 1997): 155–159.

Ott, Mark P. *A Sea of Change: Ernest Hemingway and the Gulf Stream: A Contextual Biography*. Kent, OH: Kent State University Press, 2008.
Palin, Michael. *Michael Palin's Hemingway Adventure*. London: Weidenfeld & Nicolson, 1999.
Poole, Sean, and Teresa A. Cabral. *Gattorno*. Miami, FL: American Art Corporation, 2004.
Raeburn, John. *Fame Became of Him: Hemingway as Public Writer*. Bloomington: Indiana University Press, 1984.
Reiger, George. *Profiles in Salt Water Angling*. Engelwood Cliffs, NJ: Prentice-Hall, 1973.
Reynolds, Charles B. *Standard Guide to Havana and Cuba: A Complete Handbook for Visitors, with Maps, Illustrations, History, and an English-Spanish Manual of Conversation*. Havana and New York: Foster & Reynolds, 1922.
Reynolds, Michael. *Hemingway: The Final Years*. New York: W.W. Norton, 2000.
———. *Hemingway: The Homecoming*. New York: W.W. Norton, 1999.
———. *Hemingway: The 1930s*. New York: W.W. Norton, 1997.
———. *Hemingway: The Paris Years*. New York: W.W. Norton, 1999.
———. *Hemingway's First War*. Oxford, UK: Basil Blackwell, 1987.
———. *The Young Hemingway*. New York: W.W. Norton, 1998.
Roorda, Eric Paul. *Cuba, America and the Sea: The Story of the Immigrant Boat Analuisa and 500 Years of History Between Cuba and the United States*. Mystic, CT: Mystic Seaport, 2005.
Samuelson, Arnold. *With Hemingway: A Year in Key West and Cuba*. New York: Random House, 1984.
Spainer, Sandra, and Robert W. Trogdon, eds. *The Letters of Ernest Hemingway, Volume 1, 1907–1922*. Cambridge: Cambridge University Press, 2011.
Trogdon, Robert W., ed. *Ernest Hemingway: A Literary Reference*. New York: Carroll & Graf, 2002.
Villarreal, René, and Raúl Villarreal. *Hemingway's Cuban Son: Reflections on the Writer by His Longtime Majordomo*. Kent: Kent State University Press, 2009.
Wagner-Martin, Linda, ed. *A Historical Guide to Ernest Hemingway*. New York: Oxford University Press, 2000.
Watson, William Braasch. "Hemingway in Bimini: An Introduction." *North Dakota Quarterly* 63, no. 3 (Summer 1996): 130–144.
Watts, Emily Stipes. *Ernest Hemingway and the Arts*. Urbana: University of Illinois Press, 1971.
White, William, ed. *By-Line: Ernest Hemingway: Selected Articles and Dispatches of Four Decades*. New York: Charles Scribner's Sons, 1967.

Internet Sources

"An Artist of Two Cities [Quintanilla]." http://www.catrais.org/QuintCatalogue/IntroQuint.html.
"August C. Mayhew, Jr., Photograph Collection." http://proust.library.miami.edu/findingaids/?p=collections/findingaid&id=638q=.
Baker, Christopher P. "Havana—Haunted by Hemingway's Ghost." www.christopherbaker.com/html/body_hemingway_s_havana.html.
"Battle of San Juan Hill," 1–11. http://en.wikipedia.org/wiki/Battle_of_San_Juan_hill.

"The Beret Project: Hemingway, Boina and Gattorno." http://beretbonina.blogspot.com/2009/11/hemingway-boinsa-and-gattorno.html.
Binder, David. "Philip W. Bonsal, 92, Last U.S. Envoy to Cuba." http://www.nytimes.com/1995/07/01/obituaries/philip-w-bonsal-92-last-us-envoy-to-cuba-html.
Busch, Frederick. "Reading Hemingway Without Guilt." http://www.nytimes.com/books/99/05/30/specials/busch-hemingway.html.
"El Cobre, Santiago de Cuba," http://www.cuba-junky.com/santiago-de-cuba/santiago-de-cuba-elcobre.html.
"The Collection: National Gallery of Art [Miro Painting]." http://www.nga.gov/fcgi-bintino_f?object=69660&detail=prov.
"Cuban Architecture: La Habana, the City of Columns," http://www.cubaluxuryhotels.com/Cuban-Architecture.html.
Curtis, Wayne. "The Real Old Man and the Sea." http://www.cubanet.org/CNews/yjul99/19e15.htm.
Davenport-Hines, Richard "On the Vital Importance of Being Ernest." Book Review: *The Letters of Ernest Hemingway, Volume I, 1907-1912.* http://www.spectator.co.uk/books/73424978/-the-vital-importance-of-being-Ernest-.html.
"[Deathwatch] Gregorio Fuentes, Inspiration for Hemingway," http://slick.org/deathwatch/mailarchive/ms60034.html.
DiGiantomasso, John. "Battle of Santiago, July 3, 1898," http://www.spanamwar.com/santiago.htm.
"Flashback: Remembering Martha Gellhorn," *The Atlantic Monthly*, March 11, 1998, http://www.theatlantic.com/past/docs/unbound/flashbks/gellhorn.htm.
German, Norman. "Rehabilitating Hemingway," http://www.freerepublic.com/focus/f-news/1764437/posts.
Hasslinger, Karl M. "The U-Boat War in the Caribbean: Opportunities Lost," a paper presented to the Faculty of the Naval War College in partial satisfaction of the requirements of the Department of Operations, Naval War College, Newport, RI: March 1996. www.dtc.mil/cgi-bin/GetTRDoc?AD=ADA 297938.
"Havana, Cuba 1930s." www.youtube.com/user/travelfilmarchive/videos?query=Cuba-1930s.
"Havana's Magic Ceiba Tree." http://www.havanatimes.org/?p=1975.
Hemingway, Colette C. "Ernest Hemingway (1899-1961) and Art," in "Heilbrunn Timeline of Art History." http://www.metmuseum.org/toah/hd/hemw.htm.
Hemingway, Valerie. "Hemingway's Cuba, Cuba's Hemingway." *Smithsonian Magazine*, August 2007 http://www.smithsonianmag.com/people-places/hemingway.html.
"Hemingway Home." http://www.hemingwayhome.com.
"The Hemingway Legacy." http://www.nature.org/ourinitiatives/regions/northamerica/unitedstates/idaho/exp-lore/the-hemingway-legacy.xml.
"Hemingway-Pfeiffer Timeline." hhttp://hemingway.astate.edu/timeline.html.
"José Rodríguez Fuster." http//www.cubanartspace.nt/Fuster/fuster.php.
"Key West to Havana: Steamboat Coming In," http://www.keywest2havana.com/500%20%20steamboat.html.
Lense-Larrauri, Ana, "Officers Never Forgot Glories of Cuba's Sole Naval Academy," http://miamiherald.com/news/special-reports/mariel/article193.

Accessed March 5, 2015.
"El Malecón Havana," 1–6. http://www.destination360com/carribbean/cuba/el-malecon.
"Measuring Worth." www.measuringworth.com/.
Mitgang, Herbert. "Mary Hemingway Dies at 78; Wrote of Life with Novelist," www.nytimescom/1986/11/28/obituaries/mary-hemingway-dies-at-78-tells-of-life-with-novelist.html.
"A Moveable Feast," Taped by C-SPAN Book-TV, C-Span archives, 289184–1-DVD.
Plimpton, George. "Ernest Hemingway, The Art of Fiction No. 21. *The Paris Review*, http://www.theparisreview.org/interviews/4825/the-art-of-fiction-no-21-ernest-hemingway.
Raines, Howell. "'Hemingway's Boat: Everything He Loved in Life and Lost, 1934–1961," *Washington Post*, September 22, 2011, http://www.washingtonpost.com/entertainment/books/hemingways-boat-everything-he-loved-in-life-and-lost-1934–1961-by-Paul-Hendrickson/201.
"The Real Old Man and the Sea." Karpeles Manuscript Library. http://www.dkarpeles.com/authors/hemingway/the-real-old-man-and-the-sea/.
Robinson, Joshua. "Memories of Playing on Papa Hemingway's Ball Field," http://www.nytimes.com/2008/10/02/sports/baseball/07hemingway.html.
Rodriguez, Gisselle Morales. "Manaca Iznaga: A dream-like batey," http:www.oncubamagazine.com/magazine/manaca-iznaga-dream-batey/.
"S. Kip Farington Jr. is Dead." htttp://www.nytimes.com/1983/02/08/obituaries/s-kip-farington-jr-is-dead-was-a-sportsman-and-writer.html.
Saxon, Wolfgang. "Henry S. Villard, 95, Diplomat Who Wrote Books in Retirement." *New York Times*, January 25, 1996, http://www.nytimes.com/1996/01/25/henry-s-villard-diplomat-who-wrote-books-in-retirement.html.
Stoddart, Veronica Gould. "Our Old Friend, Gregorio Fuentes." http://www.cybercuba.com/oldman.html.
UNESCO. "Trinidad and the Valley de los Ingenios," http://whc.unesco.org/en/list/460.
"U.S. Forced Hemingway to Leave Cuba, Havana Paper Claims." Latin American *Herald Tribune*, December 25, 2011, http://www.laht.com/article.asp?CategoryId=14510&ArticleId=340704.
Wilmer, Clive. "Pound's Life and Career," http://ww.english.illinois.edu'maps/poets/m_r/pound/bio/htm.

Index

Adams, Hamilton 11
Adams, James Mead 122–123
Agassiz, Louis 163
Agramonte Street 31
Ambos Mundos (hotel) 5, 16, 19
American Big Game Fishing (book) 100
Anita (boat) 12–13, 15, 91, 94
Ansaria, Maria 5
Archipiélago de Sabana-Camagüey 112–113
Avenue del Porto 22

Bahía de Perras 111
Bahía Honda 2, 74, 113, 138–139
Baker, Prof. Carlos 168, 146
Basílica Menor de San Francisco de Asís 26
Battle of San Juan Hill 128–129
Battle of Santiago de Cuba 128
Bayamo, Cuba 124
Bernaza Street 28
Bimini 94–95
Blue Highways 91
Bobadilla, Doña Inés de 23
La Bodeguita del Medio 25
Bonsall, Ambassador Philip 167–168
Boss (shotgun) 171
Brennen, Carlene 16
Brito, Jacqueline 36
Brito, Yamilys 36
Buenos Aires, Argentina 1
Bulit, Ilse 30
Burgess, Anthony 63

Cadwalader, Charles B. 97, 98–100
Café Cubano (drink) 17
Cahiers d'art (magazine) 63–64

Caibarién, Cuba 111
Calle Florida 1
Calle Tacón 23
Camagüey, Cuba 114, 115, 120
El Capitalio 31–32
Cárdenas, Cuba 74, 108
Caro, Robert 2–3
Carpentier, Alejo 24, 39
Carretera Central (road) 57, 72
Casa Alejandro de Humboldt 39–40
Casa Lancara 120–121
Casa particular 17, 40
Casa Particulare Ana Morales 40–41, 136
Casa Particulare de Liliana Zerquera 130–131
Casa Particulare de Aleida Castro 112
Casablanca, Cuba 74–76
Castillo (Cojímar) 152–153
Castillo de Atarés 73
Castillo de la Real Fuerza 23
Castillo de San Salvador de Punta 32
Castro, Fidel 2, 37, 70, 71, 127, 157, 163, 164, 166
Cathedral of the Virgin Mary of the Immaculate Conception of Havana 24
Cathedral Plaza 24–25
Cayo Confites 113–114
Cayo Guillermo 111
Cayo Paraíso 136–137, 142
Céspedes, Carlos Manuel de 21, 115, 124
The Charge of the Rough Riders at San Juan Hill (painting) 128
Chia, Enrique 34
Chicago Sun-Times (newspaper) 128
Churchill, Winston S. 100

201

202 INDEX

Ciego de Ávila, Cuba 112, 114
Cirules, Enríque 112–113
Cojímar, Cuba 2, 5, 144–145, 150, 155, 157
College and Seminary of San Carlos 25
Columbus, Christopher 24
Common Grounds Travel 5
Crittenden, William L. 74
"Crook Factory" 102
CS-13 (Cuban patrol boat) 114
Cuba improvisation 110–111
Cuba Street 26, 28
Cuban Land and Steamship Company 121
Cuban Naval Academy 137
Cuban friendliness 41–42
Cuban vaqueros 124
Cubano sato 155

daiquiri (drink) 29
Danby-Smith, Valerie 69–71
Darby, Diane 97
Death in the Afternoon (book) 1, 13, 67
Deere, Prof. Caremen Diana 123
Dilberto, Gioia 176
Dönitz, Adm. Karl 100
Dooley, Sandra 36
Dos Passos, John 8, 11, 68
Dubic Beauty Parlor 27
Dunabeitia, Juan 104
Duporte, Jorge Pérez 44–45

Ediciones Vigía 106–107
El Cobre, Cuba 124–126
Empedrado Street 23
El Equipaje Amarillo (book) 37–38
Esmeralda (village) 115
Esquire 3, 68, 92
Las Estrellas de Gigi (boys baseball team) 79–85

A Farewell to Arms (book) 11
The Farm (painting) 63–66, 68–69
Farrington, S. Kip 92
FBI 169–170
Feldman, Prof. Andrew 29–31
Felipe 148
Fernández, Pablo Armándo 34–36
Ferreiro, Isabel I. 59–63
Figurín 155
Finca Vigía 2, 49–53, 55, 58, 78
Fischel, Dr. Washington 47

Florida Hotel 28
Floridita 28–31
For Whom the Bell Tolls (book) 12
Fornos, Raúl Corral 145–146
Fowler, Henry W. 97, 98–100
Franco, Generalissimo Francisco 68
Frommer's Cuba (book) 39
Fuente de los Leones 26
Fuentes, Gregorio 146–148, 155
Fuentes, Norberto 147
Fuster, José Rodríguez 36

Gaggini, Giuseppe 26
García, Camila 38
García, Esperanza H. 13–14
García, Guy Marinez 38–39
García, Judith 38
García, Márquez 203
García Márquez, Gabriel 45
The Garden of Eden (book) 166
Gattorno, Antonio 66–67
Gellhorn, Edna 47
Gellhorn, George 46–47
Gellhorn (Hemingway), Martha 14, 46–50, 101
George Washington (Cuban town) 135–136
Gingrich, Arnold 92
Giraldilla 23
Gómez, Gen. Máximo 33
Gonzáles, Gladys 155–157
Gran Teatro de la Habana 32
Greene, Graham 61
Gris, Juan 66, 68
Guest, Winston 66, 104
Guevara, Ernesto "Che" 2
El Guitarrista (painting) 66
Gulf Stream 10
Gutiérrez, Carlos 94–95

Hadley, Elizabeth *see* Richardson
Haley, James L. 3
Hall, Grace 63, 160–162
Hauk, Walter 93–94, 146–147
Havana 18–19
Hemingway, Clarence Edmonds "Ed" 100, 160–162
Hemingway, Collete 71
Hemingway, Ernest 1–2, 8, 9, 11–12, 18, 28, 29–31, 48–49, 63, 79–84, 91, 92–94, 102–103, 125, 105–106, 138–139, 159–171
Hemingway, Gregory 81, 84, 85
Hemingway, Hilary 15–16

Index

Hemingway, John "Bumby" "Jack" 8
Hemingway, Mary 30, 54–57, 69–71, 148
Hemingway, Patrick 81, 85
Hemingway, Pauline 10
Hemingway, Valerie 67–71, 167–168
Hemingway in Cuba (book) 16
Hemingway y Cuba: Fotos de Raúl Corrales (book) 145
Henderson, Paul 97, 170, 148
Hernández, Anselmo 145, 146, 155
Herrero, José "Pichilo" 55
Holabird, Brig. Gen. Samuel 172–173
Holy Lust (book) 37–38
"Hooligan Navy" (Corsair fleet) 103–106
Hopkins, Harry 47
Horton Bay, Michigan 9
Hotchner, A.E. 170
Hotel Isabel 22
Hotel Velasco 107–108
How It Was (book) 30, 57, 69
Hudson, Thomas 21, 27, 66, 72–77
human smuggling 2

Île de France (ship) 14
Islands in the Stream (book) 21, 66, 72, 106, 142, 157, 164
Ivancich, Adriana 182–184

Jaimanitas, Havana 36
Jane, Pablo 58
Jaronú (village) 115–116
Jay-Tee (boat) 105
Jorge, Jorge 41–42
José Martí (statue) 137
José Martí International Airport 6–7

Kalkaska, Michigan 163
Kennedy, Pres. John F. 69
Kert, Bernice 174, 180, 184
Ketchum, Idaho 56, 166
Key, Jakie 11
Key West, Florida 1, 8, 91
King, Adm. Ernest J. 103
Klee, Paul 66

La Gloria (U.S. settlement) 113, 121–123
Lam, Wifredo 23–24
Least Heat Moon, William 99
Lighthouse 32
Lil, Lucky 29
Little Review (magazine) 65
Lonja del Comercio 16, 27

López, Gen. Narciso 74
López, Reinaldo 37
López-Mesa, Sergio 21
Love, Asst. Prof. Yvonne 35

MacLeish, Archibald 10
El Malecón 33
Manca (tower) 132
Manolito 146, 148
Mariel (city) 136–137
Mariel Boatlift 137
Martin, Dr. Lawrence H. 100
Mason, George Grant 14
Mason, Jane 14–16
Masson, André 64, 66
Matanzas (city) 106–109
Matisse Gallery 68
Mayhew, Augustus C. 123
Mayo Clinic 169–170
McAbee, Beulah Nevada 123
McLain, Paula 185
Men Without Women (book) 9
Mercaderes Street 26
El Mercurio Café 27
Mercury (statue) 27
Mesa, Oscar Blas Fernández "Cayuco" 79–82, 84–85
Meyers, Jeffery 15
Miami International Airport 7
Miró, Joan 63
Modern Poetry (bookstore) 28
Mollener, Monica 169–170
Moncada Barracks 127
A Monument in Arbeit (painting) 66
Morales, Ana 40, 136
Morales, Idalberto 40
Moro Castle 16
Morris, David 142
Mort, Terry 103, 106
A Moveable Feast (book) 166
Museo de Ernesto Hemingway (Finca Vigía) 59–63, 68–71
Museo Nacional de Bellas Artes 32

National Gallery of Art, Washington, D.C. 63
Neomerinthe Hemingwayi (fish) 100
Neptuno Street 27, 40–41, 136
New Republic (magazine) 47
Nobel Prize 125
Northland (riverboat) 54
Nuevitas, Cuba 2, 113, 121

Oak Park, Illinois 8

Index

Obispo Street 27, 34
Obrapia Street 31
Office of Foreign Assets Control, Treasury Department 5
Old Havana 19
The Old Man and the Sea (book) 3, 10, 125, 151, 157
O'Reilly Street 34
Orita (ship) 8
O'Rourke, Sean 63–66
Ott, Mark P. 94, 156

Palacio de los Capitanes Generales 20–21
Palma City 113, 116–119
Paris, France 8
Paso de Martí 31
Pearl of San Francisco Café 26
Perkins, Maxwell "Max" 9
Petoskey, Michigan 8
Pfeiffer, Gustavus "Uncle Gus" 8
Pfeiffer (Hemingway), Pauline 181–182
Philadelphia Academy of Natural Sciences 97, 100
Picasso, Pablo 24, 66
Pierce, Waldo 11
Pierre Matisse Gallery 68
Piggott, Arkansas 11
Pilar (boat) 2, 5, 26, 57, 74, 92–94, 148, 152, 164, 166
Pilar del Río (province) 43
Playa Jigüey 115–116
Playa Pilar 111–112
Plaza de Armas 20, 22
Plaza San Francisco 22, 26
Portocarrero, René 24
Pound, Ezra 65
Prado (Paseo) 32–33
Prado Fine Art Gallery, Miami 67
Puig, Marcus 155
Punta El Inglés 115
Purdue University 1

Quintanilla, Luis 67–68
Quintanilla, Paul 68

Rains, Howell 164
Regla (city) 74, 76–77
Remington, Frederick 128–129
Reserva de la Biosfera Sierra del Rosario 43
Reynolds, Michael 10
Ribailagua, Constantino 29

Richardson (Hemingway), Elizabeth Hadley 8, 176–179
roads 108–109
Rodríguez, Leopoldina 29–31
Rodríguez, Maria Del Rosario "Charo" 37
Rojas, Marta 37–38
Romano Archipelago 113–114
Roosevelt, Eleanor 47–48
Roosevelt, Pres. Franklin D. 47, 103
Roosevelt, Pres. Theodore 127–128
Rosales, Rosa Alfonso 59
Rotunda (Cojímar) 153–155
Running with the Bulls: My Years with the Hemingways (book) 167
Russell, Joe "Josie" 10–11, 91

Salón de los Espejos 21
Samuelson, Arnold "Mice" 95–97
San Cristóbal Medal 146, 155
San Francisco de Paula 2, 50, 18
Sánchez, Alejandro 120–121
Sánchez, Dinorah 120
Santa Clara (city) 135
Santería (religion) 31
Santiago 146
Santiago de Cuba (city) 126, 127–129
El Santuario de Nuestra Señora de Caridad del Cobre 25
Saunders, Burge 11
Saunders, Eddie "Bra" 10–11
Savon, Sgt. Don 104
The Scream of Shrapnel at San Juan Hill (painting) 128
Scribner, Charles 30
Serrano, Prof. Elisa 58, 58, 62
Shipman, Evan 63–65
Sierra de Sancti Spiritus 132–134
Sierra del Escambray 132–134
Sierra del Rosario 42–43
Silvia, María (cartoon) 135–136
Smith, Bill 11
"The Snows of Kilimanjaro" (short story) 92
Sombrero Mel (painting) 36
El Sordo 155
Soroa 43–45
Soto, Herman de 23
Spanish-American War 127–129
Spanish Civil War 68
Stein, Gertrude 63
Steinhart, Frank, Jr. 50
Strater, Henry 11
Sullivan, J.B. 11

The Sun Also Rises (book) 8, 9, 171, 179
Sun Valley, Idaho 166
Tabio, Víctor Pina 2, 27–28, 57, 72, 76, 106, 109, 115, 117, 119, 121, 124, 129, 131, 134, 150, 151
El Templete 22–23
Terminal San Maestra Puerto 26
La Terraza (Cojímar) 150–152, 157
Thomason, Col. John W. 3, 104, 140–142
Thompson, Charles 11
Thompson, Lorin 10
Throw of the Dice (painting) 65
Tin Kid (boat) 56, 148
To Have and Have Not (book) 26, 157
La Torre (book) 184
transportation 110–115
Trinidad, Cuba 129–131
Tropas Guardia Fronteras 111
The Trouble I've Seen (book) 48
Twysden, Lady Duff 179–181

U-boat war 100–109
U-67 (submarine) 101
U-156 101
U-176 114
U-333 105

United Nations Educational, Scientific and Cultural Organization (UNESCO) 16, 39, 43, 130, 131, 157
United States Coast Guard 1
United States Embassy and Consulate (former) 21

Valdés, Elpido (cartoon) 133–136
Valle de los Ingenios 131–132
Varadaro 107–108
Villarreal, Oscar 66
Villarreal, René 63, 85–90, 184
Visa, Cuban 7
Von Kurowsky, Agnes Hanna 172–176
Voort, Paul 121

Walloon Lake, Michigan 8
Welsh, Jane 14
What Mad Pursuit (book) 47
Wheeler Boatyard 92–93
Wilson, Earl 77
With Hemingway: A Year in Key West and Cuba 97
Wolf: The Lives of Jack London 3

Ximeno, Marta 37

Zaldívar, Ivon Leyva 118–119
Zerquera, Liliana 130–131

www.ingramcontent.com/pod-product-compliance
Ingram Content Group UK Ltd.
Pitfield, Milton Keynes, MK11 3LW, UK
UKHW042002140426
5217IPUK00015B/937